U·X·L Encyclopedia of
Drugs & Addictive Substances

U·X·L Encyclopedia of
Drugs & Addictive Substances

Volume 4:
Marijuana to Nitrous Oxide

Barbara C. Bigelow, MAT
Kathleen J. Edgar, Project Editor

U·X·L
An imprint of Thomson Gale, a part of The Thomson Corporation

THOMSON
★
GALE

U·X·L Encyclopedia of Drugs & Addictive Substances

Barbara C. Bigelow, MAT

Project Editor
Kathleen J. Edgar

Editorial
Stephanie Cook, Madeline Harris, Melissa Hill, Kristine Krapp, Paul Lewon, Elizabeth Manar, Heather Price

Rights and Acquisitions
Ron Montgomery, Shalice Shaw-Caldwell

Imaging and Multimedia
Leitha Etheridge-Sims, Lezlie Light, Dan Newell, Christine O'Bryan

Product Design
Pamela A. E. Galbreath, Tracy Rowens

Composition
Evi Seoud, Mary Beth Trimper

Manufacturing
Rita Wimberely

Permissions Hotline:
248-699-8006 or 800-877-4253, ext. 8006
Fax: 248-699-8074 or 800-762-4058

While every effort has been made to ensure the reliability of the information presented in this publication, Thomson Gale does not guarantee the accuracy of the data contained herein. Thomson Gale accepts no payment for listing; and inclusion in the publication of any organization, agency, institution, publication, service, or individual does not imply endorsement by the editors or publisher. Errors brought to the attention of the publisher and verified to the satisfaction of the publisher will be corrected in future editions.

LIBRARY OF CONGRESS CATALOGING-IN-PUBLICATION DATA

Bigelow, Barbara C.
 UXL encyclopedia of drugs & addictive substances / Barbara C. Bigelow, Kathleen J. Edgar.
  p. cm.
 Includes bibliographical references and index.
 ISBN 1-4144-0444-1 (set hardcover : alk. paper) – ISBN 1-4144-0445-X (volume 1) – ISBN 1-4144-0446-8 (volume 2) – ISBN 1-4144-0447-6 (volume 3) – ISBN 1-4144-0448-4 (volume 4) – ISBN 1-4144-0449-2 (volume 5)
 1. Drugs–Encyclopedias, Juvenile. 2. Drugs of abuse–Encyclopedias, Juvenile. 3. Substance abuse–Encyclopedias, Juvenile. I. Title: Encyclopedia of drugs & addictive substances. II. Title: UXL encyclopedia of drugs and addictive substances. III. Edgar, Kathleen J. IV. Title.
  RM301.17.B54 2006
  615'.1'03–dc22
                                                2005017640p

This title is also available as an e-book.
ISBN: 1414406193 (set).
Contact your Gale sales representative for ordering information.

Printed in the United States of America
10 9 8 7 6 5 4 3

Table of Contents

Volume 1

Volume 2

Volume 3

Volume 4

Alternative Drug Names

45-minute psychosis *see* **Dimethyltryptamine (DMT)**
714s *see* **Methaqualone**

A

A-bomb *see* **Marijuana**
A2 *see* **Benzylpiperazine/Trifluoromethyl-phenylpiperazine**
Abyssinian tea *see* ***Catha Edulis***
Acapulco gold *see* **Marijuana**
Ace *see* **Marijuana**
Acid *see* **LSD (Lysergic Acid Diethylamide)**
ADAM *see* **Designer Drugs** and **Ecstasy (MDMA)**
African black *see* **Marijuana**
African salad *see* ***Catha Edulis***

Afro *see* **2C-B (Nexus)** and **Designer Drugs**
Ah-pen-yen *see* **Opium**
AIP *see* **Heroin**
Air blast *see* **Inhalants**
Allium sativum see **Herbal Drugs**
Amp *see* **Amphetamines**
Amys *see* **Amyl Nitrite, Inhalants,** and **Tranquilizers**
Andro *see* **Steroids**

Angel dust *see* **Designer Drugs** and **PCP (Phencyclidine)**
Antifreeze *see* **Heroin**
Antipsychotics *see* **Tranquilizers**
Anxiolytics *see* **Tranquilizers**
Apache *see* **Fentanyl**
Aries *see* **Heroin**
Aunt Hazel *see* **Heroin**
Aunt Mary *see* **Marijuana**

Aunti *see* **Opium**
Aunti Emma *see* **Opium**

B

Backbreaker *see* **LSD (Lysergic Acid Diethylamide)**
Balloons *see* **Inhalants** and **Nitrous Oxide**
Bang *see* **Inhalants**

Barbs *see* **Barbiturates** and **Tranquilizers**

Barr *see* **Codeine**

Battery acid *see* **LSD (Lysergic Acid Diethylamide)**

Batu *see* **Methamphetamine**

Bees *see* **2C-B (Nexus)** and **Designer Drugs**

Bennies *see* **Amphetamines**

Benzos *see* **Benzodiazepines** and **Tranquilizers**

Bhang *see* **Marijuana**

Bidis *see* **Nicotine**

Big chief *see* **Mescaline**

Big d *see* **Hydromorphone**

Big H *see* **Heroin**

Big Harry *see* **Heroin**

Big O *see* **Opium**

Black *see* **Opium**

Black hash *see* **Opium**

Black pearl *see* **Heroin**

Black pill *see* **Opium**

Black Russian *see* **Opium**

Black stuff *see* **Opium**

Black tar *see* **Heroin**

Blanche *see* **Marijuana**

Blind squid *see* **Ketamine**

Block *see* **Opium**

Blotter *see* **LSD (Lysergic Acid Diethylamide)**

Blow *see* **Cocaine**

Blue cap *see* **Mescaline**

Blue dolls *see* **Barbiturates**

Blue Nitro *see* **GBL**

Blues *see* **Barbiturates** and **Tranquilizers**

Blunt *see* **Marijuana**

Boat *see* **PCP (Phencyclidine)**

Bonita *see* **Heroin**

Boo *see* **Marijuana**

Boom *see* **Marijuana**

Boomers *see* **LSD (Lysergic Acid Diethylamide)** and **Psilocybin**

Booty juice *see* **Ecstasy (MDMA)**

Booze *see* **Alcohol**

Bozo *see* **Heroin**

Brain damage *see* **Heroin**

Brew *see* **Alcohol**

Brick gum *see* **Heroin**

Bromo *see* **2C-B (Nexus)** and **Designer Drugs**

Brown acid *see* **LSD (Lysergic Acid Diethylamide)**

Brown sugar *see* **Heroin**

Buddha *see* **Opium**

Bull dog *see* **Heroin**

Bundle *see* **Heroin**

Bush *see* **Marijuana**

Bushman's tea *see* ***Catha Edulis*** and **Dimethyltryptamine (DMT)**

Butterbur *see* **Herbal Drugs**

Buttons *see* **Mescaline** and **Methaqualone**

Buzz bombs *see* **Inhalants** and **Nitrous Oxide**

BZDs *see* **Tranquilizers**

BZP *see* **Benzylpiperazine/Trifluoromethyl-phenylpiperazine**

C

C *see* **Cocaine**

Cactus buttons *see* **Mescaline**

Cactus head *see* **Mescaline**

Cadillac *see* **Designer Drugs**

Camellia sinensis see **Herbal Drugs**

Caps *see* **Psilocybin**

Cartridges *see* **Nitrous Oxide**

Cat valium *see* **Designer Drugs** and **Ketamine**

Chalk *see* **Designer Drugs** and **Methamphetamine**

Chamaemelum nobile see **Herbal Drugs**

Chamomile *see* **Herbal Drugs**

Chandoo/Chandu *see* **Opium**

Charas *see* **Marijuana**

Charley *see* **Heroin**

Chat *see* ***Catha Edulis***

Cherry meth *see* **Designer Drugs** and **GHB**

Chew *see* **Nicotine**

Chewing tobacco *see* **Nicotine**

Chicken powder *see* **PMA and PMMA**

Chicken yellow *see* **PMA and PMMA**

Chief *see* **Mescaline**

China girl *see* **Fentanyl**

China town *see* **Fentanyl**

China white *see* **Fentanyl** and **Heroin**

Chinese molasses *see* **Opium**

Chinese tobacco *see* **Opium**

Chronic *see* **Marijuana**

Cid *see* **LSD (Lysergic Acid Diethylamide)**

Cigarettes *see* **Nicotine**

Cigars *see* **Nicotine**

Circles *see* **Rohypnol**

Cloud-9 *see* **2C-B (Nexus)** and **Designer Drugs**

Coffin nails *see* **Nicotine**
Coke *see* **Cocaine**
Comfrey *see* **Herbal Drugs**
Contact lenses *see* **LSD (Lysergic Acid Diethylamide)**
Copilots *see* **Dextroamphetamine**
Coties *see* **Codeine**
Crack cocaine *see* **Cocaine**
Crank *see* **Designer Drugs** and **Methamphetamine**
Crystal *see* **Designer Drugs** and **Methamphetamine**
Crystal meth *see* **Designer Drugs** and **Methamphetamine**
Cubes *see* **Psilocybin**

D

D-ball *see* **Steroids**
D-bol *see* **Steroids**
D's *see* **Hydromorphone**
Dagga *see* **Marijuana**
Dance fever *see* **Fentanyl**
Death *see* **PMA and PMMA**
Deca *see* **Steroids**
Deca-D *see* **Steroids**
Delantz *see* **Hydromorphone**
Delaud *see* **Hydromorphone**
Delida *see* **Hydromorphone**
Demmies *see* **Meperidine**
Depo-T *see* **Steroids**
DET *see* **Dimethyltryptamine (DMT)**
Dex *see* **Dextromethorphan**
Dexies *see* **Dextroamphetamines**
Diesel *see* **Heroin**
Dietary supplements *see* **Creatine**
Dillies *see* **Hydromorphone**
Disco biscuit *see* **Designer Drugs**
Disco biscuits *see* **Ecstasy** and **Methaqualone**
Discorama *see* **Inhalants**
Diviner's sage *see* ***Salvia Divinorum***
DM *see* **Dextromethorphan**
Dollies *see* **Methadone**
Dolls *see* **Barbiturates** and **Methadone**
Dope *see* **Marijuana**
Dopium *see* **Opium**
Dors and fours *see* **Codeine**
Doses *see* **LSD (Lysergic Acid Diethylamide)**
Dots *see* **LSD (Lysergic Acid Diethylamide)**

Double-stacked *see* **PMA and PMMA**
Dover's deck *see* **Opium**
Down *see* **Codeine**
Downers *see* **Barbiturates, Benzodiazepines, Over-the-Counter Drugs,** and **Tranquilizers**
Drank *see* **Codeine**
Dream gun *see* **Opium**
Dream stick *see* **Opium**
Dreams *see* **Opium**
Drex *see* **Dextromethorphan**
Drug store heroin *see* **Hydromorphone**
Dust *see* **Designer Drugs, Hydromorphone,** and **PCP (Phencyclidine)**
DXM *see* **Dextromethorphan**

E

E *see* **Designer Drugs** and **Ecstasy (MDMA)**
Easing powder *see* **Opium**
Easy lay *see* **GHB**
Echinacea *see* **Herbal Drugs**
Echinacea purpurea *see* **Herbal Drugs**
Elderberry *see* **Herbal Drugs**
Electric kool-aid *see* **LSD (Lysergic Acid Diethylamide)**
Elephant *see* **PCP (Phencyclidine)**
Embalming fluid *see* **Designer Drugs**
Empathy *see* **Ecstasy (MDMA)**
Ephedra *see* **Herbal Drugs**
Ephedra sinica *see* **Herbal Drugs**
Essence *see* **Ecstasy (MDMA)**
Eve *see* **2C-B (Nexus)** and **Designer Drugs**

F

Fags *see* **Nicotine**
Fantasia *see* **Dimethyltryptamine (DMT)**
Fi-do-nie *see* **Opium**
Firewater *see* **GBL**
Fizzies *see* **Methadone**
Footballs *see* **Hydromorphone**
Forget-me pill *see* **Rohypnol**
Foxy *see* **Dimethyltryptamine (DMT)**
Foxy methoxy *see* **Dimethyltryptamine (DMT)**
Friend *see* **Fentanyl**
Fry *see* **Designer Drugs** and **Marijuana**

Fry sticks *see* **Marijuana**
Fungus *see* **Psilocybin**

G

G *see* **GHB**
G-riffick *see* **GHB**
G3 *see* **GBL**
Gamma G *see* **GBL**
Gamma X *see* **GBL**
Gangster *see* **Marijuana**
Ganja *see* **Marijuana**
Garlic *see* **Herbal Drugs**
Gas *see* **Inhalants**
Gat *see* ***Catha Edulis***
Gear *see* **Steroids**
Gee *see* **Opium**
Georgia home boy *see* **Designer Drugs** and **GHB**
GH Revitalizer *see* **GBL**
Ginkgo *see* **Herbal Drugs**
Ginkgo biloba see **Herbal Drugs**
Ginseng *see* **Herbal Drugs**
Glass *see* **Designer Drugs** and **Methamphetamine**
Glue *see* **Inhalants**
Go-pills *see* **Dextroamphetamine**
God's medicine *see* **Opium**
Gondola *see* **Opium**
Goodfellas *see* **Fentanyl**
Goofballs *see* **Tranquilizers**
Goop *see* **Designer Drugs**
Goric *see* **Opium**
Grass *see* **Marijuana**
Great bear *see* **Fentanyl**
Great tobacco *see* **Opium**
Green tea *see* **Herbal Drugs**
Grievous bodily harm *see* **Designer Drugs** and **GHB**
Gum *see* **Opium**
Guma *see* **Opium**

H

H *see* **Heroin**
Happy pills *see* **Antidepressants** and **Tranquilizers**
Harry *see* **Heroin**
Hash *see* **Marijuana**

Hash oil *see* **Marijuana**

He-man *see* **Fentanyl**

Herb *see* **Marijuana**

Herbal ecstasy *see* ***Salvia Divinorum*** and **Benzylpiperazine/ Trifluoromethyl-phenylpiperazine**

Herbal speed *see* **Benzylpiperazine/Trifluoromethyl-phenylpiperazine**

Hierba Maria *see* ***Salvia Divinorum***

Hillbilly heroin *see* **Oxycodone**

Hippie crack *see* **Inhalants** and **Nitrous Oxide**

Hippy flip *see* **Psilocybin**

Hog *see* **PCP (Phencyclidine)**

Honey oil *see* **Inhalants** and **Ketamine**

Hooch *see* **Alcohol**

Hop/Hops *see* **Opium**

Huff *see* **Inhalants**

Hug drug *see* **Designer Drugs** and **Ecstasy (MDMA)**

Hypericum perforatum *see* **Herbal Drugs**

I

Ice *see* **Designer Drugs** and **Methamphetamine**

Indian snakeroot *see* **Tranquilizers**

Invigorate *see* **GBL**

J

Jackpot *see* **Fentanyl**

Jet *see* **Designer Drugs** and **Ketamine**

Joint *see* **Marijuana**

Jolt *see* **GBL**

Joy plant *see* **Opium**

Juice *see* **Hydromorphone** and **Steroids**

Junk *see* **Steroids**

K

K *see* **Designer Drugs** and **Ketamine**

Karo *see* **Codeine**

Kat *see* ***Catha Edulis***

Kava *see* **Herbal Drugs**

Kef *see* **Marijuana**

Ket *see* **Designer Drugs** and **Ketamine**

Khat *see* ***Catha Edulis***

Kick *see* **Inhalants**

Kief *see* **Marijuana**

Kif *see* **Marijuana**

Killer *see* **PMA and PMMA**

Killer joints *see* **PCP (Phencyclidine)**

Killer weed *see* **PCP (Phencyclidine)**

Killers *see* **Oxycodone**

King ivory *see* **Fentanyl**

Kit kat *see* **Ketamine**

Kreteks *see* **Nicotine**

L

La rocha *see* **Rohypnol**

Laughing gas *see* **Inhalants** and **Nitrous Oxide**

Lean *see* **Codeine**

Leaves of Mary *see* ***Salvia Divinorum***

Legal E *see* **Benzylpiperazine/Trifluoromethyl-phenylpiperazine**

Legal X *see* **Benzylpiperazine/Trifluoromethyl-phenylpiperazine**

Liberty caps *see* **Psilocybin**

Liquid E *see* **GHB**

Liquid ecstasy *see* **GHB**

Liquid gold *see* **Amyl Nitrite**

Liquid X *see* **GHB**

Little d *see* **Hydromorphone**

Locker room *see* **Amyl Nitrite** and **Inhalants**

Looney tunes *see* **LSD (Lysergic Acid Diethylamide)**

Lords *see* **Hydromorphone**

Love drug *see* **Methaqualone**

Lovelies *see* **PCP (Phencyclidine)**

Lucy in the sky with diamonds *see* **LSD (Lysergic Acid Diethylamide)**

Ludes *see* **Methaqualone** and **Tranquilizers**

Lunch money *see* **Rohypnol**

M

M *see* **Morphine**

Ma huang see **Ephedra**

Magic mushrooms *see* **Psilocybin**

Mahuang see **Ephedra**

Mandies *see* **Methaqualone**

Mandrakes *see* **Methaqualone**

Mandrax *see* **Methaqualone**

Manteca *see* **Heroin**

Mary Jane *see* **Marijuana**

Matricaria recutita see **Herbal Drugs**

Max *see* **Designer Drugs**

Medusa *see* **Inhalants**

Mel *see* **Melatonin**

Melliquid *see* **Melatonin**

Mellow tonin *see* **Melatonin**

Mentha pulegium see **Herbal Drugs**

Mesc *see* **Mescaline**

Mescal *see* **Mescaline**

Meth *see* **Designer Drugs** and **Methamphetamine**

Mexican brown *see* **Fentanyl**

Mexican mint *see* ***Salvia Divinorum***

Mexican mud *see* **Heroin**

Mexican mushrooms *see* **Psilocybin**

Mexican Valium *see* **Rohypnol**

Microdots *see* **LSD (Lysergic Acid Diethylamide)**

Midnight oil *see* **Opium**

Mind erasers *see* **Rohypnol**

Miraa *see* ***Catha Edulis***

Miss Emma *see* **Morphine**

Mitsubishi *see* **PMA and PMMA**

Mitsubishi double-stack *see* **PMA and PMMA**

MLT *see* **Melatonin**

Monkey *see* **Morphine**

Moon *see* **Mescaline**

Moon gas *see* **Inhalants**

Moonshine *see* **Alcohol**

Mormon tea *see* **Ephedra**

Morph *see* **Morphine**

Mud *see* **Heroin**

Murder 8 *see* **Fentanyl**

Mushies *see* **Psilocybin**

Mushrooms *see* **Psilocybin**

MX missile *see* **Psilocybin**

N

Neuroleptics *see* **Tranquilizers**

Nexus *see* **2C-B (Nexus)** and **Designer Drugs**

Nice and easy *see* **Heroin**

Nickel *see* **Marijuana**

Nitrous *see* **Nitrous Oxide**

Nods *see* **Codeine**

Noise *see* **Heroin**

Nose candy *see* **Cocaine**

Number 4 *see* **Heroin**

Number 8 *see* **Heroin**

Nurse *see* **Heroin**

O

O *see* **Opium**

O.P. *see* **Opium**

Oat *see* *Catha Edulis*

OCs *see* **Oxycodone**

Oil *see* **Marijuana**

Old man *see* **Marijuana**

Ope *see* **Opium**

Oxies *see* **Oxycodone**

Oxycons *see* **Oxycodone**

Oz *see* **Inhalants**

Ozone *see* **PCP (Phencyclidine)**

P

P-dope *see* **Fentanyl**

P-funk *see* **Fentanyl**

Panax ginseng see **Herbal Drugs**

Panes *see* **LSD (Lysergic Acid Diethylamide)**

Party pill *see* **Benzylpiperazine/Trifluoromethyl-phenylpiperazine**

Pastora *see* *Salvia Divinorum*

PCE *see* **PCP (Phencyclidine)**

Pearls *see* **Amyl Nitrite** and **Inhalants**

Peg *see* **Heroin**

Pen yan *see* **Opium**

Pennyroyal *see* **Herbal Drugs**

Pep pills *see* **Amphetamines** and **Dextroamphetamine**

Perc-o-pop *see* **Fentanyl**

Percs *see* **Oxycodone**

Perks *see* **Oxycodone**

Persian white *see* **Fentanyl**

Petasites hybridus see **Herbal Drugs**

Pin gon *see* **Opium**

Pin yen *see* **Opium**

Pink spoons *see* **Oxycodone**

Piper methysticum see **Herbal Drugs**

Piperazine *see* **Benzylpiperazine/Trifluoromethyl-phenylpiperazine**

Poison *see* **Fentanyl**

Poor man's cocaine *see* **Methamphetamine**

Poor man's heroin *see* **Oxycodone**

Poor man's pot *see* **Inhalants**

Poppers *see* **Amyl Nitrite** and **Inhalants**
Pot *see* **Marijuana**
Powder *see* **Cocaine**
Pox *see* **Opium**
Psilcydes *see* **Psilocybin**
Psychedelic mushrooms *see* **Psilocybin**
Purple haze *see* **LSD (Lysergic Acid Diethylamide)**
Purple hearts *see* **Barbiturates**
Purple passion *see* **Psilocybin**

Q

Qaadka *see* ***Catha Edulis***
Qat *see* ***Catha Edulis***
Quaalude *see* **Methaqualone**
Quads *see* **Methaqualone**
Quat *see* ***Catha Edulis***
Quay *see* **Methaqualone**

R

R-2 *see* **Rohypnol**
R-ball *see* **Ritalin and Other Methylphenidates**
Ragers *see* **Steroids**
Rainbows *see* **Barbiturates** and **Tranquilizers**
Rauwolfia *see* **Tranquilizers**
Rave *see* **Ecstasy (MDMA)**
ReActive *see* **GBL**
Red birds *see* **Barbiturates**
Red death *see* **PMA and PMMA**
Red devils *see* **Barbiturates, Dextromethorphan, Over-the-Counter Drugs,** and **Tranquilizers**
Red mitsubishi *see* **PMA and PMMA**
Reds *see* **Barbiturates**
Reefer *see* **Marijuana**
REMForce *see* **GBL**
RenewTrient *see* **GBL**
Rest-eze *see* **GBL**
Revivarant *see* **GBL**
Rib *see* **Rohypnol**
Ro *see* **Rohypnol**
Roach *see* **Marijuana**
Roaches *see* **Rohypnol**
Roachies *see* **Rohypnol**
Roapies *see* **Rohypnol**

Robo *see* **Dextromethorphan**
Robo-tripping *see* **Dextromethorphan**
Roche *see* **Rohypnol**
Rock *see* **Cocaine**
Rocket fuel *see* **PCP (Phencyclidine)**
Roids *see* **Steroids**
Roll *see* **Ecstasy (MDMA)**
Roofies *see* **Rohypnol**
Rope *see* **Rohypnol**
Rophies *see* **Rohypnol**
Rophy *see* **Rohypnol**
Ruffies *see* **Rohypnol**
Ruffles *see* **Rohypnol**
Rush *see* **Amyl Nitrite** and **Inhalants**

S

Salty dog *see* **GHB**
Salty water *see* **GHB**
Salvia *see* ***Salvia Divinorum***
Sambucus nigra *see* **Herbal Drugs**
Sauce *see* **Alcohol**
Saw palmetto *see* **Herbal Drugs**
Schoolboy *see* **Codeine**
Scooby snacks *see* **Ecstasy (MDMA)**
Scoop *see* **GHB**
Sedative-hypnotics *see* **Tranquilizers**
Semilla de la Virgen *see* ***Salvia Divinorum***
Sensi *see* **Marijuana**
Serenoa repens *see* **Herbal Drugs**
Shabu *see* **Methamphetamine**
Shays *see* **Rohypnol**
Shepherdess *see* ***Salvia Divinorum***
Sherm *see* **PCP (Phencyclidine)**
Shermans *see* **PCP (Phencyclidine)**
Sh#t *see* **Heroin**
Shoot the breeze *see* **Inhalants**
Shrooms *see* **Psilocybin**
Sillies *see* **Psilocybin**
Silly putty *see* **Psilocybin**
Simple Simon *see* **Psilocybin**
Sinsemilla *see* **Marijuana**
Ska Maria Pastora *see* ***Salvia Divinorum***
Skag *see* **Heroin**
Skee *see* **Opium**

Skittles *see* **Dextromethorphan** and **Over-the-Counter Drugs**
Skunk *see* **Marijuana**
Sleeping pills *see* **Barbiturates**
Smack *see* **Heroin** and **Hydromorphone**
Smoke *see* **Marijuana**
Smokes *see* **Nicotine**
Snappers *see* **Amyl Nitrite** and **Inhalants**
Sniff *see* **Inhalants**
Snow *see* **Cocaine**
Snuff *see* **Nicotine**
Soap *see* **Designer Drugs** and **GHB**
Somniset *see* **Melatonin**
Sopors *see* **Tranquilizers**
Special K *see* **Designer Drugs** and **Ketamine**
Speed *see* **Adderall, Amphetamines, Designer Drugs, Dextroampheta-
     mine,** and **Methamphetamine**
Spirits *see* **Alcohol**
Spit *see* **Nicotine**
Splif *see* **Marijuana**
St. John's wort *see* **Herbal Drugs**
Stacy *see* **Designer Drugs**
Stuff *see* **Heroin** and **Steroids**
Stupefi *see* **Rohypnol**
Suds *see* **Alcohol**
Sunshine *see* **LSD (Lysergic Acid Diethylamide)**
Supergrass *see* **PCP (Phencyclidine)**
Superweed *see* **PCP (Phencyclidine)**
Supps *see* **Creatine**
Symphytum officinale see **Herbal Drugs**
Synthetic heroin *see* **Fentanyl**
Syrup *see* **Codeine**

T

T-threes *see* **Codeine**
Tango & Cash *see* **Fentanyl**
Tar *see* **Marijuana**
Texas shoeshine *see* **Inhalants**
TFMPP *see* **Benzylpiperazine/Trifluoromethyl-phenylpiperazine**
Thai sticks *see* **Marijuana**
Thrust *see* **Amyl Nitrite** and **Inhalants**
Tic tac *see* **PCP (Phencyclidine)**
Tina *see* **Methamphetamine**
TNT *see* **Fentanyl**
Toilet water *see* **Inhalants**

Tombstone *see* **Fentanyl**

Toonies *see* **2C-B (Nexus)** and **Designer Drugs**

Tootsie roll *see* **Heroin**

Topi *see* **Mescaline**

Toxy *see* **Opium**

Toys *see* **Opium**

Tranks *see* **Benzodiazepines** and **Tranquilizers**

Tranx *see* **Tranquilizers**

Trash *see* **Methamphetamine**

Triple-C *see* **Dextromethorphan** and **Over-the-Counter Drugs**

Tschat *see* ***Catha Edulis***

Tussin *see* **Dextromethorphan**

U

Uppers *see* **Adderall, Amphetamines, Dextroamphetamine,** and **Over-the-Counter Drugs**

Utopia *see* **2C-B (Nexus)** and **Designer Drugs**

V

V35 *see* **GBL**

Valerian *see* **Herbal Drugs** and **Tranquilizers**

Valeriana officinalis see **Herbal Drugs**

Velvet *see* **Dextromethorphan**

Venus *see* **2C-B (Nexus)** and **Designer Drugs**

Verve *see* **GBL**

Vino *see* **Alcohol**

Virgin Mary's herb *see* ***Salvia Divinorum***

Virgin's seed *see* ***Salvia Divinorum***

Vitamin D *see* **Dextromethorphan**

Vitamin K *see* **Designer Drugs** and **Ketamine**

Vitamin R *see* **Ritalin and Other Methylphenidates**

W

Wack *see* **PCP (Phencyclidine)**

Water pills *see* **Diuretics**

Weed *see* **Marijuana**

West Coast *see* **Ritalin and Other Methylphenidates**

Wets *see* **PCP (Phencyclidine)**

When-shee *see* **Opium**

Whip-its *see* **Nitrous Oxide**

Whippets *see* **Inhalants** and **Nitrous Oxide**

Whippits *see* **Nitrous Oxide**
White mitsubishi *see* **PMA and PMMA**
White stuff *see* **Heroin** and **Morphine**
Whiteout *see* **Inhalants**
Windowpanes *see* **LSD (Lysergic Acid Diethylamide)**
Wolfies *see* **Rohypnol**

X

X *see* **Designer Drugs** and **Ecstasy (MDMA)**
XTC *see* **Designer Drugs** and **Ecstasy (MDMA)**

Y

Ya ba see **Methamphetamine**
Yellow jackets *see* **Barbiturates** and **Tranquilizers**
Yellow sunshine *see* **LSD (Lysergic Acid Diethylamide)**
Yellows *see* **Barbiturates**

Z

Ze *see* **Opium**
Zen *see* **LSD (Lysergic Acid Diethylamide)**
Zero *see* **Opium**
Zip *see* **Methamphetamine**
Zonked *see* **GHB**

Please Read — Important Information

The *U•X•L Encyclopedia of Drugs & Addictive Substances* is a medical reference product designed to inform and educate readers about a wide variety of drugs and controlled substances. Thomson Gale believes the product to be comprehensive, but not necessarily definitive. It is intended to supplement, not replace, consultation with a physician or other health care practitioner.

Although Thomson Gale has made substantial efforts to provide information that is accurate, comprehensive, and up-to-date, Thomson Gale makes no representations or warranties of any kind, including without limitation, warranties of merchantability or fitness for a particular purpose, nor does it guarantee the accuracy, comprehensiveness, or timeliness of the information contained in this product. Readers should be aware that the universe of medical knowledge is constantly growing and changing, and that differences of medical opinion exist among authorities. Readers are also advised to seek professional diagnosis and treatment of any possible substance abuse problem, and to discuss information obtained from this book with their health care provider.

Preface

Education is the most powerful tool an individual can have when facing decisions about drug use. The *U•X•L Encyclopedia of Drugs & Addictive Substances* puts clear, comprehensive, and current information on fifty-two drugs at readers' fingertips. The set was designed with middle-school students in mind but can serve as a useful resource for readers of all ages. Each of the entries in this five-volume encyclopedia offers insights into the history, usage trends, and effects of a specific drug or addictive substance.

What Does "Addiction" Mean?

According to the National Institute on Drug Abuse's *NIDA InfoFacts: Understanding Drug Abuse and Addiction,* dated March 2005, drug addiction is more than just "a lot of drug use." The term "addiction" is described as:

- an overpowering desire, craving, or need to take a certain drug
- a willingness to obtain the drug by any means
- a tendency to keep increasing the dose that is consumed
- a psychological and/or physical dependence on the effects of the drug
- an inability to stop using the drug without treatment
- an illness that has harmful effects on the individual and on society.

What Can Readers Expect to Find in This Encyclopedia?

Every entry in the *U•X•L Encyclopedia of Drugs & Addictive Substances* has been painstakingly researched and is based on data from the latest government and university studies on the use and abuse of drugs and other addictive substances. In fact, the results of certain studies were first released to the public while this project was being researched. We are pleased to be able to pass along to readers some of the most up-to-date information on drug use available as this project went to press.

Please note that every effort has been made to secure the most recent information available. Readers should bear in mind that many major studies take years to conduct. Also, several additional years may pass before the data from these studies are made available to the public. As such, in some cases, the most recent information available in 2005 dated from 2001 or 2002. We've presented older statistics as well if they are of particular interest and no more recent data exist.

Some of the substances profiled in the *U•X•L Encyclopedia of Drugs & Addictive Substances* are legal. Examples of legal—but nevertheless addictive—substances are caffeine, nicotine, and certain over-the-counter medications. Many other substances described in this set are illicit, or illegal. Drugs that fall into this category include cocaine, ecstasy (MDMA), and heroin, among many others.

One of the leading concerns of the late 1990s and early 2000s was the spike in methamphetamine abuse. Methamphetamine, or "meth," is a highly addictive drug that can kill. It is interesting to note that methamphetamine is available by prescription for a limited number of medical uses. However, the bulk of the illicit meth that is sold on the streets is smuggled in from Mexico or manufactured by so-called "bathtub chemists" in the United States. This nickname is given to amateur drug makers working in illegal, makeshift labs. These drug makers are out to make a quick buck. They produce their drugs as cheaply as possible, often adding other dangerous substances or filler ingredients to their homemade concoctions. The risks involved in making and taking laboratory-produced mind-altering substances are discussed at length in this encyclopedia.

The Coining of a Brand-New Term: "Generation Rx"

Among the most notable trends in drug use during the first five years of the twenty-first century was the growing abuse of two types of substances: 1) inhalants, including glue, nitrous oxide, and spray paint, and 2) prescription drugs, especially painkillers and stimulants. Drugs such as oxycodone (OxyContin), Adderall, and methylphenidate (Ritalin) have been approved by the U.S. Food and Drug Administration (FDA) for legitimate uses when prescribed by a physician. Increasingly, however, these drugs have made their way from home medicine cabinets to schools and dance clubs. Because of the sizable increase in prescription drug abuse among young people, the term "Generation Rx" is frequently used to describe the teens of the early 2000s.

The magnitude of inhalant and prescription drug abuse problems first became apparent with the release of the 2004 Monitoring the Future (MTF) study results. MTF is a survey of drug use and attitudes conducted by the University of Michigan with funds from the National Institute on Drug Abuse (NIDA). In late April of 2005, the Partnership for a Drug-Free America released its 2004 Partnership Attitude Tracking Study (PATS). At that time, the extent of

Vicodin abuse, in particular, became apparent. Vicodin is the brand name of the prescription painkiller hydrocodone. To ensure that information on this growing Vicodin trend was available to readers of this encyclopedia, we have included an informative sidebar and other information on the drug within the Meperidine entry. Please consult the master index for a complete list of pages that address the topic of Vicodin.

Format

The *U•X•L Encyclopedia of Drugs & Addictive Substances* is arranged alphabetically by drug name over five volumes. Each entry follows a standard format and includes the following sections:

- What Kind of Drug Is It?
- Overview
- What Is It Made Of?
- How Is It Taken?
- Are There Any Medical Reasons for Taking This Substance?
- Usage Trends
- Effects on the Body
- Reactions with Other Drugs or Substances
- Treatment for Habitual Users
- Consequences
- The Law
- For More Information

Each entry also includes the official drug name, a list of street or alternative names for the drug, and the drug's classification according to the U.S. government's Controlled Substances Act (1970). Important glossary terms are highlighted in the text in small caps with the definitions of the words appearing in the margin.

Features

All entries contain informative sidebars on historical, social, legal, and/or statistical aspects of the drugs. This encyclopedia contains nearly 200 sidebars. In addition, the encyclopedia features more than 300 graphics, including black and white photos, maps, tables, and other illustrations.

The *U•X•L Encyclopedia of Drugs & Addictive Substances* also includes:

- Alternative Drug Names guide. As most students recognize drugs by their common rather than official names, this guide to street and other alternative names points students to the correct entry name.

- Chronology. This section presents important historical moments in the history of drugs, from the discovery of dried peyote buttons in c. 5000 BCE to the withdrawal of the prescription drug Palladone in 2005.
- Words to Know. This master glossary defines difficult terms to help students with words that are unfamiliar to them.
- Color insert. Included in each volume, the insert visually informs readers about various drug topics discussed in the set, such as natural sources of drugs, herbal and dietary supplements, older illicit drugs, prescription drugs, public service announcement posters, and the rave culture.
- Highlights of the U.S. Controlled Substances Act (CSA) of 1970. This section discusses the various drug schedules created by the U.S. government and what they mean.
- Where to Learn More. This bibliography presents important sources (books, periodicals, Web sites, and organizations) where more information on drugs and addictive substances can be obtained.
- Cumulative Index. The master index points readers to topics covered in all five volumes of the encyclopedia.

Special Thanks

Various individuals are to be thanked for aiding in the creation of the *U•X•L Encyclopedia of Drugs & Addictive Substances*. These include the following writers and editors: Pamela Willwerth Aue, Denise Evans, Joan Goldsworthy, Margaret Haerens, Anne Johnson, Jane Kelly Kosek, Mya Nelson, Diane Sawinski, and Les Stone.

In addition, special thanks go out to the project's advisory board members. Thomson Gale would like to express its appreciation to the following board members for their time and valuable contributions:

- Carol M. Keeler, Media Specialist, Detroit Country Day Upper School, Beverly Hills, Michigan
- Nina Levine, Library Media Specialist, Blue Mountain Middle School, Cortlandt Manor, New York
- Toni Thole, Health Educator, Vicksburg Middle School, Vicksburg, Michigan
- Susan Vanneman, NBPTS, Robin Mickle Middle School, Lincoln Public Schools, Lincoln, Nebraska

Comments and Suggestions

We welcome your comments on the *U•X•L Encyclopedia of Drugs & Addictive Substances* and suggestions for other topics to consider. Please write: Editors, *U•X•L Encyclopedia of Drugs & Addictive Substances,* Thomson Gale, 27500 Drake Rd., Farmington Hills, MI 48331-3535; call toll free: 1-800-877-4253; fax to 248-699-8097; or send e-mail via http://www.gale.com.

Chronology

c. 5000 BCE Dried peyote buttons dating from this era are later found in Shumla Cave, Texas.

c. 4000 BCE Opium poppies are cultivated in the Fertile Crescent (now Iran and Iraq) by the ancient cultures of Mesopotamia.

1552 BCE An ancient Egyptian papyrus text from the city of Thebes lists 700 uses for opium.

c. 1300 BCE A Peruvian carving depicting a San Pedro cactus, a source of mescaline, is made on stone tablets.

c. 700 BCE Archaeological tablets record that Persians and Assyrians used cannabis as a drug.

c. 199 Galen (129–c. 199), a medical authority during late Antiquity and the Middle Ages, creates a philosophy of medicine, anatomy, and physiology that remains virtually unchallenged until the sixteenth and seventeenth centuries.

c. 200 Chinese surgeons boil hemp in wine to produce an anesthetic called *ma fei san*.

c. 400 Hemp is cultivated in Europe and in England.

600-900 Arabic traders introduce opium to China.

1000 In Coahuila, Mexico, corpses are buried with beaded necklaces of dried peyote buttons.

c. 1200 Peoples of pre-Hispanic America throughout the Inca Empire (1200–1553) chew coca leaves for their stimulating effects and view the plant as a divine gift of the Sun God.

c. 1300 Arabs develop the technique of roasting coffee beans (native to the Kaffa region of Ethiopia), and cultivation for medicinal purposes begins.

c. 1350 Germany bans the sale of alcohol on Sundays and other religious holidays.

c. 1500 Following the Spanish conquest of the Aztecs, unsuccessful attempts are made to prohibit the use of the "magic mushroom" (*Psilocybe* mushrooms) in Central America.

c. 1500 With the rise of national navies during the sixteenth century, hemp farming is encouraged in England and continental Europe to meet the demand for rope and naval rigging.

1524 Paracelsus (1493–1541), Swiss physician and alchemist, mixes opium with alcohol and names the resulting product laudanum.

1556 Andre Thevet brings tobacco seeds to France from Brazil, thus introducing tobacco to Western Europe. Jean Nico suggests that tobacco has medicinal properties in 1559 at the French court, and the plant is renamed nicotina in his honor. By 1565, tobacco seeds are brought to England, where smoking is later made popular by Sir Walter Raleigh.

1612 Tobacco cultivation begins in America and soon becomes a major New World crop. Exports to England begin in 1613, with the first shipment by John Rolfe.

1640 First distillery is established in the United States.

1772 Nitrous oxide is discovered by British scientist, theologian, and philosopher Joseph Priestly (1733–1804).

1775 William Withering, a British physician with a strong interest in botany, introduces the drug digitalis (Foxglove *Digitalis purpurea*) into common medical practice for the treatment of dropsy. Dropsy is a now-obsolete term for edema (fluid retention or swelling) due to heart failure.

1798 Government legislation is passed to establish hospitals in the United States devoted to the care of ill sailors. This initiative leads to the establishment of a Hygenic Laboratory that eventually grows to become the National Institutes of Health.

1799 Chinese emperor Kia King's ban on opium fails to stop the profitable British monopoly over the opium trade.

1799 British scientist Humphry Davy (1778–1829) suggests nitrous oxide can be used to reduce pain during surgery.

c. 1800 Records show that chloral hydrate is used in the "Mickey Finn" cocktail—a drink used to knock people out. The Mickey Finn was used by people wanting to abduct or lure sailors to serve on ships bound for sea.

1803 German scientist Friedrich Sertürner isolates morphine as the most active ingredient in the opium poppy.

1824 Performances in London of "M. Henry's Mechanical and Chemical Demonstrations" show the effects of nitrous oxide on audience volunteers.

1827 Caffeine from tea, originally named "theine," is isolated.

1828 Nicotine ($C_{10} H_{14} N_2$, beta-pyridyl-alpha-N methylpyrrolidine), a highly poisonous alkaloid, is first isolated from tobacco.

1829 Salicin, the precursor of aspirin, is purified from the bark of the willow tree.

1832 French chemist Michel-Eugène Chevreul (1786–1889) isolates creatine from muscle tissue.

1832 Pierre-Jean Robiquet (1780–1840) discovers codeine. Codeine is an alkaloid found in opium that is now used in prescription pain relievers and cough medicines.

1837 Edinburgh chemist and physician William Gregory discovers a more efficient method to isolate and purify morphine.

1839 The First Opium War begins between Britain and China. The conflict lasts until 1842. Imperial Chinese commissioner Lin Tse-Hsu seizes or destroys vast amounts of opium, including stocks owned by British traders. The Chinese pay compensation of more than 21 million silver dollars, and Hong Kong is ceded to Britain under the Treaty of Nanking.

1841 The anesthetic properties of ether are first used by Dr. Crawford W. Long as he surgically removes two tumors from the neck of an anesthetized patient.

1844 The first recorded use of nitrous oxide in U.S. dentistry occurs and involves Quincy Colton, a former medical student, and dentist Horace Wells.

1848 The hypodermic needle is invented, allowing for quicker delivery of morphine to the brain.

1856 The Second Opium War begins between Britain and China. The conflict lasts until 1860. Also known as the Arrow War, or the Anglo-French War in China, the war breaks out after a British-flagged ship, the *Arrow*, is impounded by China. France joins Britain in the war after the murder of a French missionary. China is again defeated and made to pay another large compensation. Under the Treaty of Tientsin, opium is again legalized.

1860 German chemist, Albert Niemann, separates cocaine from the coca leaf.

1861–1865 Morphine gains wide medical use during the American Civil War. Many injured soldiers return from the war as morphine addicts. Morphine addiction becomes known as the "soldiers' disease."

1862 The Department of Agriculture establishes the Bureau of Chemistry, the forerunner of the U.S. Food and Drug Administration (FDA).

1863 German chemist Adolf von Baeyer (1835–1917) discovers barbituric acid.

1864 Amyl nitrite is first synthesized. During the last decades of the twentieth century, amyl nitrite and similar compounds (e.g., butyl, isobutyl, isoamyl, isopropyl, and cyclohexyl nitrates and nitrites) become the chemical basis of "poppers."

1864 German scientists Joseph von Mering (1849-1908) and Nobel prizewinner Emil Hermann Fischer (1852-1919) synthesize the first barbiturate.

1867 Thomas Lauder Brunton (1844–1916), a medical student in Scotland, discovers that amyl nitrite relieves angina by increasing blood flow to the heart. A few years later, nitroglycerine is discovered to have a similar dilating effect. Although both can still be prescribed for angina, nitroglycerine became more commonly prescribed because it is more easily administered and has fewer side effects.

1871 Companies in both the United States and the United Kingdom succeed in producing compressed and liquid nitrous oxide in cylinders.

1874 British chemist Alder Wright uses morphine to create diacetyl-morphine (heroin), in an effort to produce a less addictive painkiller.

1879 The Memphis, Tennessee, public health agency targets opium dens by making it illegal to sell, own, or borrow "opium or any deleterious drug." Critics point out that it is unfair to deny opium to Chinese immigrants while allowing white citizens to freely purchase morphine. In fact, people could legally inhale, drink, or inject morphine at that time. It wasn't until 1909 that federal law outlawed smoking or possessing opium.

1882 Production of the drug barbital begins, and doctors start using the barbiturate in various treatments.

1887 Amphetamines are first synthesized.

1889 French-born scientist Charles Edouard Brown-Sequard (1817–1894) reports that he has injected himself with a compound taken from the testicles of dogs. He says the compound made him feel stronger and more energetic.

1891 *The British Medical Journal* reports that Indian hemp was frequently prescribed for "a form of insanity peculiar to women."

1893 The first diet pills (e.g., thyroid extracts) are marketed in United States.

1895 Heinrich Dreser, working for the Bayer Company in Germany, produces a drug he thinks is as effective as morphine in reducing pain, but without its harmful side effects. Bayer began mass production of diacetylmorphine, and in 1898 begins marketing the new drug under the brand name "Heroin" as a cough sedative.

1896 More than 300 opium "dens" are in operation in New York City alone.

1897 German chemist Arthur Heffter identifies mescaline as the chemical responsible for peyote's hallucinogenic effects.

1898 German chemical company Bayer aggressively markets heroin as a cough cure for the rampant disease of the time, tuberculosis.

1901 Jokichi Takamine (1854–1922), Japanese American chemist, and T. B. Aldrich first isolate epinephrine from the adrenal gland. Later known by the trade name Adrenalin, it is eventually identified as a neurotransmitter.

1903 Barbiturate-containing Veronal is marketed as a sleeping pill.

1903 Barbiturates (a class of drugs with more effective sedative-hypnotic effects) replace the use of most sedative bromides.

1903 To determine the safety of additives and preservatives in foods and medicines, the U.S. government establishes a "poison squad," a group of young men who volunteer to eat foods treated with chemicals such as borax, formaldehyde, and benzoic acid. The poison squad was established by Dr. Harvey W. Wiley (1844–1930), head of the U.S. Bureau of Chemistry, the precursor to the FDA.

1906 The U.S. Congress passes the Pure Food and Drug Act.

1909 Congressional legislation stops U.S. imports of smokable opium or opium derivatives except for medicinal purposes.

1910 Britain signs an agreement with China to dismantle the opium trade. However, the profits made from its cultivation, manufacture, and sale are so enormous that no serious interruption occurs until World War II (1939–1945) closes supply routes throughout Asia.

1912 Casimir Funk (1884–1967), Polish American biochemist, coins the term "vitamine." Because the dietary substances he discovers are in the amine group, he calls all of them "life-amines" (using the Latin word *vita* for "life").

1912 Ecstasy, 3,4-Methylenedioxymethamphetamine (MDMA), is developed in Germany.

1912 Phenobarbital is introduced under the trade name Luminal.

1912 The U.S. Public Health Service is established.

1912 The U.S. Congress enacts the Shirley Amendment that prohibits false therapeutic claims in advertising or labeling medicines.

1913 The U.S. Congress passes the Gould Amendment requiring accurate and clear labeling of weights, measures, and numbers on food packages.

1914 The Harrison Narcotic Act bans opiates and cocaine in the United States. Their use as local anesthetics remains legal, however.

1916 Oxycodone is first developed in Germany and marketed under the brand name Eukodal.

1918 The Native American Church (NAC) is founded and combines Christian practices with the use of peyote rituals. Ultimately, the U.S. government exempts the NAC from its ban on peyote if the drug is used as part of a bona fide religious ceremony. This point remains a center of legal controversy in states that want to limit peyote use or outlaw it completely.

1919 The Eighteenth Amendment to the U.S. Constitution (ratified on January 29, 1919) begins the era of Prohibition in the United States. It prohibits the sale and consumption of alcohol in the nation.

1919 Methamphetamine is first manufactured in Japan.

1925 The League of Nations adopts strict rules governing the international heroin trade.

1926 Phencyclidine (PCP) is first synthesized.

1927 Albert Szent-Györgyi (1893–1986), Hungarian American physicist, discovers ascorbic acid, or vitamin C, while studying oxidation in plants.

1929 Scottish biochemist Alexander Fleming (1881–1955) discovers penicillin. He observes that the mold *Penicillium notatum* inhibits the growth of some bacteria. This is the first antibiotic, and it opens a new era of "wonder drugs" to combat infection and disease.

1930 The U.S. Food, Drug, and Insecticide Administration is renamed the U.S. Food and Drug Administration (FDA).

1932 Pharmaceutical manufacturer Smith, Kline and French introduces Benzedrine, an over-the-counter amphetamine-based inhaler for relieving nasal congestion.

1933 The Twenty-first Amendment to the U.S. Constitution repeals the Eighteenth Amendment and makes it legal to sell and consume alcohol in United States again.

1935 The Federal Bureau of Narcotics, forerunner of the modern Drug Enforcement Administration (DEA), begins a campaign that portrays marijuana as a drug that leads users to addiction, violence, and insanity. The government produces films such as *Marihuana* (1935), *Reefer Madness* (1936), and *Assassin of Youth* (1937).

1935 The first Alcoholics Anonymous (AA) group is formed in Akron, Ohio.

1935 Testosterone is first isolated in the laboratory.

1936 The U.S. government begins to open a series of facilities to help deal with the rising number of opiate addicts in the nation.

1937 Amphetamine is used to treat a condition known as minimal brain dysfunction, a disorder later renamed attention-deficit/hyperactivity disorder (ADHD).

1937 Diethylene glycol, an elixir of sulfanilamide, kills 107 people, including many children. The mass poisoning highlights the need for additional legislation regarding drug safety.

1937 The Marijuana Tax Act effectively makes it a crime to use or possess the drug, even for medical reasons.

1938 The Federal Food, Drug, and Cosmetics Act gives regulatory powers to the FDA. It also requires that new drugs be clinically tested and proven safe.

1938 Meperidine is synthesized. Other synthetic opioids soon follow.

1938 Swiss chemist Albert Hofmann (1906–) at Sandoz Laboratories synthesizes LSD. After initially testing it on animals, Hofmann accidentally ingests some of the drug in 1943, revealing LSD's hallucinogenic properties.

1938 The Wheeler-Lea Act empowers the U.S. Federal Trade Commission to oversee non-prescription drug advertising otherwise regulated by the FDA.

1939 Ernest Chain (1906–1979) and H. W. Florey (1898–1968) refine the purification of penicillin, allowing the mass production of the antibiotic.

1939 Methadone, a synthetic opioid narcotic, is created in Germany. Originally named Amidon, early methadone was used mainly as a pain reliever.

1942 The Opium Poppy Control Act outlaws possession of opium poppies in United States.

1944 To combat battle fatigue during World War II, nearly 200 million amphetamine tablets are issued to American soldiers stationed in Great Britain during the war.

1944 The U.S. Public Health Service Act is passed.

1945 After World War II, anabolic-androgenic steroids (AASs) are given to many starving concentration camp survivors to help them add skeletal muscle and build up body weight.

1948 A U.S. Supreme Court ruling allows the FDA to investigate drug sales at the pharmacy level.

1948 The World Health Organization (WHO) is formed. The WHO subsequently becomes the principal international organization managing public health related issues on a global scale. Headquartered in Geneva, Switzerland, the WHO becomes, by 2002, an organization of more than 190 member countries. The organization contributes to international public health in areas including disease prevention and control, promotion of good health, addressing disease outbreaks, initiatives to eliminate diseases (e.g., vaccination programs), and development of treatment and prevention standards.

1949 The FDA publishes a "black book" guide about the toxicity of chemicals in food.

1950 A U.S. Court of Appeals rules that drug labels must include intended regular uses of the drug.

1951 The U.S. Durham-Humphrey Amendment defines conditions under which drugs require medical supervision and further requires that prescriptions be written only by a licensed practitioner.

1952 The tranquilizer Reserpine rapidly begins replacing induced insulin shock therapy (injecting patients with insulin until their blood sugar levels fall so low that they become comatose), electroconvulsive (ECT) therapy (inducing seizures by passing an electric current through the brain), and lobotomy (making an incision in the lobe of the brain) as treatments for certain types of mental illness.

1953 British novelist Aldous Huxley (1894–1963) publishes *The Doors of Perception*, a book in which he recounts his experiences with peyote.

1953 Jonas Salk (1915–1995) begins testing a polio vaccine comprised of a mixture of killed viruses.

1953 Narcotics Anonymous (NA) is founded.

1953 The U.S. Federal Security Agency becomes the Department of Health, Education, and Welfare (HEW).

1954 Veterinarians begin using piperazines, which are designed to rid the lower intestinal tract of parasitic worms.

1955 Scientists in India first synthesize methaqualone.

1956 The American Medical Association defines alcoholism as a disease.

1956 Dimethyltriptamine (DMT) is recognized as being hallucinogenic.

1957 Researchers John Baer, Karl Beyer, James Sprague, and Frederick Novello formulate the drug chlorothiazide, the first of the thiazide diuretics. This groundbreaking discovery marks a new era in medicine as the first safe and effective long-term treatment for chronic hypertension and heart failure.

1958 Aaron B. Lerner isolates melatonin from the pineal gland.

1958 The FDA publishes a list of substances generally recognized as safe.

1958 The Parke-Davis pharmaceutical company synthesizes and patents PCP. After testing, Parke-Davis sells the drug as a general anesthetic called Sernyl.

1958 The U.S. government passes food additives amendments that require manufacturers to establish safety and to eliminate additives demonstrated to cause cancer.

1959 Fentanyl, first synthesized in Belgium by Janssen Parmaceutica, is used as a pain management drug.

1960 The FDA requires warnings on labels of potentially hazardous household chemicals.

1960 Gamma butyrolactone (GBL) is first synthesized.

1960 GBH, a fast-acting central nervous system depressant, is developed as an alternative anesthetic (painkiller) for use in surgery because of its ability to induce sleep and reversible coma.

1961 Commencing a two-year study, Harvard professor Timothy Leary attempts to reform criminals at the Massachusetts Correctional Institute. The inmates are given doses of psilocybin and psychological therapy. Ultimately, the psilocybin-subjected inmates have the same rate of return to prison as the inmates who were not part of the study. In addition to this, they have more parole violations than the general parolees.

1961 Ketamine (originally CI581) is discovered by Calvin Stevens of Wayne State University in Detroit, Michigan.

1962 The American Medical Association publishes a public warning in its journal *JAMA* regarding the increasingly widespread use of LSD for recreational purposes.

1962 Thalidomide, a sleeping pill also used to combat morning sickness in pregnant women, is discovered to be the cause of widespread and similar birth defects in babies born in Great

Britain and western Europe. Earlier, Dr. Frances Kelsey of the FDA had refused to approve the drug for use in the United States pending further research. Due to her steadfast refusal, countless birth defects are prevented in the United States.

1962 The U.S. Congress passes the Kefauver-Harris Drug Amendments that shift the burden of proof of clinical safety to drug manufacturers. For the first time, drug manufacturers have to prove their products are safe and effective before they can be sold.

1964 The first Surgeon General's Report on Smoking and Health is released. The U.S. government first acknowledges and publicizes that cigarette smoking is a leading cause of cancer, bronchitis, and emphysema.

1965 At the height of tobacco use in the United States, surveys show 52 percent of adult men and 32 percent of adult women use tobacco products.

1965 Because of disturbing side effects including horrible nightmares, delusions, hallucinations, agitation, delirium, disorientation, and difficulty speaking, PCP use on humans is stopped in the United States. PCP continued to be sold as a veterinary anesthetic under the brand name Sernylan.

1965 The manufacture of LSD becomes illegal in the United States. A year later it is made illegal in the United Kingdom. The FDA subsequently classifies LSD as a Schedule I drug in 1970.

1965 The U.S. Congress passes the Drug Abuse Control Amendments— legislation that forms the FDA Bureau of Drug Abuse Control and gives the FDA tighter regulatory control over amphetamines, barbiturates, and other prescription drugs with high abuse potential.

1966 The FDA and the National Academy of Sciences begin investigation of the effectiveness of drugs previously approved because they were thought to be safe.

1966 The U.S. Narcotic Addiction Rehabilitation Act gives federal financial assistance to states and local authorities to develop a local system of drug treatment programs. Methadone clinic treatment programs begin to rise dramatically.

1967 A "Love-In" in honor of LSD is staged at Golden Gate Park in San Francisco, California. Before LSD was made illegal, more than 40,000 patients were treated with LSD as part of psychiatric therapy.

1967 News accounts depict illicit use of PCP, then sometimes known as the "Peace Pill," in the Haight-Ashbury district of San Francisco during the "Summer of Love." PCP reemerges in the early 1970s as a liquid, crystalline powder, and tablet.

1968 Psilocybin and *Psilocybe* mushrooms are made illegal in United States.

1970 The U.S. Congress passes the Controlled Substance Act (CSA). It puts strict controls on the production, import, and prescription of amphetamines. Many amphetamine forms, particularly diet pills, are removed from the over-the-counter market.

1970 Ketamine is used as a battlefield anesthetic agent during the Vietnam war (1954–1975).

1970 The U.S. Comprehensive Drug Abuse Prevention and Control Act classifies drugs in five categories based on the effect of the drug, its medical use, and potential for abuse.

1970 Widespread use of peyote is halted by the Comprehensive Drug Abuse Prevention and Control Act of 1970. During the 1950s and 1960s, peyote was legal throughout most of the United States. During the peak of the psychedelic era, dried peyote cactus buttons were readily available through mail-order catalogs.

1971 Cigarette advertising is banned from television and radio. The nonsmokers' rights movement begins.

1971 The United Kingdom passes the Misuse of Drugs Act.

1974 2C-B is first produced by American chemist and pharmacologist Alexander Shulgin.

1974 The first hospice facility opens in the United States.

1975 Anabolic-androgenic steroids (AASs) are added to the International Olympic Committee's list of banned substances.

1975 Rohypnol, developed by the pharmaceutical firm of Hoffmann-La Roche, is first sold in Switzerland as a sleeping aid for the treatment of insomnia. Reports begin surfacing that Rohypnol is abused as a recreational or "party" drug, often in combination with alcohol and/or other drugs. It also becomes known as a date rape drug.

1976 The FBI warns that "crack" cocaine use and cocaine addiction are on the rise in the United States.

1976 Oxycodone is approved by the FDA. Various formulations follow, including drugs that combine oxycodone with either aspirin or acetaminophen.

1976 The U.S. Congress passes the Proxmire Amendments to stop the FDA from regulating vitamin and mineral supplements as drugs based on their potency or strength. This legislation also prohibits the FDA from regulating the potency of vitamin and mineral supplements.

1978 The American Indian Religious Freedom Act is passed and protects the religious traditions of Native Americans, including the use of peyote.

1978 Because of escalating reports of abuse, PCP is withdrawn completely from the U.S. market. Since 1978, no legal therapeutic use of PCP exists.

1980 The FDA proposes removing caffeine from its Generally Recognized as Safe list. Subsequently, the FDA concludes in 1992 that, after reviewing the scientific literature, no harm is posed by a person's intake of up to 100 milligrams (mg) of caffeine per day.

1980 World Health Organization (WHO) classifies khat as a drug of abuse that may produce mild to moderate psychological dependency.

1981 Alprazolam (Xanax) is introduced and subsequently becomes the most widely prescribed benzodiazepine.

1982 The FDA issues regulations for tamper-resistant packaging after seven people die in Chicago from ingesting Tylenol capsules laced with cyanide. The following year, the federal Anti-Tampering Act is passed, making it a crime to tamper with packaged consumer products.

1983 The U.S. Congress passes the Orphan Drug Act, which allows the FDA to research and market drugs necessary for treating rare diseases.

1984 Methaqualone (Quaalude, Sopor), a nonbarbiturate hypnotic that is said to give a heroin-like high without drowsiness, is banned in the United States.

1984 Nicotine gum is introduced.

1985 The FDA approves synthetic THC, or dronabinol (Marinol), to help cancer patients undergoing chemotherapy.

1985 Ecstasy (MDMA) becomes illegal in the United States.

1985 The United Kingdom passes the Intoxicating Substances (Supply) Act, making it an offense to supply a product that will be abused. Subsequent legislation, the Cigarette Lighter Refill (safety) Regulations, passed in 1999, regulates the sale of purified liquefied petroleum gas, mainly butane. Butane is the substance most often involved in inhalant deaths in the United Kingdom.

1986 The United Kingdom passes the Medicines Act.

1986 The U.S. Congress passes the Anti-Drug Abuse Act. This federal law includes mandatory minimum sentences for first-time offenders with harsher penalties for possession of crack cocaine than powder cocaine.

1986 The U.S. Surgeon General's report focuses on the hazards of environmental tobacco smoke to nonsmokers.

1987 The legal drinking age is raised to 21 years in United States.

1988 Canadian sprinter Ben Johnson (1961–) tests positive for anabolic-androgenic steroids (AASs) at the Seoul Olympic games and forfeits his gold medal to the second-place finisher, American Carl Lewis (1961–).

1990 The FDA bans the use of GHB, a drug related to GBL, a central nervous system depressant with sedative-hypnotic and hallucinogenic properties.

1990 The U.S. Supreme Court decision in *Employment Division v. Smith* says that the religious use of peyote by Native Americans is not protected by the First Amendment.

1991 Anabolic-androgenic steroids (AASs) are listed as Schedule III drugs in accord with the U.S. Controlled Substances Act (CSA).

1991 Nicotine skin patches are introduced.

1992 The Karolinska Institute publishes a study that finds subjects who take creatine supplements can experience a significant increase in total muscle creatine content. Creatine is thrust onto the global athletic scene as British sprinters Linford Christie and Sally Gunnel win Olympic gold in Barcelona after reportedly training with the aid of creatine supplementation. Subsequently, a lack of well-designed clinical studies of creatine's long-term effects combined with loose regulatory standards for creatine supplement products causes some athletic associations, including the U.S. Olympic Committee (USOC), to caution against its use without banning it outright.

1993 2C-B becomes widely known as a "rave" drug in United States.

1993 The first news accounts that cite the use of Rohypnol as a "date rape" drug are published. Rohypnol becomes one of more than 20 drugs that law enforcement officials assert are used in committing sexual assaults.

1993 The U.S. Religious Freedom Restoration Act and the American Indian Religious Freedom Act Amendments (AIRFA) restore the rights of Native Americans to use peyote in religious ceremonies.

1994 Cigarette industry secrets are revealed causing a storm of controversy. The list of some 700 potential additives shows 13 additives that are not allowed to be used in food.

1994 The U.S. Congress passes the Dietary Supplement Health and Education Act (DSHEA) in an effort to standardize the manufacture, labeling, composition, and safety of botanicals, herbs, and nutritional supplements. It expressly defines a dietary supplement as a vitamin, a mineral, an herb or other botanical, an amino acid, or any other "dietary substance." The law prohibits claims that herbs can treat diseases or disorders, but it allows more general health claims about the effect of herbs on the "structure or function" of the body or about the "well-being" they induce. Under the Act, supplement manufacturers are allowed to market and sell products without federal regulation. As a result, the FDA bears the burden of having to prove an herbal is unsafe before it can restrict its use.

1995 2C-B is classified as a Schedule I drug under the U.S. Controlled Substances Act (CSA).

1995 A study published by the *British Journal of Urology* asserts that khat (*Catha edulis*) chewing inhibits urine flow, constricts blood vessels, and promotes erectile dysfunction.

1995 A study by the Rand Corporation finds that every dollar spent in drug treatment saves society seven dollars in crime, policing, incarceration, and health services.

1995 The National Household Survey on Drug Abuse finds inhalants to be the second most commonly abused illicit drug by American youth ages 12–17 years, after marijuana.

1996 Anabolic-androgenic steroids (AASs) and other performance-enhancing drugs are added to the United Kingdom Misuse of Drugs Act.

1996 Nicotine nasal spray is introduced.

1996 The U.S. Drug-Induced Rape Prevention and Punishment Act makes it a felony to give an unsuspecting person a drug with the intent of committing violence, including rape. The law also imposes penalties of large fines and prison sentences of up to 20 years for importing or distributing more than one gram of date-rape drugs.

1997 2C-B is banned in Great Britain.

1997 The FDA proposes new rules regarding some ephedra dietary supplements and seeks to regulate certain products containing the drug. The FDA claims that certain ephedrine alkaloids resemble amphetamine, which stimulates the heart and nervous system. Congress rejects the FDA's attempt to subject ephedra products to regulation. In 2000, an ephedra study published in the *New England Journal of Medicine* shows a link between heart attacks, strokes, seizures, and mental side effects (including anxiety, tremulousness, and personality changes) with ephedra intake. Other possible mental side effects associated with ephedra are depression and paranoid psychosis.

1997 The FDA investigates the link between heart valve disease in patients using the Fen-Phen drug combination for weight loss. The FDA notes that the Fen-Phen treatment had not received FDA approval.

1997 The Institute of Medicine (IOM), a branch of the National Academy of Sciences, publishes the report *Marijuana: Assessing the Science Base*, which concludes that cannabinoids show significant promise as analgesics, appetite stimulants, and antiemetics. It states that further research into producing such medicines was warranted.

1997 Oregon voters approve the Death with Dignity Act, allowing terminally ill people to receive prescriptions for lethal doses of drugs to end their lives.

1997 Rohypnol is banned in the United States.

1997 The *Journal of the American Medical Association (JAMA)* publishes a study indicating that ginkgo dietary supplements might be useful in treating Alzheimer's disease, sparking additional research interest.

1997 The National Institutes of Health (NIH) estimate that approximately 600,000 people in the United States are opiate-dependent, meaning they use an opiate drug daily or on a frequent basis.

1998 A study at the Psychiatric University Hospital in Zurich, Switzerland, demonstrates that psilocybin produces a psychosis-like syndrome in healthy humans that is similar to early schizophrenia.

1998 Amendments made to the U.S. Higher Education Act make anyone convicted of a drug offense ineligible for federal student loans for one year up to an indefinite period of time. Such convictions may also render students ineligible for state aid.

1998 The nicotine inhaler (Nicotrol Inhaler) is introduced.

1998 The tobacco industry settles lengthy lawsuits by making a historic agreement with the States' Attorneys General called the Master Settlement Agreement (MSA). In exchange for protection from further lawsuits, the industry agrees to additional advertising restrictions and to reimburse the states billions of dollars over 25 years to pay for smoking-related illnesses.

1998 The U.S. Drug Free Communities Act offers federal money to communities to help educate citizens on the dangers on methamphetamine use and production.

1998 The U.S. Speed Trafficking Life in Prison Act increases penalties for the production, distribution, and use of methamphetamine.

1999 The Drug Enforcement Administration (DEA) lists GBL as a scheduled (controlled) substance.

1999 The FDA lists ketamine as a Schedule III drug.

1999 National Household Survey on Drug Abuse (NHSDA) estimates that a third of the American population (then an estimated 72 million people) had tried marijuana at least once.

1999 DEA agents seize 30 gallons (113.5 liters) of a dimethyltriptamine (DMT) tea called "hoasca" from the office of the O Centro Espirita Beneficente Uniao do Vegetal (UDV), a New Mexico-based religious organization with approximately 500 members. The organization subsequently sued the U.S. Government, alleging a violation of their constitutional right of freedom of religion.

2000 The *Journal of Pharmacy and Pharmacology* concludes that khat (*Catha edulis*), like amphetamines and ibuprofen, can relieve pain.

2000 The National Cancer Institute (NCI) estimates that 3,000 lung cancer deaths, and as many as 40,000 cardiac deaths per year among adult nonsmokers in the United States can be attributed to passive smoke or environmental tobacco smoke (ETS).

2000 The U.S. Congress considers but does not pass the Pain Relief Promotion Act, which would have amended the Controlled Substances Act to say that relieving pain or discomfort—within the context of professional medicine—is a legitimate use of controlled substances. The bill died in the Senate.

2000 The U.S. Congress Ecstasy Anti-proliferation Act increases federal sentencing guidelines for trafficking and possessing with intent to sell ecstasy (MDMA). It drastically increases jail terms for fewer numbers of pills in personal possession.

2000   The U.S. Congress passes a transportation spending bill that includes creating a national standard for drunk driving for adults at a 0.08 percent blood alcohol concentration (BAC) level. States are required to adopt this stricter standard by 2004 or face penalties. By 2001, more than half the states adopt this stricter standard.

2000   U.S. President William J. Clinton (1946–) signs the Hillory J. Farias and Samantha Reid Date-Rape Drug Prohibition Act into law.

2001   The *American Journal of Psychiatry* publishes studies providing evidence that methamphetamine can cause brain damage that results in slower motor and cognitive functioning—even in users who take the drug for less than a year.

2001   *International Journal of Cancer* researchers assert that khat (*Catha edulis*) chewing, especially when accompanied by alcohol and tobacco consumption, may cause cancer.

2001   National Football League (NFL) joins the National Collegiate Athletic Association (NCAA) and the International Olympic Committee (IOC) in issuing a ban on ephedrine use. The NFL ban on ephedrine prohibits NFL players and teams from endorsing products containing ephedrine or companies that sell or distribute those products.

2001   National Institute of Drug Abuse (NIDA) research reveals that children exposed to cocaine prior to birth sustained long-lasting brain changes. Eight years after birth, children exposed to cocaine prior to birth had detectable brain chemistry differences.

2001   A thoroughbred race horse wins a race at Suffolk Downs in Massachusetts but then tests positive for BZP (also known as Equine Ecstasy).

2001   The U.S. Supreme Court rules (unanimously) in *United States vs. Oakland Cannabis Buyers' Cooperative* that the cooperatives permitted under California law to sell medical marijuana to patients who had a physician's approval to use the drug were unconstitutional under federal law.

2002   Companies begin developing drink coasters and other detection kits that allow consumers to test whether drinks have been drugged. If date-rape drugs are present, a strip on the testing kit changes color when a drop of the tampered drink is placed on it.

2002 A Florida physician is convicted of manslaughter for prescribing OxyContin to four patients who died after overdosing on the powerful opiate. News reports allege that he is the first doctor ever convicted in the death of patients whose deaths were related to OxyContin use.

2002 Health Canada, the Canadian health regulatory agency, requests a voluntary recall of products containing both natural and chemical ephedra.

2002 The U.S. military's use of go-pills (dextroamphetamine) comes under fire after two U.S. Air Force pilots are involved in a friendly fire incident in Afghanistan. Four Canadian soldiers are killed and eight wounded when one of the American pilots bombs them from his F-16 after mistaking them for the enemy.

2002 In the aftermath of the September 11, 2001, terrorist attacks on the United States, the U.S. government dramatically increases funding to stockpile drugs and other agents that can be used to counter a bioterror attack.

2002 Several states, including Connecticut and Minnesota, pass laws that ban teachers from recommending psychotropic drugs, especially Ritalin, to parents.

2002 A U.S. federal district court judge rejects a U.S. Justice Department attempt to overturn Oregon's physician-assisted suicide law. The Justice Department had claimed that the state law violated the federal Controlled Substances Act.

2002-2003 During the severe acute respiratory syndrome (SARS) scare, many people visit Chinese herbalists to purchase a mixture of herbs to help protect them from the disease.

2003 More than 2,200 pounds (998 kilograms) of khat are seized at the Dublin Airport in Ireland. The bundles were being sent to New York from London.

2003 The FDA approves the use of Prozac in depressed children as young as seven years old.

2003 The U.S. government implements the Reducing Americans' Vulnerability to Ecstasy Act.

2003 Steve Bechler, a pitcher with the Baltimore Orioles, collapses during a preseason workout in Florida and dies the next day. His death is linked to the use of ephedra.

2003 More than 3,500 children in the United States are involved in meth lab incidents during the year.

2004 Australian police begin stopping motorists randomly to conduct saliva tests to check for various illegal drugs, including marijuana and amphetamines.

2004 Adderall XR is approved by the FDA for use by adults with ADHD.

2004 The FDA announces that "black box" labeling of antidepressants will become mandatory.

2004 The federal court case regarding the O Centro Espirita Beneficiente Uniao do Vegetal religious sect concludes with the group winning the right to use an hallucinogenic tea in its religious services.

2004 The FDA bans the use of ephedra in the United States following reports of more than 150 deaths linked to the supplement.

2004 The Warner Bros. movie *Scooby-Doo 2: Monsters Unleashed* contains a scene showing Shaggy taking a hit of nitrous oxide off a whipped cream can. The scene angers many parents who have lost children due to inhalant abuse.

2004-2005 BZP is still being sold over-the-counter in New Zealand as an herbal party pill. In 2005, the DEA officially classifies BZP as a Schedule I drug in the United States.

2004-2005 After the fall of the Taliban government in Afghanistan in late 2001, opium poppy production begins to soar by 2004. Street heroin becomes purer and available in larger quantities. Prices reach a twenty-year low.

2005 Baseball players and managers are called to testify before Congress about steroid use in the Major Leagues.

2005 The Partnership for a Drug-Free America releases a study showing that prescription drug abuse among teens is growing rapidly. Teens are dubbed "Generation Rx."

2005 The U.S. Supreme Court agrees to hear a case involving Oregon's physician-assisted suicide law.

2005 Utah-based Nutraceutical International successfully challenges the FDA ban on ephedra in federal court. U.S. judge Tena Campbell rules that the FDA has failed to prove that the company's ephedra-based product is unsafe.

2005 The FDA launches a pilot program using high-tech radio frequency identification (RFID) tags to track the movement of bottles of the most addictive prescription painkillers.

2005 The Canadian government joins several European nations (most notably the Netherlands) in a pilot program to give free heroin to heroin addicts to help them stabilize their lives, eventually overcome addiction, and prevent them from contracting diseases by sharing dirty needles.

2005 The U.S. Supreme Court rules against the use of medical marijuana. At the time of the ruling, ten states allow medical marijuana to be used by cancer, AIDS, and other patients suffering severe pain when prescribed by a physician.

2005 The FDA issues a public health advisory about the use of fentanyl skin patches after receiving reports that people have died or experienced serious side effects after overdosing on the drug.

2005 The new opiate drug Palladone is pulled off the market for further research by its maker, Purdue Pharma.

2005 Oregon lawmakers vote to make over-the-counter cold and allergy remedies containing pseudoephedrine available by prescription only beginning in mid-2006. The move is taken to make it harder for illegal methamphetamine "cooks" to obtain the ingredient. A dozen other states move the product "behind the counter."

Words to Know

A

acetaminophen: Pronounced uh-SEE-tuh-MINN-uh fenn; a non-aspirin pain reliever, such as Tylenol.

acetylcholine: Pronounced uh-settle-KOH-leen; a neurotransmitter that forms from a substance called choline, which is released by the liver.

acquired immunodeficiency syndrome (AIDS): An infectious disease that destroys the body's immune system, leading to illness and death.

active ingredient: The chemical or substance in a compound known or believed to have a therapeutic, or healing, effect.

adenosine triphosphate (ATP): An important energy-carrying chemical, created with the assistance of creatine.

adrenaline: Pronounced uh-DREN-uh-linn; a natural stimulant produced by the human body; also known as epinephrine (epp-ih-NEFF-run).

adverse reactions: Side effects, or negative health consequences, reported after taking a certain substance.

aerobic exercises: Exercises performed to increase heart health and stamina, such as jogging, biking, and swimming, usually lasting between twenty minutes and an hour.

aerosol: Gas used to propel, or shoot out, liquid substances from a pressurized can.

alchemists: Those who study or practice medieval chemical science aimed at discovering a cure for all illnesses.

alcoholism: A disease that results in habitual, uncontrolled alcohol abuse; alcoholism can shorten a person's life by damaging the brain, liver, and heart.

alkaloid: A nitrogen-containing substance found in plants.

Alzheimer's disease: A brain disease that usually strikes older individuals and results in memory loss, impaired thinking, and personality changes; symptoms worsen over time.

amines: Organic (or carbon-containing) chemical substances made from ammonia.

amino acids: Any of a group of chemical compounds that form the basis for proteins.

ammonia: A strong-smelling colorless gas made of nitrogen and hydrogen; often used as a cleaning agent in its liquid form.

amnesia: The loss of memory.

amphetamines: Pronounced am-FETT-uh-meens; stimulant drugs that increase mental alertness, reduce appetite, and help keep users awake.

anabolic agents: Substances that promote muscle growth.

anaerobic exercise: Short, strenuous exercises that require sudden bursts of strength, such as weight lifting and batting a baseball.

analgesics: Pain relievers or the qualities of pain relief.

analogs: Drugs created in a laboratory, having a slightly different chemical composition than a pharmaceutical, yet having the same effects on the brain as the pharmaceutical.

anemia: A blood condition that results in the decreased ability of the blood to transport enough oxygen throughout the body.

anesthesiologists: Medical doctors trained to use medications to sedate a surgery patient.

anesthetic: A substance used to deaden pain.

angina pectoris: Pronounced an-JINE-uh peck-TOR-ess; a feeling of suffocation and pain around the heart that occurs when the blood supply to the heart is not adequate.

anhedonia: Pronounced ann-heh-DOE-nee-uh; the inability to experience pleasure from normally enjoyable life events.

anorectics: Pronounced ah-nuh-RECK-ticks; diet pills that cause a loss of appetite; they were developed to replace amphetamines.

anorexia: Pronounced ah-nuh-REK-see-uh; a severe eating disorder characterized by an intense fear of gaining weight, a refusal to eat, a distorted sense of self-image, and excessive weight loss.

antagonist: Pronounced ann-TAG-uh-nist; a drug that opposes the action of another drug.

anthelmintic: Pronounced ant-hel-MINN-tick; a substance that helps destroy and expel parasitic worms, especially worms located in the intestines.

antidote: A remedy to reverse the effects of a poison.

antihistamines: Drugs that block *histamine,* a chemical that causes nasal congestion related to allergies.

antioxidant: A chemical that neutralizes free radicals (chemicals with an unpaired electron) that can damage other cells.

antitussants: Pronounced an-ty-TUH-sihvs; medicines that quiet coughs.

anxiety: A feeling of being extremely overwhelmed, restless, fearful, and worried.

anxiety disorders: A group of mental disorders or conditions characterized in part by extreme restlessness, uncontrollable feelings of fear, excessive worrying, and panic attacks.

aphrodisiac: Pronounced aff-roh-DEE-zee-ack; a drug or other substance that excites or increases sexual desire.

arthritis: Painful swelling of joints caused by abnormal bone growth or wear and tear on the joint.

asphyxiation: Death or unconsciousness caused by one of three things: 1) a lack of adequate oxygen, 2) the inhalation of physically harmful substances, or 3) the obstruction of normal breathing.

asthma: Pronounced AZ-muh; a lung disorder that interferes with normal breathing.

ataxia: Pronounced uh-TAKS-ee-uh; loss of control of muscle coordination.

attention-deficit/hyperactivity disorder (ADHD): A disorder characterized by impulsive behavior, difficulty concentrating, and hyperactivity that interferes with social and academic functioning.

autism: Pronounced AW-tizm; a psychological disorder, usually diagnosed in children, that affects emotional development, social interactions, and the ability to communicate effectively.

ayahuasca: One of several teas of South American origin used in religious ceremonies, known to contain dimethyltryptamine (DMT); also a plant.

B

barbiturates: Pronounced bar-BIH-chuh-rits; drugs that act as depressants and are used as sedatives or sleeping pills; also referred to as "downers."

bathtub chemists: Inexperienced and illegal drug makers who concoct homemade drugs; also referred to as "kitchen chemists" or "underground chemists."

behavior modification: A type of therapy that changes behavior by substituting desired responses for undesired ones.

benzodiazepines: A type of drug used to treat anxiety.

binge drinking: Consuming a lot of alcohol in a short period of time.

bipolar disorder: A psychological disorder that causes alternating periods of depression and extreme elevation of mood.

black market: The illegal sale or trade of goods; drug dealers are said to carry out their business on the "black market."

boils: Large pimples that are inflamed and filled with pus.

bone marrow: Soft tissue in the center of bones where blood cell formation occurs.

bronchitis: An illness that affects the bronchial tubes in the lungs, leading to shortness of breath and coughing.

bronchodilator: A drug that relaxes breathing muscles, allowing air to flow more easily through the tubes that lead to the lungs.

bufotenine: The component of venom from the toad genus *Bufo* that contains dimethyltryptamine (DMT).

bulimia: Pronounced bull-EEM-eeh-yuh; an eating disorder that involves long periods of bingeing on food, followed by self-induced vomiting and abuse of laxatives.

C

cancer: Out-of-control cell growth leading to tumors in the body's organs or tissues.

cannabinoids: Chemical compounds found in cannabis plants and in small amounts in the brains of humans and animals.

carbon monoxide: A poisonous gas with no odor; carbon monoxide is released when cigarettes burn.

carcinogens: Chemicals that can cause cancer in the body.

cardiovascular illnesses: Illnesses involving the heart and blood vessels.

carries: Doses of methadone given to users to take home for another day.

chemotherapy: A medically supervised regimen of drugs used to kill cancer cells in the body. The drugs have potential side effects including nausea, vomiting, and other reactions.

cholesterol: Pronounced kuh-LESS-tuhr-ol; an essential substance made of carbon, hydrogen, and oxygen that is found in animal cells and body fluids; in high amounts, it may be deposited in blood vessels, resulting in dangerous blockages of blood flow.

cirrhosis: Pronounced sir-OH-sis; destruction of the liver, possibly leading to death.

clinical trials: Scientific experiments that test the effect of a drug in humans.

club drugs: Mostly synthetic, illegal substances found at raves and nightclubs, including the drugs ecstasy, GHB, ketamine, LSD, methamphetamines, PCP, and Rohypnol.

coca paste: An impure freebase made from coca leaves and used mainly in South America; coca paste is smoked and is highly addictive.

cocaethylene: A substance formed by the body when cocaine and alcohol are consumed together; it increases the chances of serious adverse reactions or sudden death from cocaine.

cognitive behavioral therapy (CBT): A type of therapy that helps people recognize and change negative patterns of thinking and behavior.

coma: A state of unconsciousness from which a person cannot be aroused by noise or other stimuli.

congestive heart failure (CHF): Inability of the heart to circulate, or pump, the blood throughout the body with sufficient force.

constipation: An inability to have a bowel movement.

control group: In a drug test, the group that does *not* receive the drug being tested.

controlled substance analog: Any chemical compound that acts on the body the same way a controlled substance does.

coroner: An official who investigates unexplained deaths.

corticosteroids: Pronounced kor-tih-koh-STEH-roydz; medications widely prescribed to treat inflammation.

crack cocaine: A highly addictive, smokable freebase cocaine made by combining powder cocaine with water and sodium bicarbonate.

cravings: Overwhelming urges to do something, such as take an illegal drug.

Crohn's disease: A serious disease of the intestines that causes inflammation, along with severe pain, diarrhea, nausea, and sometimes extreme weight loss.

cutting: Adding other ingredients to a powdered drug to stretch the drug for more sales.

cyanide: A poisonous chemical compound that shuts down the respiratory system, quickly killing people who have been exposed to it.

cyanosis: Bluish or purplish skin caused by a lack of oxygen in the blood.

D

decongestant: A drug that relieves nasal congestion.

dehydration: An abnormally low amount of fluid in the body.

delirium: A mental disturbance marked by confusion, hallucinations, and difficulty focusing attention and communicating.

delusions: False, unshakable beliefs indicating severe mental difficulties; "delusional" refers to the inability to distinguish between what is real and what seems to be real.

dementia: Pronounced dih-MENN-shuh; a brain disorder that causes a reduction in a person's intellectual functioning, most often affecting memory, concentration, and decision-making skills.

dependent: When a user has a physical or psychological need to take a certain substance in order to function.

depressants: Substances that slow down the activity of an organism or one of its parts.

depression: A mood disorder that causes people to have feelings of hopelessness, loss of pleasure, self-blame, and sometimes suicidal thoughts.

designer drugs: Harmful and addictive substances that are manufactured illegally in homemade labs.

detoxification: Often abbreviated as detox; a difficult process by which substance abusers stop taking those substances and rid their bodies of the toxins that accumulated during the time they consumed such substances.

diabetes: A serious disorder that causes problems with the normal breakdown of sugars in the body.

dietary supplements: Products including vitamins, herbal extractions, and synthetic amino acids sold for specific uses such as weight loss, muscle building, or prevention of disease.

dilate: Expand or open up.

dissociation: A psychological syndrome in which the mind seems detached from the body; sometimes referred to as an "out of body" experience.

dissociative anesthetics: Pronounced dih-SOH-shee-uh-tiv ANN-ess-THET-iks; drugs that cause users to feel as if their minds are separated from their bodies.

diuretic: Pronounced die-er-EH-tik; substances that reduce bodily fluids by increasing the production of urine.

divination: The mystical experience of seeing into the future, witnessing a hidden truth, or gaining a deep insight.

doctor shopping: A practice in which an individual continually switches physicians so that he or she can get enough of a prescription drug to feed an addiction; this makes it difficult for physicians to track whether the patient has already been prescribed the same drug by another physician.

dopamine: Pronounced DOPE-uh-meen; a combination of carbon, hydrogen, nitrogen, and oxygen that acts as a neurotransmitter in the brain.

dysphoria: Pronounced diss-FOR-ee-yuh; an abnormal feeling of anxiety, discontent, or discomfort; the opposite of euphoria.

E

edema: Pronounced ih-DEEM-uh; water buildup in the body's tissues that causes swelling.

electrolytes: Charged atoms such as sodium, potassium, chloride, calcium, and magnesium that conduct electrical impulses in the body, and therefore are essential in nerve, muscle, and heart function.

elixirs: Pronounced ih-LIK-suhrs; medicines made of drugs in a sweetened alcohol solution.

emaciated: Pronounced ee-MASE-ee-ate-ed; very thin and sickly looking.

endocrine system: The bodily system made of glands that secrete hormones into the bloodstream to control certain bodily functions.

endogenous: Pronounced en-DAH-juh-nuss; produced within the body.

endorphins: A group of naturally occurring substances in the body that relieve pain and promote a sense of well-being.

enkephalins: Pronounced en-KEFF-uh-linz; naturally occurring brain chemicals that produce drowsiness and dull pain.

enzymes: Substances that speed up chemical reactions in the body.

ephedrine: Pronounced ih-FEH-drinn; a chemical substance that eases breathing problems.

epilepsy: A disorder involving the misfiring of electrical impulses in the brain, sometimes resulting in seizures and loss of consciousness.

epinephrine: Pronounced epp-ih-NEFF-run; a hormone that increases heart rate and breathing; also called adrenaline.

ergot: Pronounced URH-got; a fungus that grows on grains, particularly rye, and contains lysergic acid, a chemical used to make LSD.

esophagus: The muscular tube connecting the mouth to the stomach.

essential amino acid: An amino acid that is only found in food; amino acids make up proteins.

estrogen: A hormone responsible for female reproductive traits.

ethanol: The colorless flammable liquid in alcoholic drinks; ethanol is the substance that gets people drunk.

ether: A flammable liquid used as an anesthetic.

euphoria: Pronounced yu-FOR-ee-yuh; a state of extreme happiness and enhanced well-being; the opposite of dysphoria.

expectorant: A cough remedy used to bring up mucus from the throat or bronchial tubes; expectorants cause users to spit up thick secretions from their clogged breathing passages.

F

fetal alcohol effects (FAE): The presence of some—but not all—of the symptoms of fetal alcohol syndrome (FAS).

fetal alcohol syndrome (FAS): A pattern of birth defects, learning deficits, and behavioral problems affecting the children of mothers who drank heavily while pregnant.

fix: A slang term referring to a dose of a drug that the user highly craves or desires.

forensics: The scientific analysis of physical evidence.

freebase: Term referring to the three highly addictive forms of cocaine that can be smoked: 1) coca paste, which is made from processed coca leaves, 2) freebase, which is made with powder cocaine, ammonia, and ether, and 3) crack, which is made with powder cocaine and sodium bicarbonate.

fry sticks: Marijuana cigarettes laced with formaldehyde, a chemical used to keep dead tissues from decaying.

G

general anesthetic: Anesthetics that cause a loss of sensation in the entire body, rather than just a specific body part, and bring on a loss of consciousness.

glaucoma: An eye disease that causes increased pressure within the eyeball and can lead to blindness.

glycerin: A syrupy form of alcohol.

Golden Triangle: The highlands of Southeast Asia, including parts of Burma, Laos, Vietnam, and Thailand, where opium poppies are grown illegally.

gynecomastia: Pronounced GY-nuh-koh-MASS-tee-uh; the formation of female-type breasts on a male body.

H

hallucinations: Visions or other perceptions of things that are not really present.

hallucinogen: A substance that brings on hallucinations, which alter the user's perception of reality.

hangover: An uncomfortable set of physical symptoms caused by drinking too much alcohol; symptoms include headache, upset stomach, and trembling feelings and are caused by an expansion of blood vessels in the brain.

hashish: Concentrated, solidified cannabis resin.

heat exhaustion: A condition that results from physical exertion in extreme heat; symptoms range from clammy and cool skin, tiredness, nausea, weakness, confusion, and vision problems to a possible loss of consciousness.

heat stroke: A condition resulting from longtime exposure to high temperatures; symptoms include an inability to sweat, a very high body temperature, and, eventually, passing out.

hemp: Cannabis plant matter used to make fibers.

hepatitis: A group of viruses that infect the liver and cause damage to that organ.

herniated disk: A rupture of a spinal disk that puts painful pressure on nerves in the spinal column.

high: Drug-induced feelings ranging from excitement and joy to extreme grogginess.

hippocampus: A part of the brain that is involved in learning and memory.

histamines: Pronounced HISS-tuh-meenz: chemicals released by the body during an allergic reaction; they cause: 1) an increase in gastric secretions, 2) the dilation, or opening up of capillaries, 3) constriction of the muscles around the airway, and 4) a decrease in blood pressure.

hormone: (from the Greek word *hormo,* meaning "to set in motion") a chemical messenger that is formed in the body and transported by the blood to a certain target area, where it affects the activity of cells.

hospice: A special clinic for dying patients where emphasis is placed on comfort and emotional support.

huffing: Inhaling through the mouth, often from an inhalant-soaked cloth.

hydrocarbon: A compound containing only two elements: carbon and hydrogen; hydrocarbons are found in petroleum and natural gas.

hydrochloride: A chemical compound composed of the elements hydrogen and chlorine, often in the form of a crystallized salt.

hyperkalemia: A dangerous build-up of excess potassium in the body.

hypertension: Long-term elevation of blood pressure.

hyperthermia: A dangerous rise in body temperature.

hypogonadism: Pronounced high-poh-GO-nad-izm; a lack of activity in the male testicles, which can be caused by low testosterone levels.

hypokalemia: A loss of potassium in the body.

hyponatremia: Pronounced HY-poh-nuh-TREE-mee-uh; a potentially fatal condition brought on by drinking too much water; can cause swelling of the brain or sodium imbalance in the blood and kidneys.

hypothalamus: A region of the brain that secretes hormones.

hypoxia: A dangerous condition brought on by an inadequate amount of oxygen circulating throughout the body.

I

illicit: Unlawful.

impulsive behavior: (sometimes called impulsivity) Acting quickly, often without thinking about the consequences of one's actions.

incontinence: The loss of bladder and/or bowel control.

infertility: The inability to have children.

inflammation: A physical reaction to injury, infection, or exposure to an allergen characterized by redness, pain or swelling.

ingest: To take in for digestion.

inhalant: A chemical that gives off fumes or vapors that are sniffed, or breathed in.

inhibitions: Inner thoughts that keep people from engaging in certain activities.

insomnia: Difficulty falling asleep or an inability to sleep.

intermediaries: Chemical compounds that are intended for use in the manufacture of more complex substances.

intoxicating: Causing drunkenness, but not necessarily from alcohol; the loss of physical or mental control due to the use of any drug is termed "intoxication."

intramuscular: Injected into a muscle.

intravenous: Injected into a vein.

intubation: Putting a plastic tube into the lungs through the nose and throat, thus opening the airway of a person unable to breathe independently.

K

kidney: The body's urine-producing organ.

L

laxatives: Drugs that help produce bowel movements.

levomethorphan: A synthetic substance that mimics the behavior of opiates such as heroin, morphine, or codeine; levomethorphan is the parent drug of dextromethorphan.

lipase: A substance that speeds up the breakdown of fats in the body.

local anesthetic: A painkiller applied directly to the skin or mucus membranes.

loop of Henle: The U-shaped part of the nephron (tiny filtering unit of the kidney) where reabsorption processes take place.

M

mania: A mental disorder characterized by intense anxiety, aggression, and delusions.

menopause: A hormonal process associated with aging in females that results in an inability to become pregnant; also known as the "change of life."

menstrual cycle: Commonly referred to as a woman's "period"; the monthly discharge of blood and other secretions from the uterus of nonpregnant females.

metabolism: The process by which food is converted to energy that the body uses to function.

methylation: Pronounced meh-thuh-LAY-shun; the process of synthesizing or transforming codeine from morphine.

microgram: A millionth of a gram; there are 28 grams in 1 ounce.

miscarry: When a pregnancy ends abruptly because a woman is physically unable to carry the fetus (unborn baby) until it is able to survive on its own.

morphine: An addictive opiate that is used to kill pain and bring on relaxation and sleep.

mucus: A secretion released by the body to prevent germs and allergens from entering the bloodstream.

multiple sclerosis: A progressive illness that affects muscle tissue, leading to pain and inability to control body movements.

muscle dysmorphia: Pronounced muh-SUL diss-MORE-fee-uh; a mental disorder leading to a desire for larger and larger muscles.

mycologist: A person who studies mushrooms.

N

narcolepsy: A sleep disorder characterized by daytime tiredness and sudden attacks of sleep.

narcotic: A painkiller that may become habit-forming; in a broader sense, any illegally purchased drug.

nausea: Upset stomach, sometimes with vomiting.

nephrons: Tiny working units of the kidney; each kidney has more than a million nephrons.

neurological: Related to the body's nervous system.

neuron: A cell in the central nervous system that carries nerve impulses.

neurotransmitter: A substance that helps spread nerve impulses from one nerve cell to another.

nitrite: A negatively charged molecule of nitrogen and oxygen.

nitroglycerin: A heavy, oily, highly explosive liquid that—when used in very small doctor-prescribed amounts—relieves the pain of angina pectoris in heart patients.

nitrous oxide: A gas given to surgical patients to induce sleep.

norepinephrine: Pronounced nor-epp-ih-NEFF-run; a natural stimulant produced by the human body.

noxious: Physically harmful.

nurse anesthetist: (full title is certified registered nurse anesthetist, or CRNA) Nurses who receive special training in the administration of anesthesia.

O

obsessive-compulsive disorder (OCD): An anxiety disorder that causes people to dwell on unwanted thoughts, act on unusual urges, and perform repetitive rituals such as frequent hand washing.

obstetrician: A physician specializing in the birthing process.

opiate: Any drug derived from the opium poppy or synthetically produced to mimic the effects of the opium poppy; opiates tend to decrease restlessness, bring on sleep, and relieve pain.

opioid: A substance created in a laboratory to mimic the effects of naturally occurring opiates such as heroin and morphine.

opium dens: Darkly lit establishments, often in the Chinatown section of big cities, where people went to smoke opium; many dens had beds, boards, or sofas upon which people could recline while experiencing the effects of the drug.

organic: A term used to describe chemical compounds that contain carbon.

osteoporosis: A loss in bone density resulting in thinned and fragile bones.

ovulation: The release of an egg from an ovary.

P

panic attacks: Unexpected episodes of severe anxiety that can cause physical symptoms such as shortness of breath, dizziness, sweating, and shaking.

paranoia: Abnormal feelings of suspicion and fear.

parasitic infections: Infection with parasites, which are organisms that must live with, in, or on other organisms to survive.

Parkinson's disease: An incurable nervous disorder that worsens with time and occurs most often after the age of fifty; it is generally caused by a loss of dopamine-producing brain cells; symptoms include overall weakness, partial paralysis of the face, trembling hands, and a slowed, shuffling walk.

passive smoking: Inhaling smoke from someone else's burning cigarette.

pesticide: A chemical agent designed to kill insects, plants, or animals that threaten gardens, crops, or farm animals.

phenethylamine: A type of alkaloid, or nitrogen-containing molecule.

phenylketonuria: Pronounced fenn-uhl-keet-uh-NORR-ee-yuh; an inherited disorder that interferes with the breakdown of a certain protein called phenylalanine (fenn-uhl-AL-uh-neen). Phenylalanine is found in milk, eggs, and other foods. Without treatment, this protein builds up in the bloodstream and causes brain damage.

phlegm: Pronounced FLEM; thick, germ-filled mucus secreted by the respiratory system.

phobias: Extreme and often unexplainable fears of certain objects or situations.

piperazines: Pronounced pih-PAIR-uh-zeens; chemical compounds made of carbon, hydrogen, and nitrogen that are used medically to destroy worms and other parasites in humans and animals.

placebo: Pronounced pluh-SEE-boh; a "sugar pill" or "dummy pill" that contains no medicine.

placebo effect: A psychological effect noted by researchers in which patients' conditions improve if they *believe* they are taking a medication that will relieve their symptoms.

pneumonia: A disease of the lung, usually brought on by infection, that causes inflammation of the lung tissue, fluid buildup inside the lungs, lowered oxygen levels in the blood, and difficulty breathing.

postmortem examinations: Examining the body after death; also called an autopsy.

postpartum depression: A form of depression that affects more than one in ten new mothers; symptoms include sadness, anxiety, irritability, tiredness, interrupted sleep, a loss of enjoyment or desire to do anything, and guilt over not being able to care properly for their babies.

post-traumatic stress disorder (PTSD): An illness that can occur after experiencing or witnessing life-threatening events, such as serious accidents, violent assaults, or terrorist attacks; symptoms include reliving the experience through nightmares and flashbacks, having problems sleeping, and feeling detached from reality.

potent: Powerful.

powder cocaine: (cocaine hydrochloride) an addictive psychoactive substance derived from coca leaves; it is either snorted into the nose or mixed with water and injected into the veins.

premenstrual syndrome: Symptoms that occur in some women about a week before the start of their monthly period and may include irritability, fatigue, depression, and abdominal bloating.

propellant: A gas that pushes out the contents of a bottle, can, or cylinder.

prostate: A male reproductive gland.

pseudoephedrine: Pronounced SUE-doh-ih-FEH-drinn; a chemical similar to ephedrine that is used to relieve nasal congestion.

psychedelic: The ability to produce hallucinations or other altered mental states.

psychoactive: Mind-altering; a psychoactive substance alters the user's mental state or changes one's behavior.

psychological addiction or psychological dependence: The belief that a person needs to take a certain substance in order to function, whether that person really does or not.

psychosis: Pronounced sy-KOH-sis; a severe mental disorder that often causes hallucinations and makes it difficult for people to distinguish what is real from what is imagined.

psychostimulant: Pronounced SY-koh-STIM-yew-lent; a stimulant that acts on the brain.

psychotherapy: The treatment of emotional problems by a trained therapist using a variety of techniques to improve a patient's outlook on life.

psychotic behavior: A dangerous loss of contact with reality, sometimes leading to violence against self or others.

psychotropic: Having an effect on the mind.

pulmonary hypertension: A life-threatening condition of continuous high blood pressure in the blood vessels that supply the lungs.

Q

quarantined: Isolated in order to prevent the spread of disease.

R

raves: Overnight dance parties that typically involve huge crowds of people, loud techno music, and illegal drug use.

receptors: Group of cells that receive stimuli.

recreational drug use: Using a drug solely to achieve a high, not to treat a medical condition.

respiratory depression: A slowed breathing rate; severe cases can cause a person to slip into a coma or even stop breathing entirely.

retina: A sensory membrane in the eye.

rhabdomyolysis: Pronounced rabb-doh-my-OLL-uh-sis; destruction of muscle tissue leading to paralysis.

rush: A feeling of euphoria or extreme happiness and well-being.

S

schizophrenia: A mental disease characterized by a withdrawal from reality and other intellectual and emotional disturbances.

screw music: An engineered music inspired by codeine use that uses existing songs but slows them down and makes certain segments repetitive.

secondhand smoke: The smoke from a cigarette user and breathed in by someone nearby.

sedation: Drowsiness or lowered levels of activity brought on by a drug.

sedative: A drug used to treat anxiety and calm people down.

sedative-hypnotic agents: Drugs that depress or slow down the body.

self-mutilation: Deliberately cutting or injuring oneself in some way.

senility: Pronounced suh-NILL-ih-tee; a condition associated with old age; symptoms include a decrease in the ability to think clearly and make decisions.

serotonin: A combination of carbon, hydrogen, nitrogen, and oxygen; it is found in the brain, blood, and stomach lining and acts as a neurotransmitter and blood vessel regulator.

shaman: Spiritual leader who cures the sick and uncovers hidden truths.

sinsemilla: Literally, "without seeds"; buds from female marijuana plants carrying the highest concentration of THC.

sodium bicarbonate: A fizzy, liquid, over-the-counter antacid taken by mouth to relieve upset stomachs.

sodium pentathol: A drug given to surgical patients to induce sleep, usually administered by injection.

solvent: A substance, usually liquid, that dissolves another substance.

speed: The street name for amphetamines.

speedball: A combination of cocaine (a stimulant) and heroin (a depressant); this combination increases the chances of serious adverse reactions and can be more toxic than either drug alone.

steroids: Drugs that mimic the actions of testosterone, a hormone found in greater quantities in males than in females, and help build muscle mass and strength.

stimulant: A substance that increases the activity of a living organism or one of its parts.

stroke: A loss of feeling, consciousness, or movement caused by the breaking or blocking of a blood vessel in the brain.

sudden sniffing death (SSD) syndrome: Death that occurs very quickly after inhaled fumes take the place of oxygen in the lungs; SSD is most often caused by butane, propane, and aerosol abuse.

suffocate: Unable to breathe; death caused by a blockage of air to the lungs.

sulfuric acid: A strong and oily compound made of hydrogen, sulfur, and oxygen; it is capable of eating away at other substances.

suppository: Medicine that is delivered through the anus.

sympathomimetics: Pronounced SIMM-path-oh-muh-MEH-ticks; medications similar to amphetamines but less powerful and with less potential for addiction.

synapses: Junctions between two nerve cells where signals pass.

synthetic: Made in a laboratory.

T

tactile: Pronounced TAK-tuhl; relating to the sense of touch.

testicular atrophy: Pronounced tess-TIK-you-lar AH-truh-fee; the shrinking of the male testicles, which sometimes results from overdoses of testosterone or anabolic-androgenic steroids.

testosterone: Pronounced tess-TOS-tuhr-own; a hormone—found in greater quantities in males than in females—that is responsible for male traits and the male sex drive.

THC: The main active ingredient in cannabis.

thebaine: pronounced thee-BAIN; one of the active alkaloids in opium, used to create synthetic painkillers.

theobromine: Pronounced THEE-uh-BROH-meen; a xanthine found in cacao (kah-KOW) beans (the source of chocolate).

theophylline: Pronounced thee-AFF-uh-lun; a xanthine found in tea leaves.

thyroid: An important gland, or group of cells, in the body that secretes chemical messengers called hormones; these hormones control metabolism, the process by which food is converted to energy that the body uses to function.

tics: Repetitive, involuntary jerky movements, eye blinking, or vocal sounds that patients cannot suppress on their own.

tinctures: Combinations of an active drug and a liquid alcohol.

tolerance: A condition in which higher and higher doses of a drug are needed to produce the original effect or high experienced.

toluene: Pronounced TOL-yuh-ween; a household and industrial solvent common in many inhaled substances, including model airplane glue, spray paint, correction fluid, paint thinners, and paint removers.

Tourette's syndrome: A severe tic disorder that causes distress and significant impairment to those affected by it.

toxic: Harmful, poisonous, or capable of causing death.

trafficking: Making, selling, or distributing a controlled drug.

trance: A sleep-like state in which important body functions slow down.

tranquilizers: Drugs such as Valium and Librium that treat anxiety; also called benzodiazepines (pronounced ben-zoh-die-AZ-uh-peens).

traumatic: Dangerous, life-threatening, and difficult to forget.

trip: An intense and usually very visual experience produced by an hallucinogenic drug.

tuberculosis: Pronounced tuh-burk-yuh-LOH-siss; a highly contagious disease of the lungs.

tryptamine compound: A crystalline compound of carbon, hydrogen, and nitrogen that is made in plant and animal tissues.

U

ulcers: The breakdown of mucus membranes, usually in the stomach.

V

vapors: Gas or fumes that can be irritating or physically harmful when inhaled.

venom: A liquid poison created by an animal for defense against predators or for killing prey.

W

withdrawal: The process of gradually cutting back on the amount of a drug being taken until it is discontinued entirely; also the accompanying physiological effects of terminating use of an addictive drug.

X

xanthine: Pronounced ZAN-thene; a compound found in animal and plant tissue.

Highlights of the U.S. Controlled Substances Act (CSA) of 1970

The Controlled Substances Act (CSA) is part of a larger piece of legislation called the Comprehensive Drug Abuse Prevention and Control Act of 1970. It provides the legal basis for the U.S. government to fight the ongoing war against drugs.

Under the CSA, all drugs are categorized into one of five "schedules." A substance's scheduling is based on three factors: 1) its medicinal value; 2) its possible harmfulness to human health; and 3) its potential for abuse or addiction. Schedule I is reserved for the most dangerous drugs that have no recognized medical use, while Schedule V is the classification used for the least dangerous drugs.

Schedule I Drugs

- have no known medical use in the United States
- have a very high potential for abuse
- are too dangerous to be used even under medical supervision

Drugs classified as Schedule I include 2C-B (Nexus), dimethyltryptamine (DMT), ecstasy (MDMA), GHB, heroin, LSD, mescaline, PMA, and psilocybin.

Schedule II Drugs

- are accepted for medical use in the United States
- may cause severe psychological and/or physical dependence
- have a high potential for abuse

Drugs classified as Schedule II include Adderall, cocaine, hydromorphone, methylphenidates such as Concerta and Ritalin, morphine, and oxycodone.

Schedule III Drugs

- are accepted for medical use in the United States
- may lead to moderate psychological and/or physical dependence
- are less likely to be abused than drugs categorized as Schedule I or Schedule II

Drugs classified as Schedule III include certain barbiturates such as aprobarbital (Alurate), butabarbital (Butisol), and butalbital

(Fiorinal and Fioricet), as well as muscle-building steroids and testosterone.

Schedule IV Drugs

- are accepted for medical use in the United States
- may lead to limited psychological and/or physical dependence
- have a relatively low potential for abuse

Drugs classified as Schedule IV include various benzodiazepines, including alprazolam (Xanax) and diazepam (Valium).

Schedule V Drugs

- are accepted for medical use in the United States
- are less likely to cause psychological and/or physical dependence than drugs in any other Schedule
- have a low potential for abuse

Drugs classified as Schedule V include various over-the-counter medicines that contain codeine.

Source: Compiled by Thomson Gale staff from data reported in "Controlled Substances Act," U.S. Drug Enforcement Administration (DEA), http://www.usdoj.gov/dea/agency/csa.htm (accessed September 4, 2005); and "Controlled Substance Schedules," U.S. Department of Justice, Drug Enforcement Administration (DEA) Office of Diversion Control, http://www.deadiversion.usdoj.gov/schedules/alpha/alphabetical.htm (accessed September 4, 2005).

Marijuana

What Kind of Drug Is It?

Marijuana is the most widely used illegal controlled substance in the world. Although the drug has been illegal in the United States since the 1930s, an estimated 40.6 percent of the U.S. population over twelve years of age (forty out of every one hundred people) has tried it at least once. As recently as 2003, 25.2 million people—basically one in ten Americans—reported using the drug at least once that year, as reported by the Office of National Drug Control Policy.

Marijuana, or the plant *Cannabis sativa*, has been used as a medicine, as a part of religious ceremonies, and even as a fiber for making clothing, rope, and paper for many thousands of years. It has also been used RECREATIONALLY in many cultures, both ancient and modern. Still, its effects on the brain and body are not yet completely understood. Scientists differ on how to classify the drug: Is it a hallucinogen like LSD (lysergic acid diethylamide), a narcotic like opium, or does it belong in a class by itself? (Entries on LSD and opium are included in this encyclopedia.) To further confuse matters, some scientists call marijuana a *stimulant*, or a substance that makes the brain and body more active, and some call it a *depressant*, or a substance that slows down brain and body processes. Whatever its properties, ORGANIC—or plant-derived—marijuana is illegal to possess or sell as a recreational substance.

The controversy over marijuana's role as a medicine for certain illnesses highlights the drug's strange history in American society. A small minority of Americans wants the drug to be made legal and sold under controlled circumstances, similar to the sale of alcohol. The U.S. government has made no move to legalize marijuana possession and, in fact, has tightened laws against it since the 1980s. People who buy, sell, or use marijuana for recreational purposes face many penalties if caught, including a permanent criminal record.

Overview

The earliest archeological evidence of marijuana comes from China. Twelve thousand years ago the plant was CULTIVATED there for many uses. Its fibers, known as HEMP, could be woven into

Official Drug Name: *Cannabis sativa;* hashish; hemp; marijuana

Also Known As: More than 200 street names, including A-bomb, Acapulco gold, ace, African black, Aunt Mary, bhang, blunt, blanche, boo, boom, bush, charas, chronic, dagga, dope, fry (laced with embalming fluid), fry sticks (laced with embalming fluid), gangster, ganja, grass, hash, hash oil, herb, joint, kef, kief, kif, Mary Jane, nickel, oil, old man, pot, reefer, roach, sinsemilla, sensi, skunk, smoke, splif, tar, Thai sticks, weed

Drug Classifications: Schedule I, hallucinogen; Schedule III, prescription synthetic THC, dronabinol (brand name Marinol)

recreationally: to get high, not to treat a medical condition

organic: a term used to describe chemical compounds that contain carbon

cultivated: planted and tended with the intention of harvesting

hemp: cannabis plant matter used to make fibers

Marijuana, or the plant *Cannabis sativa,* has been used as a medicine, as a part of religious ceremonies, and even as a fiber for making clothing, rope, and paper for many thousands of years. *AP/Wide World Photos.*

sturdy clothing or rope, or even processed as paper. The Chinese also used the plant as a medicine for anxiety and physical pain. From China the use of the plant spread to India, where by 2000 BCE it had become part of religious ceremonies. The *Vedas,* a series of Indian religious writings, credits the god Shiva with introducing cannabis to humankind, to help relieve the soul from suffering. To this day, a mild marijuana preparation called *bhang* is used during holidays in India, just like Americans might toast in the New Year with champagne.

An Ancient History

In his book *Illegal Drugs: A Complete Guide to Their History, Chemistry, Use and Abuse,* Paul M. Gahlinger noted that Europeans had discovered and were using cannabis by the fifth century BCE. By the time Venetian traveler Marco Polo (c. 1254–1324) made his famous expedition to the Far East in the late thirteenth century, the drug was widespread throughout the Middle East, Asia, Europe, and Africa.

Different cultures used it in varied ways even then. Marco Polo records the legend of the "Old Man of the Mountain," a Muslim Middle Easterner said to have recruited assassins by intoxicating them with HASHISH, which is the solidified form of the drug. (The very word "assassin" is said to have roots in "hashish," but the story Marco Polo reports has never been verified.) In Europe as early as the Middle Ages (c. 500–c. 1500), hemp was planted for use as clothing and rope, and cannabis was used as medicine for illnesses as varied as menstrual cramps, labor pains, and head-aches. Its recreational uses were understood as well, and in 1484 Pope Innocent VIII (1432–1492) said that hashish consumption was linked to Satanic rituals.

Grown on Plantations

As cannabis fell out of favor as a recreational drug, it grew in importance as a plant fiber. The era of exploring the world by sailing ship had dawned, and demand for canvas—another word derived from cannabis—grew rapidly. In 1533, King Henry VIII (1491–1547) commanded all English farmers to set aside part of their holdings to grow hemp. The plant was exported to the Americas, where it was first grown in Canada in 1606 and in Virginia in 1611. In the United States, it was used for making canvas and rope. However, written documents note that George Washington (1732–1799), the first U.S. president, not only grew cannabis but also used it to soothe his toothaches. According to the 1850 U.S. Census, the plant was grown on 8,327 plantations in the nation.

The renewed interest in recreational use of cannabis dates to the 1840s, when Egyptian hashish spread among the artistic communities in France and England as a drug of enlightenment (enhanced intelligence). At the same time, the medical community in Europe renewed its interest in the substance, recommending it for a wide variety of ailments from asthma and depression to EPILEPSY. Cannabis was also recommended to the mentally ill and to alcoholics and people with opium addiction. In the heyday of "cure-all" medicines during the early 1900s, marijuana extracts could be found in many over-the-counter remedies, sometimes mixed with opiates like morphine. (An entry for morphine is available in this encyclopedia.)

The Tide Turns

In time, the tide of American opinion turned against marijuana. Some historians credit business tycoon William Randolph Hearst (1863–1951) with launching this crusade. Hearst, who

hashish: concentrated, solidified cannabis resin

epilepsy: a disorder involving the misfiring of electrical impulses in the brain, sometimes resulting in seizures and loss of consciousness

Marijuana Chronology

2737 BCE The emperor Shen-Nung of China composes an herbal encyclopedia, recommending cannabis as a painkiller.

2000-1400 BCE Indian priests compile the *Vedas,* a series of writings that detail the use of marijuana in religious ceremonies.

C. 500 BCE A funeral urn of this date, found in Germany by archeologists, contains cannabis seeds.

1307 CE In *The Book of Marco Polo,* Venetian traveler Marco Polo describes hashish use among religious sects in the Middle East.

1533 King Henry VIII of England commands his subjects to grow hemp (cannabis) for use in making ropes and canvas.

1611 Cannabis is first cultivated in Virginia.

1776 The U.S. Declaration of Independence is published on paper made from hemp.

1900 Cannabis extracts are available in more than thirty over-the-counter medications, used as painkillers, cough suppressants, and to soothe babies.

1936 The film *Reefer Madness* is released, showing teenagers becoming violent criminals under the influence of marijuana.

1937 The Marijuana Tax Act effectively ends legal production of hemp in the United States.

1970 The Controlled Substances Act places marijuana, hashish, and hash oil on the Schedule I list of controlled substances.

1985 Chemists create dronabinol, a synthetic version of the most powerful chemical in marijuana. Pill forms of dronabinol are sold as Marinol.

2004 Ten U.S. states have passed "medical marijuana" laws, allowing certain patients to possess small amounts of marijuana for relief of medical symptoms. Use of "medical marijuana" is challenged by the federal government in a case that reaches the U.S. Supreme Court.

2005 The U.S. Supreme Court, in the case of *Gonzalez v. Raich*, rules 6-3 that Congress has the authority to prohibit the possession of medical marijuana.

owned many major newspapers, also owned many thousands of acres of trees that he planned to turn into paper. As late as the 1880s, almost all American paper was made from hemp, and a great deal of hemp was still grown in the United States. (The U.S. Declaration of Independence was published on hemp paper.) Hearst capitalized on anti-Mexican prejudice and, through his newspapers, linked marijuana use to Mexican immigrants, crime, violent behavior, and poor job performance. It was the Hearst newspaper chain that changed the spelling of marijuana from its older form, marihuana. During this time, use of the word *cannabis* faded as well.

According to Hugh Downs, in a commentary for *ABC News* in 1990: "Nobody was afraid of hemp—it had been cultivated and processed into usable goods, and consumed as medicine, and burned in oil lamps, for hundreds of years. But after a campaign to discredit hemp in the Hearst newspapers, Americans became afraid of something called marijuana." Downs also noted that the crusade against hemp "misled the public into thinking that marijuana and hemp were different plants."

Hearst's campaign was one of many waged against marijuana in the 1930s. Another important figure who changed American attitudes toward the drug was Harry Anslinger (1892–1975), head of the Commission of Narcotics during the Great Depression (1929–1941). Bolstered by scientific studies published in credible journals, Anslinger was able to convince state governments that marijuana use caused an increase in crime and violence, that it was addictive, and that its attraction to young people could lead to a lifetime of trouble. Hollywood seemed to support this view, issuing a series of hour-long dramas about marijuana, of which *Reefer Madness* (1936) is the best known. In *Reefer Madness* and other similar films, young, innocent people become violent, dishonest—or at least rather hysterical—victims of the "devil weed."

Following a series of congressional hearings, the U.S. government passed the Marijuana Tax Act of 1937. The act did not outlaw marijuana outright, but "created a tax structure around the cultivation, distribution, sale, and purchase of cannabis products, which made it virtually impossible to have anything to do with the drug without breaking some part of the tax law," wrote Cynthia Kuhn and her coauthors in *Buzzed: The Straight Facts about the Most Used and Abused Drugs from Alcohol to Ecstasy*. In other words, the 1937 law made it impossible to reap a legal profit from growing cannabis.

Illegal Experimentation

After World War II (1939–1945), a new generation of young people began to frequent urban jazz clubs, where the musicians often used marijuana and other drugs. Interest in recreational marijuana increased. As the teenagers of the 1960s and 1970s began using the drug in record numbers, they showed that many of the "scientific" claims made against marijuana in the 1930s were untrue. Marijuana, it appeared, did not cause violence or hysterical behavior. It was not particularly addictive, and it appeared to have few lasting effects on the user in the days and weeks following a dose. This finding led various people to mistakenly doubt *all* information they had received about illegal drugs, based on their own experiences with marijuana. This created a climate of illegal drug experimentation that has lasted into the twenty-first century.

Illegal marijuana is smuggled into the country in cars, trucks, trains, boats, and planes. This plane, used for smuggling marijuana from Jamaica, crashed into a swamp in Florida as it was being pursued by U.S. Customs and DEA officials. Some 800 pounds of the drug were onboard. © *Nathan Benn/Corbis.*

Such experimentation led to drugs flooding the BLACK MARKET and being sold illegally on the street.

Federal Government Labels Marijuana a Hazard

In 1970, the U.S. Controlled Substances Act named marijuana and its by-products, hashish and hash oil, as Schedule I controlled substances. This is the highest level of control, indicating a substance with a high probability of abuse and no medical benefit. Even in 1970 some members of the medical and scientific community felt that marijuana should not have been placed in the same category as drugs such as LSD and heroin. (Separate entries on LSD and heroin are available in this encyclopedia.)

black market: the illegal sale or trade of goods; drug dealers are said to carry out their business on the "black market"

By the end of the twentieth century, several medical uses for cannabis had been documented with full research evidence. These include being an appetite-enhancer in cancer and ACQUIRED IMMUNODEFICIENCY SYNDROME (AIDS) patients; a pain reliever in GLAUCOMA patients; and a muscle relaxant for those suffering from MULTIPLE SCLEROSIS, a degenerative disease of the central nervous system.

Chemists developed a synthetic (laboratory-made) tablet, dronabinol (manufactured as Marinol), that contains one of the chemicals found in marijuana. Dronabinol was introduced in 1985 as a Schedule II substance and has since been placed in the Schedule III category, making it as easy to prescribe as codeine. (An entry on codeine is available in this encyclopedia.) Still, some patients found that the dronabinol pills did not work as well as smoking cannabis.

Gonzalez v. Raich. By 2005, ten states had passed "medicinal marijuana" bills, allowing people with certain illnesses to grow or obtain enough marijuana for their own use. But these state laws for medical marijuana conflict with the federal laws against its possession. Late in 2004, two California women brought their petition for medical marijuana to the U.S. Supreme Court.

The Supreme Court case that concerned state laws on medical marijuana use, called *Gonzalez v. Raich,* was decided on June 6, 2005. The Supreme Court ruled 6-3 that Congress has the authority to prohibit the local cultivation of marijuana, even if it is used for medical marijuana, under federal interstate commerce laws. Under federal law, people in states that permit medical marijuana use will not be able to buy the plant form of marijuana or to grow it for their own consumption legally.

After the ruling on June 6, Oregon stopped issuing medical marijuana cards, given to patients with a doctor's prescription through the Oregon Medical Marijuana Program. However, the state continued to process applications. On June 17, 2005, Oregon's attorney general, Hardy Myers, stated that the program would begin issuing the medical marijuana cards again because the Supreme Court ruling did not affect the state's program. Myers did make it clear that though people using medical marijuana through Oregon's program will not be violating state laws, users could still be arrested and prosecuted by the federal government. In addition, Myers said that the state cannot protect patients' caregivers and those growing medical marijuana plants should the federal government decide to prosecute them.

acquired immunodeficiency syndrome (AIDS): an infectious disease that destroys the body's immune system, leading to illness and death

glaucoma: an eye disease that causes increased pressure within the eyeball and can lead to blindness

multiple sclerosis: a progressive illness that affects muscle tissue, leading to pain and inability to move

A medical marijuana patient joins other protesters in California outside the state's capitol in 2002. The group is protesting raids and arrests that have occurred in state-approved and licensed medical marijuana dispensaries.
© *Kim Kulish/Corbis.*

What Is It Made Of?

Marijuana comes from two plants that are so closely related they are probably the same species. The plants are *Cannabis sativa* (marijuana/hemp), and *Cannabis indica,* a bushier variety grown simply for its psychoactive (brain-altering) qualities. Cannabis produces male and female plants, and both of them contain delta-9-tetrahydrocannabinol or THC, the main mind-altering chemical in marijuana. Female plants, especially those that are not

THC: the main active ingredient in cannabis

allowed to pollinate, or fertilize another plant, contain the highest concentrations of THC.

Marijuana smoke contains sixty-one different chemical compounds, called CANNABINOIDS, that are unique to the plant. Scientists are not sure exactly how these compounds interact with THC to produce the effects associated with a marijuana high. They do know that the most important mind-altering compound in cannabis is THC.

The cannabinoid compounds in marijuana can be found throughout the plant—in the leaves and stems, for instance. But the strongest concentrations of THC and other cannabinoids are found in the buds and flowering tops of the female plants. The time of harvest determines the amount of THC in the buds. Female plants that are kept away from male plants will not pollinate and produce seeds. Instead they keep producing flowers that contain a powerful resin—the plant's signal that it wants to pollinate. These resinous buds are the strongest form of marijuana, called SINSEMILLA (the Spanish term for "without seeds").

Purchased on the street, marijuana and sinsemilla are green or brown buds, leaves, or stems. The leaves and stems do not contain the concentrations of THC found in the buds and flowers, but people smoke them to get high.

Hashish is another product of the cannabis plant. It consists of the dried resin from the flower buds and is also very high in THC content. The resin is gathered by hand from the cannabis buds and rolled into gummy balls. Once a quantity of the balls has been collected, they are pressed together into larger cakes or sheets that resemble dark-colored dough. A highly powerful product, hash oil, is produced by boiling hashish or marijuana in a liquid that absorbs THC, such as alcohol, gasoline, or kerosene. The remaining plant material is filtered out, leaving behind thick oil. The color varies from clear to black, with yellows and browns in between. Hash oil contains the highest concentrations of THC. Just a drop or two on an ordinary tobacco cigarette will have an effect similar to smoking a whole dose of marijuana.

Marijuana Growers

Marijuana is grown throughout the United States, even though it is illegal. It is rare to find a state forest or national park anywhere

---

Chemicals in Cannabis

Cannabis contains 421 chemical compounds. Sixty-one of these are unique to the cannabis plant. When smoked, these chemicals work together in ways that scientists do not completely understand. The most important compound is delta-9-tetrahydro-cannabinol (THC). A marijuana cigarette also contains tar, carbon monoxide, and cyanide—similar to a tobacco cigarette.

---

cannabinoids: chemical compounds found in cannabis plants and in small amounts in the brains of humans and animals

sinsemilla: literally, "without seeds"; buds from female marijuana plants carrying the highest concentration of THC

Members of the U.S. Navy and Marines inspect a small boat in the North Arabian Sea near the Persian Gulf in 2004. The military discovered more than 2,800 pounds of narcotics, including hashish, onboard. The raid was planned and carried out by U.S. and coalition forces during the war in Iraq. *AP/Wide World Photos.*

that has not been put to use by anonymous growers. Still, the bulk of the marijuana bought on America's streets comes from Mexico and—increasingly—Canada, where it is grown indoors under ideal conditions.

Hashish also arrives in the United States from Pakistan, Nepal, Afghanistan, and the Middle East. Since it is a federal crime to bring these drugs across U.S. borders, smugglers find many alternative ways to deliver the product into dealers' hands. Most of the Mexican marijuana that arrives in America comes by car or truck, hidden among legal products or even within the upholstery of a vehicle. One group of smugglers got caught trying to bring marijuana into Texas inside coffins.

How Is It Taken?

In order to produce psychoactive effects, marijuana must be heated. People cannot get high just by eating the raw plant material, unless they eat hashish or buds with the highest concentration of THC. Even so, the high produced will be lessened and will establish itself slowly, over a period of hours. Marijuana does not dissolve in water or other room-temperature solvents, so it cannot be injected.

The most common way to use marijuana is to smoke it. Small amounts of marijuana are rolled into cigarette papers and smoked. These are called "spliffs" or "joints." Pipes are also used, both the conventional sort that are made for tobacco and special ones just for marijuana or hashish. More elaborate pipes, called "bongs," pass the smoke through water as the user inhales. Bongs work with tobacco as well as marijuana, but vendors who sell them still run the risk of getting arrested for peddling drug paraphernalia (items used to deliver drugs into the system). Users also hollow out cigars and replace the tobacco with marijuana. These are called "blunts."

Marijuana, or more often hashish, is also baked into food, such as "hash brownies." The cooking process releases the same chemicals that are released while smoking. When eaten, baked hashish products can provide the strongest—and most unpredictable—high. Some users brew marijuana as a tea as well.

Are There Any Medical Reasons for Taking This Substance?

The U.S. government lists marijuana and its by-products as Schedule I substances, indicating that cannabis has no medical value. However, since the 1970s, marijuana has been used as a medicine for several specific conditions, although the legality of this use remains under debate.

Cancer patients who receive CHEMOTHERAPY, the use of chemicals to prevent or treat the disease, often suffer the side effects of nausea, vomiting, and loss of appetite. This can cause people who are already sick to lose weight and become more prone to secondary illnesses. Marijuana stimulates the appetite. Chemotherapy patients who use it are more likely to maintain body weight and suffer less from nausea.

The scientific evidence for these claims has led chemists to create a synthetic form of THC, taken as a pill called Marinol. However, the pills seem to have less effect than smoking the drug. Perhaps this is due to the fact that the pills have to be swallowed and digested, and this can be a problem for cancer sufferers. (Some cancer patients take

chemotherapy: a treatment for cancer that causes nausea, vomiting, and other side effects

A variety of medical marijuana products were offered for sale to those with prescriptions from doctors. Here, medical marijuana is shown in various formats, including cakes and cookies. © Jeff Albertson/Corbis.

Marinol pills prior to chemotherapy.) Also, the pills contain THC, but not the other cannabinoids. Most scientists believe that THC alone does not account for the appetite-enhancing qualities of marijuana.

Marijuana—and Marinol—are also used to enhance the appetite in patients suffering from acquired immunodeficiency syndrome (AIDS). People with AIDS sometimes "waste away" from lack of appetite. Maintaining nutrition can help them stay strong to fight infection. Again, doctors can prescribe Marinol, but the Schedule III drug is not as effective as smoked marijuana.

Evidence suggests that marijuana eases the pain and the symptoms of multiple sclerosis, a progressive disease that affects the muscles. It is also used for a disease of the eyes called glaucoma, where it helps to relieve painful pressure in the eye tissue.

Although it is not prescribed or indicated for use in depression or anxiety, marijuana has been used as a medication for those illnesses in the past. It is unlikely to be re-introduced for this use, however, given the number of modern prescription medications that exist for depression and anxiety.

State vs. Federal Government

The several uses for marijuana as medicine have led some states to pass "medical marijuana" laws. Such laws allow patients with proven medical conditions to possess a small amount of marijuana without facing criminal penalties. These state laws openly contradict the federal law that makes possession of marijuana for any use a crime.

In 2005, a case based on this contradiction was heard by the U.S. Supreme Court. The federal government gained a limited victory in this case on June 6, 2005. The court decided that the federal government could prosecute patients for personal possession and cultivation of marijuana despite state medical marijuana laws. Yet the court did not overturn state medical marijuana laws. This means that although it is a federal crime to possess or grow marijuana, it is not a state crime in those states where medical marijuana has been made legal. According to *CNN.com,* "along with California, nine [other] states have passed laws permitting marijuana use by patients with a doctor's approval: Alaska, Colorado, Hawaii, Maine, Montana, Nevada, Oregon, Vermont and Washington. Arizona also has a similar law, but no formal program in place to administer prescription pot."

Chemists and pharmaceutical companies continue to research delivery systems for marijuana that will be considered legal (if covered by a prescription), including inhalers similar to those used by people suffering from asthma.

Montel Williams on Medical Marijuana

Talk show host Montel Williams spoke on April 11, 2005, about how medical marijuana helps him cope with the symptoms of multiple sclerosis. "Patients struggling for their lives against such illnesses as [multiple sclerosis], cancer and AIDS should not be treated as criminals. We need to get beyond politics. We need more research into marijuana's medicinal effects, and we should heed the research already available." Williams added: "Because of medical marijuana, I am still alive—and leading a far more fruitful life than before." Shortly after making these remarks, Williams testified before Congress on May 5, 2005. One month later, the U.S. Supreme Court decided that medical marijuana use is illegal under federal law.

Usage Trends

Four in ten Americans have used marijuana at least once in their lifetimes. One in ten Americans reports using the drug at least once in the past year, and six in every one hundred Americans report using the drug at least once in the past month. These statistics come from the "2003 National Survey on Drug Use and Health (NSDUH)." According to the NSDUH report, 96.6 *million* Americans have tried marijuana at least once.

The 1999 "National Household Survey on Drug Abuse" reported that the age group *least* likely to have tried marijuana is people over seventy. The group *most* likely to have tried it is eighteen- to twenty-five-year-olds. A Youth Risk Behavior Surveillance System survey conducted in 2001 indicated that 23.9 percent, or just over two in ten people between the ages of ten and twenty-four, had used marijuana in the month before the survey took place. The 2001 survey reported that males were more likely to smoke marijuana than females, but the 2003 NSDUH report said that 53 percent of first-time marijuana users were female. The only large group showing less first-time use of marijuana was Asian Americans. Otherwise the drug is equally popular among African Americans, Caucasians, Native Americans, and Hispanic Americans.

In the 2004 *Monitoring the Future* study, 16.3 percent of eighth graders, 35.1 percent of tenth graders, and 45.7 percent of twelfth graders reported using marijuana at least once. And despite major efforts to find and punish dealers, 73.3 percent of tenth graders and 85.8 percent of twelfth graders noted that marijuana is "fairly easy" or "very easy" to obtain. Clearly, it is nearly impossible to pass through high school without meeting at least one person who uses or sells marijuana.

Although the U.S. government has maintained a policy of strong opposition to marijuana use, the drug has found an appeal across generations. People attending high school in the early part of the twenty-first century are more likely to have parents who tried marijuana than people who attended high school in the 1950s or 1960s. This translates to a more tolerant attitude among *some* parents toward marijuana use in their children. Nevertheless, the 2003 NSDUH survey did find that lifetime use of marijuana is declining among teens.

Effects on the Body

The human brain contains RECEPTORS, specifically for cannabinoids. The brain also produces its own natural cannabinoids, called anandamide (uh-NANN-duh-myd) and 2-arachidonylglycerol (AH-ruh-kid-ON-uhl-GLISS-uh-rol). These two compounds have been found in the brains of animals as well.

receptors: group of cells that receive stimuli

The most common way of using marijuana is to smoke it. Some users roll small amounts of the drug into cigarette papers. These marijuana cigarettes are called spliffs or joints. *Photo by Jim Pozarik/Getty Images.*

What Happens in the Brain

All of the cannabinoid receptors are located in the brain. There are no cannabinoid receptors in the spinal column, so using marijuana does not affect a person's ability to breathe or the function of other organs in the body.

When marijuana is smoked, THC and the other cannabinoids flow to the brain from the lungs, where the compounds are transferred into the bloodstream. The effects begin within minutes, generally with a feeling of light-headedness and euphoria (intense happiness). The user may become less inhibited, more outgoing, and laugh easily. At the same time, the user can experience a loss of motor control and difficulty concentrating. Since most of the cannabinoid receptors are located in the HIPPOCAMPUS, the center of memory and learning, people high on marijuana have difficulty learning new things or remembering what is happening at the moment. Marijuana does not destroy memories that already exist before the user gets high.

The typical marijuana experience is one of euphoria, heightened sensations of music and light, relaxation, and increased appetite.

hippocampus: a part of the brain that is involved in learning and memory

Sometimes, however, even the most experienced users will react differently. The drug can heighten anxiety and create PARANOIA—an uncomfortable feeling of danger or distress. When that happens, the user can do little but ride out the unpleasant experience, which usually happens within two to three hours.

The marijuana high gradually changes to a period of diminished physical activity and communication. The term "stoned" was coined to describe this period. In two to six hours the cannabinoid overload begins to exit the brain, usually causing a spike in appetite along the way. When users get hungry, they are said to have "the munchies."

It is not possible to smoke a fatal dose of marijuana. It *is* possible to consume too much THC by eating baked goods with hashish in them. Still this does not lead to death, but rather to a possibly unpleasant "trip" with paranoid or psychotic (extremely frightening) episodes. Again, no antidote to cannabis exists except trying to get the victim to vomit the undigested portion of the baked goods.

Effects on Judgment, Memory, and Learning

There is no such thing as a safe recreational drug. A person high on marijuana has the same lack of judgment, poor coordination, and diminished sense of fear as a person drunk on whiskey. The leading cause of death for young people is automobile crashes—and sometimes those fatal crashes are caused by marijuana, or a combination of marijuana and other drugs or alcohol. Marijuana impairs the ability to drive, operate machinery, or judge dangerous situations. As such, it can be deadly.

Because marijuana affects memory and learning, daily use can undermine a student's ability in school or a worker's capability on the job. Although scientists have debunked the old caution that marijuana affects motivation, the drug does affect short-term memory and the brain's ability to process new material. People who smoke marijuana regularly almost always experience declines in grades and difficulties in the classroom related to the drug use.

THC, the most active component of marijuana, remains in the body long after the psychoactive effects have worn off. The body stores THC in its fat cells. After one use, a person will test positive for THC for as many as three days. With regular use, a person can test positive for THC even after abstaining from marijuana for four weeks. The drug tests available at the turn of the twenty-first century were sophisticated enough that they do not yield a positive result for "passive" marijuana smoking (just being around other people who

paranoia: abnormal feelings of suspicion and fear

In late 2004 Australian police began stopping motorists randomly to conduct saliva tests. The test checks salivia for various illegal drugs, including marijuana and amphetamines. *Photograph by Trevor Pinder/Newspix/ Getty Images.*

are using the drug). Thus, law enforcement officers will not accept that as a defense. As Paul M. Gahlinger stated in his book, "If the drug test is positive for marijuana, the only legitimate excuse is either the use of dronabinol or, if allowed, the use of medically prescribed marijuana."

What Happens in the Lungs

Marijuana smoke contains the same cancer-causing compounds as tobacco, including tar, benzanthrene (ben-ZANN-threen), and benzpyrene (benz-PIE-reen). Since marijuana smokers inhale more deeply—and because joints, pipes, and blunts do not contain filters—the user exposes the lungs to more of the cancer-causing agents. Smoking marijuana daily or even occasionally for a period of years increases the risk of lung cancer. Smoking both marijuana *and* tobacco greatly increases that risk.

Link to Mental Illness?

A study released in 2005 by the Office of National Drug Control Policy found that people who begin smoking marijuana at a young age—between ten and fourteen—run a high risk of mental problems later in life. The study found that between 8 and 9 percent of the general population develop serious mental illnesses in adulthood. For people who begin using marijuana before the age of twelve, the chances of developing mental illness leap to 21 percent. Two reasons could account for this. First, marijuana could have a bad effect on the developing brain. Second, someone tempted to use marijuana at such a young age might already be predisposed to have emotional or psychological problems. Also, a significant percentage of heavy marijuana users may be "self-medicating" to treat a variety of mental conditions. These conditions include anxiety, phobias, or depression.

Withdrawal from marijuana is not terribly difficult, even after heavy use. The symptoms of marijuana withdrawal include insomnia, anxiety, decreased appetite, and irritability. Usually these symptoms go away within a few weeks if the user does not return to the drug.

A "Gateway Drug"?

For several decades marijuana has been described as a "gateway drug"—one that leads users to experiment with more dangerous, more addictive substances. That theory has been dismissed, however. Most people use marijuana and then stop taking *any* illegal drugs. Far fewer progress to other substances. So it could just as easily be said that marijuana is an "end stage" drug. Again, the individual person's mental makeup determines whether or not marijuana use will lead to harder drugs. People with family histories of mental problems, alcoholism, anxiety, or depression should try to avoid *every* psychoactive substance, including legal ones like alcohol and nicotine. (Entries for alcohol and nicotine are available in this encyclopedia.) For anxious or depressed people, better treatments exist than marijuana use.

Reactions with Other Drugs or Substances

One of the biggest problems with any illegal substance is the variation in quality. Some sources say that marijuana produced in the twenty-first century is far stronger than that smoked in previous decades. Others say the doses are about the same. Whatever the case, each purchase of illegal marijuana carries dangers related to the strength of the product, the possible by-products, and the methods of preparation. Outdoor-grown marijuana might have been sprayed with pesticides that still linger on the leaves and buds. The plants might also have fungus or even bacteria from the unclean hands that picked or packed them.

Dealers sell marijuana joints containing PCP, a hallucinogen, or crack cocaine. FRY STICKS are joints dipped in formaldehyde, a chemical compound used as a preservative and disinfectant. All of these combinations have proven fatal in users. In November of 2004, the Newark *Star-Ledger* reported the death of a seventeen-year-old who ran naked across a busy highway and hurled himself through a glass window after smoking a fry stick. The young man died of the injuries he sustained from crashing through the glass.

Mixing marijuana and alcohol heightens the effects of each substance and can lead to reckless behavior. Mixing marijuana with amphetamines or even tobacco can increase the heart rate, possibly causing heart damage or stroke.

Treatment for Habitual Users

More people are treated in rehabilitation programs for marijuana use than for any other drug. This is partly because more people are arrested for marijuana possession and ordered into treatment by the courts. Whatever the case, marijuana users—even heavy marijuana users—can usually free themselves of the drug fairly easily if they have no history of other drug or alcohol abuse. The situation becomes more complicated when marijuana has been combined with other powerful drugs such as cocaine or an opiate, like heroin or morphine.

Some people do become physically addicted to marijuana and experience withdrawal symptoms when they stop using it. For most people, use is a psychological habit and is sometimes a form of self-treatment for anxiety, depression, phobias, panic attacks, or other serious mental illnesses. When people find themselves spending more time buying, smoking, and becoming stoned on the drug than they do studying, socializing with friends and family, or working, they should seriously consider getting professional help to stop their marijuana use. Such help includes examination by a medical doctor and therapy with a psychologist or psychiatrist who can help find the root causes and proper treatment for the drug abuse. Self-help twelve-step programs such as Narcotics Anonymous also provide opportunities to beat the drug with the help of others who have experienced similar addiction problems.

fry sticks: marijuana cigarettes laced with formaldehyde, a chemical used to keep dead tissue from decaying

Consequences

Buying, selling, and using recreational marijuana is illegal. Penalties for marijuana possession vary from state to state and from country to country. The penalties are often based on the amount of marijuana found; whether the person intended to sell the marijuana; and whether the person was intoxicated at the time of the arrest. However, even first-time marijuana convictions can wreck a life. For instance, someone convicted of marijuana possession will lose any federal financial aid they might be receiving to attend college. (In contrast, theft conviction—perhaps of a laptop—does not automatically result in loss of financial aid.) In some states, employers are notified when someone is caught with marijuana. Almost half the states in the nation suspend the driver's license of anyone convicted of marijuana possession, though the length of the suspension varies from state to state and depends on the circumstances and number of offenses.

Judges usually sentence marijuana users to high fines, community service, and drug tests for up to a year, just with a first conviction. Second convictions, or possession with intent to sell, can land a person in jail. Judges can also order marijuana users into treatment programs. Whatever the penalties, the marijuana user has earned a criminal record that will impact future job opportunities, the ability to drive legally, and educational choices.

Legal consequences aside, long-term users of marijuana will find that it affects their ability to learn, remember, and concentrate. THC stays in the body long after the high has worn off, and it can continue to impact the brain. Additionally, some of the ingredients in a marijuana cigarette are known CARCINOGENS, or cancer-causing agents. People who smoke marijuana run a higher risk of lung cancer than those who do not.

Habitual use of marijuana can either mask or aggravate symptoms of mental illness. People prone to PSYCHOSIS, a severe mental disorder, can have bad reactions to a marijuana high. People who are depressed or anxious may lean on the drug to ease their symptoms, rather than find the professional help they need for their illnesses.

carcinogens: chemicals that can cause cancer in the body

psychosis: pronounced sy-KOH-sis; a severe mental disorder that often causes hallucinations and makes it difficult for people to distinguish what is real from what is imagined

The Law

By the end of 2004, ten American states had passed "medical marijuana" laws. The details of these laws vary from state to state, but they usually require a doctor's written prescription for marijuana use and documentation of the illness for which the marijuana is

In the News: Marijuana Lollipops and a Secret Tunnel

In the summer of 2005, two marijuana-related stories made the headlines. The first involved manufacturers of marijuana-flavored lollipops. Sold under names such as Chronic Candy, Pot Suckers, and Purple Haze, these lollipops are flavored with hemp oil. The oil makes the candies taste like pot, but it does not bring on a high when consumed. Even though the products are considered legal, some convenience stores throughout the United States reportedly agreed to stop selling them. This action came after the city of Chicago banned them in mid-July.

Around the same time, a 360-foot-long tunnel used for transporting marijuana between Canada and the United States was shut down. The secret tunnel led from a hut on Canadian land to an opening underneath a house in Lynden, Washington, a town very close to the border separating the two countries. Canadian authorities knew about the tunnel's construction for several months and tipped off U.S. officials, who monitored activity in the area throughout the spring and early summer.

U.S. agents moved in and sealed off the tunnel after capturing evidence on tape of its use as a drug-smuggling passageway. Three men from British Columbia were arrested for importing marijuana into the United States. Two other individuals in the state of Washington were also arrested after being caught with approximately 100 pounds of marijuana from the tunnel in their vehicles.

---

recommended. In some states, patients carry cards that identify them as medical marijuana users. These users must either grow their own plants or find a state-sanctioned grower who can prove that the marijuana is only grown for medical use, and only distributed within the boundaries of that state. Doctors who misidentify patients and permit medical marijuana use where it does not apply face criminal penalties.

On June 6, 2005, the U.S. Supreme Court ruled that under federal law, even in states where "medical marijuana" laws existed, all use of medical marijuana was illegal. Yet later that month, Hardy Myers, Oregon's attorney general, said that under Oregon state law, medical marijuana cultivation and medical use was still legal. This meant that the state would not prosecute growers and users of medical marijuana, but that the federal government could, and the state could not offer protection against the federal laws.

All other use of marijuana in all states is considered a crime. Some states have very stiff penalties even for first-time users. Other states allow first-time users to pay fines and undergo drug testing and counseling. In New Jersey, for instance, the 2003 penalty for a first arrest on marijuana possession was $1,000 and a year of drug testing. Students caught with marijuana lose any federal financial aid they might be receiving for college. If still in high school, the student will not qualify for federal financial aid.

Because marijuana is such a popular recreational drug, federal and state prisons are full of people who have been caught dealing it. Sometimes these dealers face longer jail terms than people convicted of armed robbery or manslaughter. Repeat offenders can be sent to jail for life.

For More Information

Books

Earleywine, Mitch. *Understanding Marijuana: A New Look at the Scientific Evidence.* New York: Oxford University Press, 2002.

Gahlinger, Paul M. *Illegal Drugs: A Complete Guide to Their History, Chemistry, Use and Abuse.* Las Vegas, NV: Sagebrush Press, 2001.

Kuhn, Cynthia, Scott Swartzwelder, and Wilkie Wilson. *Buzzed: The Straight Facts about the Most Used and Abused Drugs from Alcohol to Ecstasy,* 2nd ed. New York: W.W. Norton Company, 2003.

Zimmer, Lynn, and John P. Morgan. *Marijuana Myths, Marijuana Facts: A Review of the Scientific Evidence.* New York: The Lindesmith Center, 1997.

Periodicals

Agar, John. "Driver Sent to Prison for Teen's Death." *Grand Rapids Press* (January 22, 2005): p. 3.

Bauer, Jeff. "Marijuana Abuse and Dependence Is on the Rise." *RN* (July, 2004), p. 18.

"Counseling to Prevent Motor Vehicle Injuries." *American Family Physician* (May, 1990), p. 1465.

"Employee's Use of Medical Marijuana May Justify Dismissal." *Fair Employment Practices Guidelines* (February, 2005), p. 6.

Gluck, Gabriel H. "Police Test for Drugs after Teen's Death: Laced Marijuana Possible in Mountainside Incident." *Star-Ledger* (November 12, 2004), p. 29.

Greenburg, Jan Crawford. "Supreme Court Hears Arguments on Medical Marijuana Use." *Chicago Tribune* (November 30, 2004).

Klein, Naomi. "Canada: Hippie Nation?" *The Nation* (July 21, 2003), p. 12.

"Not So Dopey: Marijuana as Medicine." *The Economist* (April 9, 2005), p. 69.

"Researchers Say Marijuana Addiction Is Up." *UPI News Track* (May 5, 2004).

Richey, Warren. "Showdown over Medical Marijuana: The Supreme Court Hears a California Case Monday That Could Become a Signature Decision of the Rehnquist Era." *Christian Science Monitor* (November 29, 2004), p. 2.

Salooja, Anjali. "A New Generation of Lollipops." *Newsweek* (July 18, 2005): p. 12.

Williams, Montel. "Turning Patients into Criminals." *Cincinnati Post* (April 11, 2005), p. A10.

"Youth Risk Behavior Surveillance: United States, 2001." *Journal of School Health* (October, 2002), p. 313.

Web Sites

"2003 National Survey on Drug Use and Health (NSDUH)." *Substance Abuse and Mental Health Services Administration (SAMHSA).* http://www.drugabusestatistics.samhsa.gov (accessed July 29, 2005).

"Admissions to Treatment for Marijuana Abuse Increase Sharply" (March 4, 2005). *U.S. Department of Health and Human Services, Substance Abuse and Mental Health Services Administration.* http://www.samhsa.gov/news/newsreleases/050304nr_mjtx.htm (accessed July 29, 2005).

"Attorney General Issues Advice on Medical Marijuana Program" (June 17, 2005). *State of Oregon, Department of Justice.* http://www.doj.state.or.us/releases/rel061705.htm (accessed July 30, 2005).

"Catholic Encyclopedia: Marco Polo." *Catholic Encyclopedia.* http://www.newadvent.org/cathen/12217a.htm (accessed July 29, 2005).

"Cops Find 610 Pounds of Pot in Coffins." *USA Today,* December 16, 2004. http://www.usatoday.com/news/offbeat/2004-12-16-caskets_x.htm (accessed July 29, 2005).

Courson, Paul. "Research: Youth Risks Mental Health with Pot Use." *CNN.com,* May 3, 2005. http://www.cnn.com/2005/HEALTH/05/03/pot.risk/ (accessed August 1, 2005).

Frieden, Terry. "Drug Tunnel Found Under Canada Border." *CNN.com,* July 22, 2005. http://www.cnn.com/2005/US/07/21/border.tunnel/index.html (accessed August 1, 2005).

Johnson, Gene. "Feds Shut Down Drug-Smuggling Tunnel." *Washington-Post.com,* July 22, 2005. http://www.washingtonpost.com/wp-dyn/content/article/2005/07/22/AR2005072200217_pf.html (accessed August 1, 2005).

"The Link Between Marijuana and Mental Illness" (May 5, 2005). *Office of National Drug Control Policy, Executive Office of the President.* http://www.mediacampaign.org/pdf/marij_mhealth.pdf (accessed August 2, 2005.

"Marijuana." *Office of National Drug Control Policy.* http://www.whitehousedrugpolicy.gov/drugfact/marijuana/index.html (accessed July 29, 2005).

"Marijuana May Increase Risk of Psychosis." *MSNBC.com,* December 1, 2004. http://www.msnbc.msn.com/id/6629828/ (accessed July 29, 2005).

Mears, Bill. "Supreme Court Allows Prosecution of Medical Marijuana." *CNN.com,* June 7, 2005. http://www.CNN.com/2005/LAW/06/06/scotus.medical.marijuana/ (accessed July 28, 2005).

"Media Campaign Fact Sheets: Marijuana and Mental Health." *Office of National Drug Control Policy, National Youth Anti-Drug Media Campaign.* http://www.mediacampaign.org/newsroom/factsheets/marij_mhealth.html (accessed August 1, 2005).

Monitoring the Future. http://www.monitoringthefuture.org/and http://www.nida.nih.gov/Newsroom/04/2004MTFDrug.pdf (both accessed August 31, 2005).

"National Household Survey on Drug Abuse: 1999." *U.S. Department of Health and Human Services, Substance Abuse and Mental Health Services Administration.* http://www.samhsa.gov/news/newsreleases/000831nrhousehold.htm (accessed August 1, 2005).

"Oregon Resumes Issuing Medical Marijuana Cards." *NorthWest Cable News,* June 17, 2005. http://www.nwcn.com/health/stories/NW_061705ORNmarijuanacardsLJ.1c1da52a.html (accessed July 30, 2005).

"Pot-Flavored Candy Takes a Licking." *MSNBC.com,* June 25, 2005. http://www.msnbc.msn.com/id/8305249/ (accessed August 1, 2005).

"Survey: Parents Mellowing over Kids' Drugs." *MSNBC.com,* February 22, 2005. http://www.msnbc.msn.com/id/7010947/ (accessed July 29, 2005).

"Teens Targeted in Drugged Driving Campaign." *MSNBC.com,* December 3, 2004. http://www.msnbc.msn.com/id/6639590 (accessed July 29, 2005).

Other

Hugh Downs Commentary on Marijuana. *ABC News,* broadcast November 1990.

See also: Nicotine

Melatonin

What Kind of Drug Is It?

Melatonin is a dietary supplement sold without a prescription at U.S. health stores or through Web sites. It is sold primarily as a sleep aid because it induces sleep. Researchers have studied melatonin's potential benefits for certain conditions, such as insomnia (difficulty sleeping); jet lag; and even cancer (the uncontrolled, abnormal growth of cells that can lead to serious illness and death).

However, taking melatonin supplements has not been proven by scientific studies to be effective for any condition. Much more research needs to be done to prove the positive claims of melatonin use. Also, because it is considered a dietary supplement, it is not regulated by the U.S. Food and Drug Administration (FDA). This means that the supplements are not produced under the strict guidelines of the FDA, so their side effects and long-term effects are not clearly known.

Melatonin is a hormone—a substance created by the body to control certain bodily functions. It is found naturally in humans and other animals. It is secreted by the pineal (PY-nee-uhl) gland, which is located in the middle of the brain. Melatonin helps to regulate when animals, including humans, fall asleep and when they wake up. This sleep/wake cycle is known as the circadian rhythm (sir-KAY-dee-in RIH-thum), the twenty-four-hour sleep/wake cycle in humans and other animals. Some people believe that taking melatonin supplements can help alleviate problems that can occur when this cycle is disrupted.

Overview

Sleeping is a part of life. It allows the body to rest and repair itself after physical activity. Ruth Winter, writing in *The Anti-Aging Hormones: That Can Help You Beat the Clock,* stated that "most people need at least seven and a half hours [of sleep] to function adequately and be fully alert the next day, but some may need as little as five while others need nine to ten hours." Lack of sleep can cause a host of problems such as fatigue and poor mood. Thus, it is important to have a normal sleep/wake cycle for good health.

Official Drug Name: Melatonin, 5-methoxy-N-acetyltryptamine
Also Known As: Mel, Melliquid, mellow tonin, MLT, somniset
Drug Classifications: Not scheduled

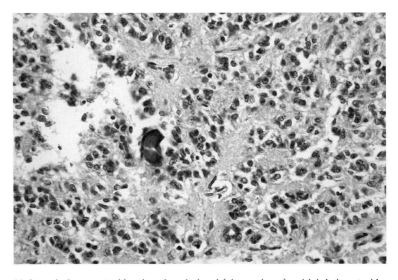

Melatonin is secreted by the pineal gland (shown here), which is located in the middle of the brain. © *Dr. Frederick Skvara/Visuals Unlimited.*

Melatonin plays an active role in maintaining a regular schedule for sleeping and waking. It induces sleep when it is secreted into the bloodstream by the pineal gland, a pea-sized gland that is part of the ENDOCRINE SYSTEM. Darkness stimulates its secretion, while light, both natural and artificial, inhibits it.

The Dracula of Hormones

Melatonin has been called the "Dracula of hormones" because, like the vampire Dracula, it only comes out at night. Usually around 9 P.M., after daylight fades away and darkness arrives, the pineal gland begins releasing melatonin, causing sleepiness and initiating a decline in body temperature. The hormone is continually released throughout the night as the body sleeps until about 9 A.M. the next morning, when it is light again. Peak production occurs approximately between 2 A.M. and 4 A.M.

In the morning, when light hits the RETINA, messages are sent to the HYPOTHALAMUS in the brain. In the hypothalamus, the messages find the suprachiasmatic (SOO-pruh-ky-uhz-MAH-tik) nucleus (SCN), prompting the SCN to send signals to the glands that control hormones, including the pineal gland. When the pineal gland receives a message from the SCN, it slows down the release of melatonin until darkness comes and it is time to sleep again. Daytime melatonin levels are so small they are usually undetectable. The decrease of melatonin in the morning signals the body temperature to rise, and the body feels awake and alert.

endocrine system: the bodily system made of glands that secrete hormones into the bloodstream to control certain bodily functions

retina: a sensory membrane in the eye

hypothalamus: a region of the brain that secretes hormones

Discovering Melatonin

For centuries, the function of the pineal gland was unknown. This was partly due to the fact that melatonin is created in very small amounts, smaller than any other hormone, and is hard to detect. In the 1950s, Yale University dermatologist Dr. Aaron Lerner was conducting research on skin pigmentation, or color. Thinking the pineal gland may be involved in skin pigmentation, he began the process of trying to isolate a molecule from this gland that he believed may be responsible for lightening skin. In 1958, Lerner was finally successful in isolating a molecule from the pineal gland.

Because the molecule is chemically related to melanin (skin pigment) and SEROTONIN, Lerner named his discovery melatonin. Though melatonin lightened the skin of frogs, it did not affect the color of the skin of humans. In the end, Lerner did not find a molecule that would help his research, but he did help answer the mystery of the pineal gland. He discovered a very powerful hormone that has helped researchers understand more about the human sleep/wake cycle.

After Lerner's discovery, other scientists began testing melatonin to see what benefits it may have. They found that injecting synthetic (human-made) melatonin into people could cause a tranquilizing effect and induce sleep. From there, more studies were done, and eventually melatonin was made into a dietary supplement that could be self-administered.

The Melatonin Craze

In the mid-1990s, when melatonin supplements became available without a prescription, a frenzy over the possible benefits of taking these supplements occurred. Some called it a "miracle" or "wonder" drug. Many praised it as an immune-booster, a youth serum, a cancer-fighter, and a cure for insomnia.

Various books were written about the wonders of melatonin. The craze eventually died down, and, as of the early twenty-first century, research has not been able to prove or disprove the benefits of melatonin. In 2000, University of Surrey's Josephine Arendt discussed the supplement. As quoted by Elizabeth Cohen in "Study Bolsters Melatonin Sleep Claims" on *CNN.com,* Arendt stated that "the hype and claims of the so-called miraculous powers of melatonin several years ago did a great disservice to a scientific field of real importance."

Melatonin as a Supplement

In 1994 melatonin became available over the counter as a dietary supplement. Manufacturers claimed melatonin could bring on sleep, ease jet lag, and more. Studies have been conducted and books written on the potential benefits of melatonin, but no one has been able to prove or disprove these claims. Most research suggests that melatonin can help regulate the sleep/wake cycle for conditions such as insomnia and jet lag, as well as problems from shift work (people working at night and sleeping during the day). It has also been regarded as an ANTIOXIDANT and an immune-booster. Some people believe it also combats aging.

serotonin: a combination of carbon, hydrogen, nitrogen, and oxygen; it is found in the brain, blood, and stomach lining and acts as a neurotransmitter and blood vessel regulator

antioxidant: a chemical that neutralizes free radicals (chemicals with an unpaired electron) that can damage other cells

The Trouble with L-tryptophan

Tryptophan is an essential amino acid from which melatonin is made in the body. It was once available as a dietary supplement, known as L-tryptophan. Much like melatonin, it was marketed as a sleep aid. However, in 1989, a batch of L-tryptophan pills (all made in Japan) was contaminated and caused 1,500 people to contract the disease eosinophilia-myalgia syndrome (EMS; pronounced ee-oh-sin-oh-FIH-lee-uh my-AL-jee-uh). EMS causes weakness, severe muscle and joint pain, headaches, fever, and shortness of breath. More than thirty people died from the disease in the United States. The FDA banned L-tryptophan, and from that point on Americans had to get tryptophan from food sources.

Some foods that contain tryptophan include the following:
- Almonds
- Bananas
- Chicken
- Cottage Cheese
- Eggs
- Ice Cream
- Milk
- Peanuts
- Shrimp
- Soy Nuts
- Tofu
- Tuna
- Turkey
- Yogurt

What Is It Made Of?

Melatonin is a hormone found naturally in the human body, in other animals, in certain plants, and even in some foods. It is made from tryptophan (TRIP-tuh-fan), an ESSENTIAL AMINO ACID. When tryptophan is ingested, the body turns it into serotonin that is then made into melatonin. The pineal gland is the primary location for melatonin production but the retina and intestines make small amounts as well.

Melatonin supplements are either synthetic (human-made) or natural (contain animal products). They are chemically identical to the melatonin that is produced by the human body. Some people think that using the natural melatonin, typically made from the pineal glands of animals such as sheep, run a greater risk of being contaminated by a virus. Therefore, the synthetic version is the most recommended and most popular form of melatonin. However, since the FDA does not regulate it, one can never be sure of the effectiveness, purity, or safety of the supplement.

As a supplement, melatonin consists of much higher amounts of the hormone than are naturally secreted at any one time in the body. A single dose is usually 500 micrograms to 5 milligrams per dose, more than 10 times higher than what is normal in the human body.

essential amino acid: an amino acid that is only found in food; amino acids make up proteins

A scientist wears a protective suit as he makes up a batch of melatonin in a laboratory in the United Kingdom. © *Bryn Colton/Assignments Photographers/Corbis.*

Studies have not shown the high doses cause greater benefit or greater risk to the body. However, a doctor should be consulted before taking any supplement.

Age Factors

Before reaching puberty, children create the largest amounts of melatonin, with the highest levels between the ages of four and seven. At puberty, melatonin production begins to slow down and gradually decreases to an average of about 30 micrograms per day. Some researchers suggest that the decrease in the level of melatonin at puberty may be related to the fact that the child is maturing sexually.

Research findings have been inconsistent about whether or not melatonin continues to diminish with age. A number of scientists believe that melatonin production decreases as the body ages, which might explain why elderly people have greater sleep problems. However, a study by Dr. J. B. Fourtillan, published in the January 2001 issue of *American Journal of Physiology,* indicated that the levels of melatonin did not differ between a group of 34 healthy adults over age 65 and a group of 101 healthy adults under age 30.

How Is It Taken?

Melatonin is sold over the counter as a dietary supplement. It is available in pill form (tablets or capsules), as a cream or tea, or as a lozenge that can be dissolved under the tongue. Time-release capsules are also sold. Such capsules release the melatonin slowly over time after the dose is ingested. Manufacturers provide a range of doses. A person should consult a physician about the proper dose and how long to take the supplement as results can vary for each individual. Typical doses fall in the range of 0.1 milligram to 10 milligrams. However, a noticeable difference in effectiveness usually is not seen in doses over 5 milligrams. A person normally takes melatonin only a few days at a time.

The time of day that the supplement is taken also plays an important role in melatonin's effectiveness. Usually, melatonin is taken right before bedtime. Taking melatonin during the day has minimal effect other than drowsiness. In the treatment of jet lag, it is recommended that melatonin be taken on the day of travel and then for a few days after arrival at the destination.

Are There Any Medical Reasons for Taking This Substance?

Many studies suggest that taking melatonin may have positive effects on a number of human ailments, especially sleep-related conditions. However, such studies have not shown that taking melatonin supplements will result in healing or prevention of these ailments. More research needs to be completed in order to really know what melatonin supplements can do for the human body.

Helping the Blind

As reported by Elizabeth Cohen on *CNN.com,* a study on the blind was conducted by scientists at Oregon Health Sciences University. The blind tend to suffer sleep problems due to their inability to detect the daily light and dark cycles. The study revealed that the blind had more regular sleep cycles after taking melatonin. The scientists concluded that melatonin could help the sleep patterns of those who can see as well. However, one of the scientists, Dr. Al Lewy, pointed out the importance of knowing when, how, and why to take melatonin.

"The concern I have," the doctor remarked, "is that people have been taking melatonin at the wrong time at the wrong dose for the wrong reasons."

Usage Trends

According to the Agency for Healthcare Research and Quality in "Melatonin for Treatment of Sleep Disorders," "Studies suggest that sleep disorders affect 50 to 70 million Americans, representing 20 percent of the population." Since naturally occurring melatonin induces sleep, many people take melatonin supplements to help combat these sleep disorders. Cohen claimed that in the year 2000 more than 20 million Americans took melatonin supplements to help regulate their sleep. In addition to taking melatonin for sleep-related problems, people may also be taking melatonin for its supposed benefits for a number of other conditions.

Insomnia

Insomnia is a sleep disorder in which a person has difficulty falling or staying asleep. As reported in "Melatonin for Treatment of Sleep Disorders," insomnia affects 6 to 12 percent of adults. Medical treatment for insomnia can include taking sleep aids, like benzodiazepines, in order to help the patient fall asleep. (A separate entry on benzodiazepine is available in this encyclopedia.) Relaxation techniques are also used. Some researchers believe that melatonin supplements can be used in the treatment of insomnia as well. However, other researchers have not found melatonin to have much effect at all on those suffering from insomnia.

There is some promising news for those who suffer from a form of insomnia called delayed sleep phase syndrome (DSPS). People with this condition have a sleep/wake cycle that has them set to fall asleep much later in the night, like 4 A.M., and rise much later the following day, like noon. According to "Melatonin for Treatment of Sleep Disorders," when taking melatonin supplements, the time it takes to fall asleep "decreased greatly in people with delayed sleep phase syndrome." This finding was considered "clinically significant." However, the time it takes to fall asleep only "decreased marginally in patients with insomnia," which was considered "clinically insignificant."

Jet Lag

People need to adjust their watches to the local time when they travel through time zones. But humans also need their body clocks, or sleep/wake cycles, to adjust to the local time as well. Being out of

Stanford University students are shown taking part in a research study on jet lag. They had their temperature and heart rate monitored after a flight from California to Tokyo. Jet lag—or being out of synch with the time zone—can result in feeling tired, being awake, or being hungry at odd hours of the day. © Louie Psihoyos/Corbis.

synch with the new time zone can result in feeling tired or awake or hungry at all the wrong times. An out-of-synch body clock, coupled with a lack of sleep during a flight that has crossed multiple time zones, can result in "jet lag." Symptoms of jet lag can include:

- Constipation or diarrhea
- Disorientation
- Dry cough, eyes, and skin
- Earache
- Fatigue
- Headache
- Impaired concentration, coordination, or vision
- Insomnia
- Irritability

- Loss of appetite
- Low mood
- Memory loss
- Nausea
- Sore throat
- Swollen feet

Melatonin supplements are thought to help reduce jet lag by helping the body clock more rapidly adjust to the new time zone.

Shift Work

A large number of people work during the hours that most people sleep. Having to be awake and alert during the time when the body normally should be sleeping can cause problems in a person's sleep/wake cycle. Melanie Johns Cupp in *American Family Physician* pointed out that in a "trial involving 27 shift workers, melatonin was found capable of 'resetting' sleep patterns to match the change in schedule in approximately one half of the patients tested."

Seasonal Affective Disorder (SAD)

Seasonal affective disorder, or SAD, is a mood disorder that causes depression in the winter months when the days are shorter and less light is available. Symptoms include low mood, irritability, fatigue, weight gain, and cravings for carbohydrates— like pasta, potatoes, or bread. Some researchers suggest that SAD is caused by elevated melatonin levels at the wrong times (i.e., not at bedtime) and that taking melatonin supplements may help regulate its production. Other studies have found melatonin does not help curb the symptoms of SAD and may actually make the symptoms worse. Light therapy (going outside in natural light or looking at artificial light) is another form of treatment for SAD sufferers.

Cancer

Researchers have studied a number of ways that melatonin may be helpful in fighting cancer. Some evidence suggests that melatonin may help regulate other hormones. Therefore, it may be helpful with cancers that are triggered by hormones like estrogen, such as breast cancer, or testosterone, such as prostate

---

Melatonin and Jet Lag

To help combat jet lag, according to *Health Services at Columbia: Go Ask Alice!*, it is suggested that a person take melatonin at the start of and during a trip at specific times in order to achieve the best results. If traveling east, a person, on the day of travel, should take one dose of melatonin between 6 and 7 P.M. of his or her normal time zone. At the destination, the person should take one dose of melatonin during the first five days at bedtime (between 9 and 10 P.M.) of the local time.

When traveling west, a person should take one dose of melatonin at the local bedtime after arriving at the destination, and continue to do so for the next four days. Melatonin has not been proven to help when traveling less than five time zones to the west.

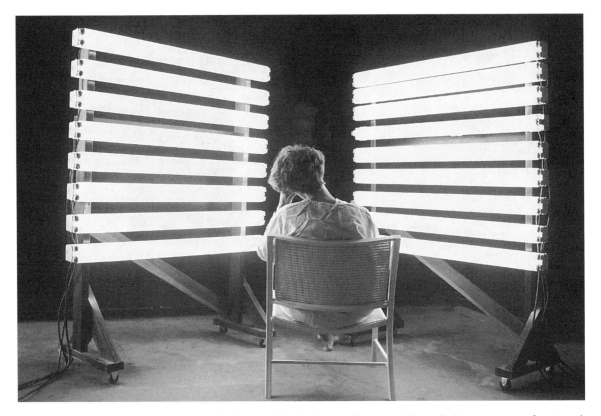

Whether melatonin does or does not help curb the symptoms of seasonal affective disorder (SAD) is still debated. Light therapy (going outside in natural light or looking at artificial light) is also used to treat SAD. A mood disorder, SAD causes depression during the wintertime when there is less sunshine. © *Louie Psihoyos/Corbis.*

cancer. Melatonin has also been described as an immune-booster and antioxidant. Having a stronger immune system and a greater ability to fight off cancer-causing free radicals can aid in fighting cancer.

According to the University of Maryland Medical Center, other conditions thought to be improved by melatonin (although with limited or no research support), include: 1) osteoporosis—fragile bones; 2) menopause—a period in a woman's life in which menstruation ends; 3) eating disorders; 4) epilepsy—a disorder causing seizures; 5) heart disease; 6) inflammatory diseases; 7) attention-deficit/hyperactivity disorder (ADHD); and 8) sunburn. Others claim that melatonin can improve life span, aid a person trying to stop smoking, and help with benzodiazepine withdrawal.

Effects on the Body

Because research has not been able to prove or disprove the benefits of supplemental melatonin, it is difficult to pinpoint all of the effects it has on the body. If taken at the proper time, usually bedtime, melatonin has been shown to help regulate sleep. However, using too much melatonin or not using it according to directions could hinder instead of help the body's sleep/wake cycle.

Though found naturally in the human body, melatonin, if taken as a supplement, can have certain side effects. These include sleepiness, headache and dizziness, nausea, stomach cramps, irritability, and depression. Users claim it causes more intense dreams, even nightmares. Melatonin has also been found to prevent OVULATION. Some women have even used it to avoid getting pregnant. Overall, no serious side effects have been reported, and no long-term effects, negative or positive, have been proven.

The Fountain of Youth?

Some researchers believe that melatonin holds the key to a longer life. Walter Pierpaoli, William Regelson, and Carol Colman reported in their book *The Melatonin Miracle: Nature's Age-Reversing, Disease-Fighting, Sex-Enhancing Hormone,* that "melatonin is a potent age-reversing compound." They added that "we are confident that melatonin's primary benefit is in its ability to prevent disease by preventing the downward spiral that leads to illness." Their beliefs stem from research with mice, including studies that revealed mice that had improved health and longer lives as a result of taking melatonin. They also cited studies that showed older mice live longer when given pineal glands from younger mice and that the younger mice with the older pineal glands die at an earlier age. However, no studies on humans have been done that conclude that melatonin helps diminish the aging process.

Reactions with Other Drugs or Substances

Melatonin is not recommended for users who are taking antidepressants, corticosteroids (steroids used to counteract inflammation), blood pressure medication, or drugs that suppress the immune system, as it may reduce the other medicine's effects. Taking melatonin along with other sleep aids should be avoided although melatonin may be helpful in getting through withdrawal from the highly addictive benzodiazepines.

ovulation: the release of an egg from an ovary

Melatonin is a dietary supplement sold without a prescription at U.S. health stores or through Web sites. Its main use is as a sleep aid. © *James Leynse/Corbis.*

Withdrawal is the process of gradually cutting back on the amount of a drug being taken until it can be stopped entirely.

Melatonin has also been suggested as an aid in quitting smoking. In addition, certain drugs and substances have been found to lower the level of melatonin in the body. These include alcohol, caffeine, tobacco, some high blood pressure medications including beta-blockers, and anti-inflammatories such as ibuprofen. Amphetamines and cocaine may raise the level of melatonin in the body.

Treatment for Habitual Users

There is no treatment available for habitual users of melatonin. This supplement has not been proven to be an addictive substance, nor have any studies been conducted on whether or not a person can build up a tolerance to it or suffer any withdrawal symptoms when stopping its use. Tolerance is a condition in which higher and higher doses of a drug are needed to produce the original effect.

Consequences

Hormones are very powerful. They control the functions of many parts of the body naturally. Even though melatonin is considered a dietary supplement and is available without a prescription, it is important to consult with a physician before taking any hormones. A press release by Robert Sanders in *UCBerkeleyNews* notes that George E. Bentley, an assistant professor of integrative biology, has conducted research on melatonin and its effects in the brain. According to Bentley: "It really amazes me that melatonin is available in any pharmacy." He continued, "It is a powerful hormone, and yet people don't realize that it's as 'powerful' as any steroid. I'm sure that many people who take it wouldn't take steroids so glibly." Bentley noted that melatonin could have many unknown effects, but few data are available about how "it interacts with other hormone systems." (A separate entry on steroids is available in this encyclopedia.)

Research has shown some benefits in taking melatonin as a supplement, primarily for sleep disorders, but its long-term effects are unknown. Therefore, people who take melatonin do not know what it may do to their bodies over time.

Melatonin is not recommended for some people. Healthy children produce large amounts of melatonin, so they should not take melatonin as a supplement. Nor is it recommended for women who are trying to become pregnant because melatonin can inhibit ovulation. Also, since the effects of melatonin on babies are not known, melatonin should not be used by pregnant or nursing mothers. People with certain immune-system conditions, like the disease leukemia, should not take melatonin either.

Because melatonin is a dietary supplement, it is not regulated by the FDA. Since the manufacturers do not have to follow strict guidelines, they can be more relaxed about ensuring a high quality product. This puts the user at risk of ingesting substances not listed on the bottle label or taking an amount of melatonin that is not reflected accurately on the label.

The Law

Melatonin is neither an illegal drug nor is it monitored by the U.S. government. It is illegal to use it without a prescription in other countries. Under the U.S. Dietary Supplement Health and Education Act (DSHEA) of 1994, it is legal to sell melatonin as a dietary supplement in the United States. According to this Act, a dietary supplement:

- is a product (other than tobacco) that is intended to supplement the diet that bears or contains one or more of the following dietary ingredients: a vitamin, a mineral, an herb or other botanical, an amino acid, a dietary substance for use by people to supplement their diet by increasing the total daily intake, or a concentrate, metabolite, constituent, extract, or combinations of these ingredients.
- is intended for ingestion in pill, capsule, tablet, or liquid form.
- is not represented for use as a conventional food or as the sole item of a meal or diet.
- is labeled as a "dietary supplement."
- includes products such as an approved new drug, certified antibiotic, or licensed biologic that was marketed as a dietary supplement or food before approval, certification, or license (unless the Secretary of Health and Human Services waives this provision).

For More Information

Books

Bock, Steven J., and Michael Boyette. *Stay Young the Melatonin Way.* New York: Plume, 1995.

Pierpaoli, Walter, William Regelson, and Carol Colman. *The Melatonin Miracle: Nature's Age-Reversing, Disease-Fighting, Sex-Enhancing Hormone.* New York: Simon & Schuster, 1995.

Reiter, Russel J., and Jo Robinson. *Melatonin: Your Body's Natural Wonder Drug.* New York: Bantam Books, 1995.

Sahelian, Ray. *Melatonin: Nature's Sleeping Pill.* Marina Del Rey, CA: Be Happier Press, 1995.

Shneerson, John. *Handbook of Sleep Medicine.* Oxford, UK: Blackwell Science Inc., 2000.

Smokensky, Michael, and Lynne Lamberg. *The Body Clock Guide to Better Health.* New York: Henry Holt & Company, Inc., 2000.

Winter, Ruth. *The Anti-Aging Hormones: That Can Help You Beat the Clock.* New York: Three Rivers Press, 1997.

Periodicals

Cupp, Melanie Johns. "Melatonin." *American Family Physician* (October 1, 1997).

Fourtillan, J. B., and others. "Melatonin Secretion Occurs at a Constant Rate in Both Young and Older Men and Women." *American Journal of Physiology: Endocrinology and Metabolism* (January, 2001): pp. E11-22.

Pray, W. Steven. "Consult Your Pharmacist—The Sleep-Wake Cycle and Jet Lag." *U.S. Pharmacist* 24, no. 3 (1999): p. 10.

"What about Melatonin?" *Nursing* (May, 2001).

Web Sites

Buscemi, N., B. Vandermeer, R. Pandya, et al. "Melatonin for Treatment of Sleep Disorders" (November, 2004). *Agency for Healthcare Research and Quality.* http://www.ahrq.gov/clinic/epcsums/melatsum.htm (accessed July 26, 2005).

Cohen, Elizabeth. "Study Bolsters Melatonin Sleep Claims." *CNN.com,* October 12, 2000. http://archives.cnn.com/2000/HEALTH/alternative/10/12/melatonin.clock/ (accessed July 26, 2005).

"Dietary Supplement Health and Education Act of 1994" (December 1, 1995). *U.S. Food and Drug Administration: Center for Food Safety and Applied Nutrition.* http://www.cfsan.fda.gov/~dms/dietsupp.html (accessed July 26, 2005).

"Melatonin." *Drug Digest.* http://www.drugdigest.org/DD/DVH/HerbsWho/0,3923,4060|Melatonin,00.html (accessed July 26, 2005).

"Melatonin." *familydoctor.org.* http://familydoctor.org/258.xml?printxml (accessed July 26, 2005).

"Melatonin." *University of Maryland Medical Center.* http://www.umm.edu/altmed/ConsSupplements/Melatonincs.html (accessed July 26, 2005).

"Melatonin: The Basic Facts." *National Sleep Foundation.* http://www.sleepfoundation.org/sleeplibrary/index.php?secid=&id=60 (accessed July 26, 2005).

"Melatonin—Jet Lag?" (September 27, 1996). *Health Services at Columbia: Go Ask Alice!* http://www.goaskalice.columbia.edu/0970.html (accessed July 26, 2005).

Sanders, Robert. "Popular Supplement Melatonin Found to Have Broader Effects in Brain Than Once Thought." *UCBerkeleyNews,* February 7, 2005. http://www.berkeley.edu/news/media/releases/2005/02/07_melatoninfin.shtml (accessed July 26, 2005).

See also: Benzodiazepine; Herbal Drugs

Meperidine

Official Drug Name: Meperidine (meh-PER-ih-deen), meperidine hydrochloride, Demerol, Pethidine (PETH-ih-deen)
Also Known As: Demmies
Drug Classifications: Schedule II, synthetic opioid

What Kind of Drug Is It?

Meperidine (meh-PER-ih-deen) is best known by its brand name, Demerol. It is a synthetic opioid, meaning that it is a drug created by chemists to imitate certain medicinal qualities of opium, a drug made from flowers called opium poppies. Opioids are NARCOTIC drugs that cause drowsiness and mood changes by interacting with the nerve cells in a person's brain. They can cause physical addiction with extended use. Physical addiction occurs when the body becomes dependent on a particular chemical substance or a combination of chemicals.

Opioids are controlled substances. This means they are available only with a doctor's prescription. Meperidine is a narcotic analgesic, or pain reliever. It is most commonly used in hospitals for patients who have just had surgery.

An analgesic is any chemical substance that has the ability to control or relieve pain. Many familiar analgesics, including acetaminophen (Tylenol), aspirin, and ibuprofen (Advil; Motrin), are sold in drugstores without a doctor's prescription. These over-the-counter (OTC) drugs must be taken with care to avoid unpleasant or dangerous side effects, but they do not have the power to create physical or PSYCHOLOGICAL ADDICTION.

By contrast, meperidine and other narcotic analgesics are highly addictive substances. They are legal but controlled substances. The only people who are supposed to have access to them are those whose doctors have prescribed the medications to treat specific medical conditions. Some other well-known prescription analgesics include hydrocodone (brand name, Vicodin) and oxycodone (brand names, OxyContin, Percocet, and Percodan). (An entry on oxycodone is also available in this encyclopedia.)

As of 2005, drug treatment counselors and law enforcement officials were alarmed at the increasing use of prescription-only opioids such as hydrocodone, meperidine, and oxycodone for illegal, nonmedical purposes. Among those most likely to abuse drugs like OxyContin, Demerol, and Vicodin are teens and young adults who engage in RECREATIONAL DRUG USE, to experience the mood-altering effects of the drugs. Other abusers of prescription drugs include

narcotic: a painkiller that may become habit-forming; in a broader sense, any illegally purchased drug

psychological addiction: the belief that a person needs to take a certain substance in order to function

recreational drug use: using a drug solely to achieve a high, not to treat a medical condition

Prescription Drug Abuse by Teens

The abuse of prescription drugs by teens has increased dramatically in the twenty-first century. Did you know that:

- Nearly one out of five teenagers has taken Vicodin to get high.
- In 2004, teens were more likely to use a prescription drug than a so-called "street" drug to get high.
- Some middle and high school students falsely believe that prescription painkillers are safe to use as recreational drugs.
- These same students also believe that using prescription drugs to get high is not illegal.

- Some students misuse prescription drugs in an attempt to enhance their athletic performance.
- Hundreds of Internet sites offer prescription drugs to anyone with a credit card; 90 percent do not always verify the age of the buyer.
- Prescription drug sales have climbed 400 percent since 1990, in part due to "doctor shopping."
- "Doctor shopping" is the practice of finding a doctor who will write illegal prescriptions, or of getting prescriptions for a particular drug from more than one doctor at a time.

individuals who have become physically addicted to an opioid after using it to treat a legitimate medical condition.

Overview

Narcotic analgesics are prescribed by doctors to treat moderate to severe pain. The first narcotics were opiates, which are any drugs derived from the opium poppy or synthetically produced to mimic the effects of the opium poppy. Opiates tend to decrease restlessness, bring on sleep, and relieve pain. Opium is a plant-based, chemically complex drug that has been used for thousands of years as medicine and as a recreational drug. Although it does block pain, it is highly addictive. The intensity of its effects is difficult to regulate from one use to the next, which makes it impractical as a pharmaceutical drug.

One of the chemical components of opium is morphine, an addictive opiate that is used to kill pain and bring on relaxation and sleep. In 1806, German chemist Friedrich Sertürner (1783–1841) was finally able to isolate pure morphine from opium. This resulted in the first pure, highly effective analgesic (painkilling) drug for medical use. In 1832, codeine, the other major chemical in opium, was isolated and used as medicine. Both drugs are still in use, individually and in combination with other drugs, because they are very effective pain relievers. However, both are also highly addictive. That is why researchers have continued to try to develop better opiate-like drugs—that is, drugs that possess the pain-relieving power of morphine and codeine, but with fewer negative effects.

One of the first wholly synthesized opioids—or opiate-like drugs—was meperidine. It was first created in the 1930s. It was produced from human-made chemicals, rather than from any part of the opium poppy. Meperidine is still in medical use today.

More About Opioids

Semi-synthetic opioids are drugs that are synthesized with one of the natural opiates, morphine or codeine. Examples of these are hydrocodone (Vicodin) and oxycodone (OxyContin). Both the synthesized and semi-synthesized opioids are drugs specifically created to produce effects similar to opium. They each have particular benefits and drawbacks. Morphine and codeine are still used, however, because researchers still have not found anything that works quite as well as the natural opiates themselves. In addition to their pain-relieving characteristics, opiates and opioids also have something else in common: They are all physically and psychologically addictive to one degree or another. Scientists are still working to try to find a chemical compound that will function as effectively as an opiate-like substance without the dangers of addiction.

What Is It Made Of?

Meperidine hydrochloride (the drug's full name) is a synthetic opioid. It is created through the reaction of two chemicals: *dichlorodiethyl methylamine* (pronounced di-KLO-ro-di-eh-thyl meh-thyl-A-mine) and *benzyl cyanide*, an oily, colorless liquid. The chemical name for the resulting white crystalline substance is *ethyl 1-methyl-4-phenyl-isonipecotate hydrochloride.*

Meperidine is synthesized exclusively from laboratory-made chemicals, and not from any part of the opium poppy. That is why it is called a totally synthetic opioid. By contrast, other well-known narcotics that imitate the effects of opium are said to be semi-synthetic opioids. These drugs are produced with one of the naturally occurring opiates as a starting material. Natural opiates include codeine and morphine. A chemical modification of codeine, another opiate, results in hydrocodone, a highly addictive but effective painkilling drug. By contrast, a chemical alteration of morphine results in heroin, a dangerous and highly addictive narcotic that has no legal use and none of the benefits of narcotic medications.

How Is It Taken?

Meperidine is taken orally or injected. The oral forms of the drug include tablets and syrup. Tablet sizes range from 25 milligrams to 100 milligrams per tablet. The syrup form contains 50 milligrams of meperidine per 5 milliliters of liquid. A typical oral dosage of meperidine is 50 milligrams to 150 milligrams every three to four hours.

The body responds to meperidine more quickly when it is injected, so those dosages are usually about half that of the oral forms of the drug. Injections may be given in the muscle, under the skin, or directly into the bloodstream. Doses are usually given every three to four hours, although an INTRAVENOUS (IV) administration of meperidine is often maintained at a low, continual therapeutic dose.

Hospitalized patients receiving meperidine for pain control after surgery sometimes use a system called patient controlled anesthesia (PCA). A PCA machine allows a specific amount of meperidine to be administered intravenously each hour. However, the patient has control over when the medicine is dispensed. This reduces the need for a nurse to give the patient an injection every three to four hours, and it keeps the drug at a more constant level in the body for better pain relief. The PCA machine is programmed so that it cannot give the patient too much of the drug. This prevents the potential for an overdose.

Meperidine is abused by people used to taking nonprescription street drugs. Sometimes they crush the meperidine tablets and then chew, snort, or dissolve the drug in a liquid and inject it. Misusing meperidine can dangerously affect the way the body processes the drug.

Are There Any Medical Reasons for Taking This Substance?

Demerol, the brand name for meperidine, is one of the most commonly used narcotic analgesics in U.S. hospitals. It is used to treat moderate to severe pain, especially immediately after surgery. It is sometimes used together with anesthesia before and during operations. Meperidine is also frequently given to pregnant women during labor and delivery. It is not recommended for treating pain in infants and small children or the elderly.

For several reasons, meperidine is used in hospitals more than it is prescribed for at-home use. First, it is more effective in treating the acute (immediate, short-term) pain that follows surgery than the chronic (longer-lasting, ongoing) pain that a patient might experience during recovery at home. It is also eliminated from the body quicker than other opioids, which means that it must be taken more often than other narcotic drugs in order to maintain pain relief. This rapid

intravenous: injected into a vein

Designer Meperidine

In the early 1980s, a new drug was created that imitated the chemistry and effects of meperidine. This so-called "designer" meperidine was known as MPPP. It was manufactured in illegal drug labs where mistakes and unreliable conditions sometimes led to unintended results. One such consequence was the contamination of MPPP with a poisonous chemical by-product called MPTP. This is a toxin that can destroy nerve cells in certain parts of the brain.

When people ingested the MPPP that had been tainted with MPTP, they suffered neurological symptoms that mimicked Parkinson's disease. Their muscles became rigid and they exhibited uncontrollable twitching. The damage was permanent.

The dangerous "designer" meperidine was one of many drugs called "analogs," which means they were created specifically to be similar to, but not exactly like, other drugs. Why was this done? Because illegal drug labs could sometimes avoid Drug Enforcement Administration (DEA) consequences by making drugs whose specific chemical formulas were not listed on the Schedule of Controlled Substances. Illegal drug manufacturers could get away with making a drug that acted like a highly controlled substance, but had a slightly different chemical structure than the regulated drug. For a time this was not illegal.

In 1986, however, legislation was passed to stop this practice and make the manufacture of analog drugs illegal. It was finally against the law to create a drug that was designed to produce effects similar to any drug already listed as a controlled substance.

---

elimination of the drug also means that its pain-relieving effects are not as consistent as those of other opioids.

Usage Trends

Meperidine is a prescription drug with both legal and illegal usage trends. Meperidine was, and is, particularly useful for the treatment of acute pain, but it is not as effective in controlling chronic pain. Newer synthetic and semi-synthetic opioids include chemical compounds that relieve pain for longer periods of time, but many of the side effects are similar.

Although meperidine is still used in hospitals and emergency treatment settings, Drug Enforcement Administration (DEA) figures show that between 1990 and 1996, the legitimate medical use of meperidine in the United States decreased by 35 percent. World-wide, the legitimate use of meperidine dropped 20 percent between the early 1980s and 1999. The decline in usage of meperidine is related to the development of newer opioids that are safer and longer lasting than meperidine.

Street usage of meperidine became a law enforcement issue during the 1980s, when it was frequently used as a substitute for heroin. In particular, two meperidine analogs, or imitation drugs, became popular: MPPP and PEPAP. Heroin users like MPPP because it produces a heroin-like EUPHORIA when it is injected. The creation of these analogs is now completely illegal. This occurred, in part, because during the 1980s street drug labs produced an analog that contained MPTP, a poison that caused serious and irreversible neurological damage in users.

Among opioids, Demerol (brand name of meperidine) is not as frequently prescribed outside hospital settings as Vicodin and OxyContin, so its abuse is not as widespread or well-publicized as the abuse of these other drugs. Demerol is more readily available to medical professionals—doctors, nurses, pharmacists or others who work in a hospital or emergency care clinic—than to others. It is sometimes stolen from ambulances or stand-alone emergency care facilities through street robberies or "inside" thefts perpetrated by employees.

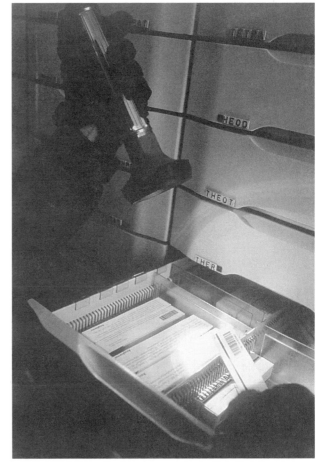

Demerol and other drugs are sometimes stolen from hospitals or emergency care clinics, ambulances, or pharmacies. © *Pinto/Gulliver/Corbis.*

Prescription Drug Abuse Grows

The illegal use of prescription drugs, including opioids like meperidine, is a large and growing segment of the complete drug abuse picture. Several nationwide studies track the use of both legal substances (prescription medications and over-the-counter, or OTC, drugs) and illegal drugs such as marijuana and cocaine. The National Household Survey on Drug Abuse (NHSDA), which is conducted by the U.S. Department of Health and Human Services, collects yearly statistical data on five drug groups. These include: 1) marijuana and hashish; 2) psychotherapeutic drugs, which are generally prescription drugs that can be used illegally to get high; 3) cocaine and crack; 4) hallucinogens, which are substances that bring on hallucinations, which alter the user's

euphoria: pronounced yu-FOR-ee-yuh; a state of extreme happiness and enhanced well-being; the opposite of dysphoria

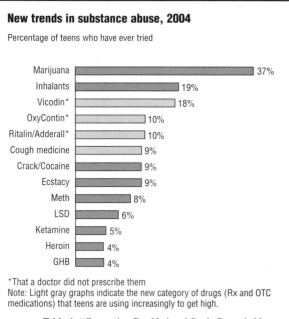

New trends in substance abuse, 2004

Percentage of teens who have ever tried

Marijuana	37%
Inhalants	19%
Vicodin*	18%
OxyContin*	10%
Ritalin/Adderall*	10%
Cough medicine	9%
Crack/Cocaine	9%
Ecstacy	9%
Meth	8%
LSD	6%
Ketamine	5%
Heroin	4%
GHB	4%

*That a doctor did not prescribe them
Note: Light gray graphs indicate the new category of drugs (Rx and OTC medications) that teens are using increasingly to get high.

SOURCE: Table 1, "Generation Rx: National Study Reveals New Category of Substance Abuse Emerging: Teens Abusing Rx and OTC Medications Intentionally to Get High," *The Partnership for a Drug-Free America Web site*, New York, NY [Online] http://www.drugfree.org/Portal/About/NewsReleases/Generation_Rx_Teens_Abusing_Rx_and_OTC_Medications [accessed May 25, 2005].

perception of reality; and 5) inhalants. Psychotherapeutic drugs include stimulants, sedatives, TRANQUILIZERS, and pain relievers. Meperidine and other opioids make up the majority of the pain relievers in that group.

In 2003, the NHSDA found that 4 percent of all people between twelve and seventeen reported that they had used some kind of psychotherapeutic medication during the previous month for a nonmedical—illegal—purpose. More than 9.2 percent in that age group reported such use at any time during the year. In 2003, 6 percent of individuals between eighteen and twenty-five reported nonmedical use of prescription drugs in the month prior to the date on which they were surveyed. That was up from 3.6 percent in 2000 and just 1.6 percent in 1994.

According to the NHSDA's 2000 study, approximately 1.6 million Americans used prescription pain relievers nonmedically for the first time in 1998. During the 1980s, there were generally fewer than 500,000 first-time users per year. The trend shows steadily rising numbers of people using prescription drugs for nonmedical use.

New Generation of Abusers

Another yearly study is conducted by the Partnership for a Drug-Free America. In April 2005, the Partnership released the results of its seventeenth annual national study of teen drug abuse. The 2004 Partnership Attitude Tracking Study (PATS) reported that one of every five teenagers has used a prescription painkiller as a recreational drug. The most frequently abused brand-name opioids were Vicodin (reported by 18 percent of respondents) and OxyContin (reported by 10 percent of respondents). These are narcotic analgesics whose nonmedical effects on users are similar to those of meperidine (brand name Demerol). Overall, teen misuse and abuse of prescription drugs, including opioids, is growing rapidly. As a result, teens were given the nickname "Generation Rx."(See chart on this page.)

Teens are drawn to the use of prescription drugs for a variety of reasons, including ease of availability, relatively low cost, and a perception that the pills are harmless because they are legal.

tranquilizers: drugs such as Valium and Librium that treat anxiety; also called benzodiazepines (pronounced ben-zoh-die-AZ-uh-peens)

Generation Rx

"Rx" is a traditional abbreviation for the word "prescription." "Generation Rx" is a term coined in 2005 to reflect the soaring popularity of prescription drugs among teens. This nonmedical, and illegal, use of drugs such as Ritalin, Vicodin, OxyContin, Xanax, and Valium is sometimes called "pharming" by drug counselors and by teens themselves.

The phenomenon is not limited to teens, however. Well-known public figures including actors Matthew Perry and Melanie Griffith and athletes Brett Favre and Darryl Strawberry have publicly battled addictions to the prescription painkiller Vicodin. In October 2003, radio personality and former ESPN sports analyst Rush Limbaugh entered a treatment center to deal with his addiction to OxyContin.

While adults often become addicted to pain pills after using them for a legitimate medical reason, teen use of the drugs is typically more recreational. If there is no legitimate medical need to get a prescription from the family doctor, some teens resort to stealing pills from medicine cabinets at home or order them from Internet pharmacy sites.

Teens mistakenly believe that because these are brand-name drugs, manufactured by legal pharmaceutical companies, they are safe. Teens often do not realize how dangerous it is to mix prescription drugs with alcohol, or to combine different drugs "to see what happens." Even adults frequently are not aware that large quantities of the over-the-counter medicine acetaminophen—commonly known as Tylenol—can cause liver damage. This is important to know because one of the main ingredients in Vicodin is acetaminophen.

Students often do not realize, either, that the nonmedical use of prescription medicines is against the law. "Generation Rx" teens who commit crimes related to the abuse of prescription drugs not only risk addiction or other physical consequences, they also face job loss, jail time, or being denied access to scholarships and other financial aid to further their post-high school education.

According to Carol Falkowski, a drug researcher at Hazelden, a well-known substance abuse treatment center in Minnesota, young drug users often prefer prescription drugs because they believe they are "cleaner, safer and less illegal." Teens also admit that they find prescription drugs more attractive than other substances because they are not as likely to leave signs of use, such as the visible disorientation of being drunk or the odor that results from smoking marijuana.

Effects on the Body

Physical pain occurs when illness or injury causes pain signals to be transmitted to the brain through nerve cells in the body. The pain-relieving effect of an opioid like meperidine is produced when

Some schools and communities seek to prevent young people from turning to drugs, alcohol, and tobacco. They offer life skills training programs so students can build self-esteem and confidence, set goals, and learn how to cope with peer pressure and avoid addiction. © *Mark Peterson/Corbis.*

the drug blocks these signals by interacting with proteins called opioid receptors that exist on the surface of nerve cells. The chemical relationship is something like keys and locks. The narcotic drug fits into the receptor proteins and opens a pathway for chemical changes that reduce the ability of the nerve cell to transmit pain signals. When this happens, fewer pain signals are received by the brain, which means that the person taking the drug feels less pain.

If opioids are used when one is not in pain, the chemical changes in the nerve cells and the brain can produce feelings of euphoria, or a state of extreme happiness and well-being. When this occurs over a period of time, the nerve cells become tolerant of the effect, which means that more of the chemical substance is needed to produce the same sensation. Over the course of time, the body also becomes addicted to the basic chemical action of the drug. Thus, if the drug is discontinued, the user experiences unpleasant physical symptoms of drug WITHDRAWAL.

Addiction Problems

Opioids can also cause psychological addiction or dependence. This is present when a person craves a drug and feels a compulsive need to take it, no matter what the consequences may be. This is what drives many people to commit crimes ranging from fraud to robbery in order to acquire the prescription drugs on which they are dependent. They become psychologically addicted to the emotional sensations that accompany the physical effects of the drug. Psychological addiction generally does not occur when people use prescription opioids for long-term, chronic pain. However, it is possible for legitimate use to turn into abuse in individuals who have developed physical dependence when their doctors decide that prescription narcotics are no longer appropriate as treatment. This is what has happened to many people who have become hooked on these painkilling drugs that were prescribed for them for long-term use after surgery or an injury of some kind.

Meperidine is generally used to treat acute pain, so medical use does not usually lead to either physical dependence or tolerance. Prescription users of meperidine do not need more and more of the drug to get the needed level of pain relief. However, when the drug is used specifically to get high, users typically develop both physical tolerance and addiction and psychological addiction. This means they not only crave the drug and physically need more of the drug just to get high, they also need to keep taking the drug to avoid the discomfort of chemical withdrawal.

When a person who is addicted to the physical aspects of a drug suddenly stops taking that drug, withdrawal symptoms occur. Opioid withdrawal is not life threatening, as is sometimes the case with the physical withdrawal from some heavily used substances, such as alcohol and barbiturates. It is unpleasant, however. Short-term withdrawal symptoms include anxiety, yawning, sweating, abdominal cramps and diarrhea, chills and "goose bumps," and a runny nose. Symptoms begin to appear about four or five hours after the last dose. They are at their most intense between thirty-six and seventy-two hours later, and are generally over within a week or ten days. Complete detoxification and recovery from physical addiction can take six months or more.

withdrawal: the process of gradually cutting back on the amount of a drug being taken until it is discontinued entirely; also the accompanying physiological effects of terminating use of an addictive drug

Side Effects of Meperidine Use

Even when meperidine and other opioids are taken under medical supervision, side effects can occur. Opioids relieve pain by temporarily altering the function of nerve cells. In addition to reducing one's pain, this may also cause mental confusion, drowsiness, dizziness and/or nausea, constipation, sweating, low blood pressure, or a slow heartbeat. More serious effects include convulsions and respiratory distress. These most frequently occur if the drug's dosage is too high, or if a patient combines meperidine with alcohol or other drugs.

Patients with kidney or liver disease may be at risk of nervous system damage if they use meperidine for a significant length of time. A by-product of meperidine called normeperidine is broken down in the liver and excreted by the kidneys. Someone with impaired function of either organ may develop high levels of normeperidine, which can be toxic (poisonous) to the nervous system.

People with a history of seizures, or those who have experienced recent head trauma, which puts them at risk of a first seizure, should avoid the use of meperidine. This is because meperidine presents a higher risk for seizures than other opioids. Other serious, but rare, neurological side effects include delirium, hallucinations, and tremors. Allergic reactions to meperidine are unusual, but severe cases can cause symptoms such as cold, clammy skin, generalized weakness, respiratory arrest, and unconsciousness or coma.

Reactions with Other Drugs or Substances

Because meperidine acts as a central nervous system depressant, no other similarly acting substance should be taken with meperidine, unless it is under the close supervision of a physician. Alcohol is a prime example of this. So are drugs known as sedatives, which are used to treat anxiety and calm people down. A large enough dose of any opioid, including meperidine, can stop a person's breathing completely, resulting in death. In combination with alcohol or sedatives, this reaction can occur at much lower doses.

Drugs to be avoided while taking meperidine include most ANTIHISTAMINES, sleeping pills, and any drugs that are in the same classification as Valium. Several types of antidepressants should be used with great caution or not at all in combination with meperidine. These include tricyclics (brand name examples include Elavil and Aventyl); SSRIs (selective serotonin reuptake inhibitors; some name brand examples include Prozac, Zoloft, and Paxil); and MAOIs (monoamine oxidase inhibitors; examples include Marplan and Nardil). Even moderate therapeutic doses of meperidine

antihistamines: drugs that block *histamine,* a chemical that causes nasal congestion related to allergies

administered up to two weeks after a patient has used an MAOI-class drug can result in unpredictable and severe reactions, including coma and death.

Treatment for Habitual Users

Meperidine is a highly addictive, Schedule II opioid narcotic. A high potential for addiction usually means that long-term use is risky. Long-term use may be measured as years of continual use, or as a repeating cycle of periods of use interrupted by times when the drug is not being used. The longer a narcotic drug is used, the more likely it is that a person may need help to quit using it. People who become addicted to drugs like meperidine or other prescription painkillers are less likely than users of street drugs to seek assistance in withdrawing from taking the drug.

When an opioid is suddenly discontinued after a long period of use, serious and uncomfortable withdrawal symptoms generally occur. Most people who manage to overcome an addiction to meperidine do it on their own, but many cases require professional help. Symptoms of physical withdrawal from meperidine may include restlessness, pain in bones and muscles, insomnia, diarrhea, a runny nose, chills with goose bumps, and involuntary leg movements. Symptoms of psychological addiction include becoming severely depressed and having an almost uncontrollable craving or desire for the drug.

For a chronic addiction, meaning drug use and addiction that has lasted more than a year, methadone may be used in a medically supervised withdrawal process. (An entry on methadone is also available in this encyclopedia.) Methadone is another opioid. It is used in progressively smaller doses to help users break free of addictions to more powerful drugs. Methadone helps reduce withdrawal symptoms, including the craving of another opioid, and it has fewer side effects than other opioids.

An Alternative Treatment

Since 2002, drug treatment specialists have experimented with a new drug called buprenorphine (BYOO-preh-NOR-feen). One day it might replace the use of methadone to treat withdrawal symptoms. Early results are promising, but access to the drug is still strictly limited by government control.

Researchers are hopeful that buprenorphine can help people break free of addiction to opiates such as heroin and codeine, and to opioid pain pills like Demerol, Vicodin, and OxyContin. Also known by the names Suboxen and Subutex, the drug has similar effects on the body as methadone but it is not as addicting as other opiate or opioid-like drugs. Controlled doses of buprenorphine help people withdraw from their addiction to drugs like heroin and Vicodin without some of the complications of methadone treatment. Doctors who have used buprenorphine consider it a successful treatment option and they wish more patients could benefit from it.

According to federal law, only doctors who earn special certification from the Drug Enforcement Administration (DEA) are allowed to prescribe buprenorphine. In addition, the law specifies that each certified doctor or group practice is limited to treating thirty patients at a time with the drug. By early 2005, only 4,850 of 600,000 U.S. doctors—fewer than 1 percent—had earned certification to dispense the drug. Of those, only 1,500 had treated patients with it.

Cost of Abuse

At between $300 and $350 per month for treatment, buprenorphine is expensive, and many insurance companies will not pay for it. However, people with pain pill addictions often spend more than $300 every month to support their habits. Plus, the true cost of addiction can include the breakup of a marriage or family, the loss of a job, and a criminal record.

What is the best balance between controlling access to the drug and making it available to all who need it in a treatment setting? The DEA wants to maintain close restrictions on the use of buprenorphine to prevent a possible new drug abuse "epidemic." Doctors who use it to treat patients with opioid addictions want to be able to help more people, and sooner, rather than later. While the waiting lists grow, doctors and other addiction treatment professionals will have to work with federal lawmakers to figure out how to best use this resource.

Consequences

Meperidine and other opioids offer specific benefits when they are used appropriately. However, the benefits of the drugs must be weighed against the possibility of abuse or addiction. An established addiction is costly to maintain—financially, emotionally, and physically. Sufferers admit that a serious opioid addiction consumes all their energy. Everything in their lives eventually revolves around obtaining more of the drug. When the drug becomes the focus of life, they lose friends, alienate family members, and often find themselves unable to hold a job.

Those who are caught committing crimes to maintain their addiction may end up serving jail or prison time. The ultimate

Healer or Dealer?

On April 14, 2005, Dr. William E. Hurwitz, a well-known pain doctor from McLean, Virginia, was sentenced to twenty-five years in prison. He was convicted in December 2004 of narcotics trafficking and running a drug conspiracy. The doctor was held responsible in the death of one patient and the serious injury of two others.

The case was watched closely because it reflected the ongoing debate over whether doctors should be allowed to prescribe large quantities of narcotic medications to patients who are in chronic pain. Critics of Dr. Hurwitz said that he continued providing patients with massive doses of highly addictive drugs, even when he knew that some of them were misusing

or abusing their medications or selling them to others. The doctor's supporters said that he was a dedicated and caring medical professional. They believed he was determined to provide chronic pain sufferers with the relief they needed, despite intense government scrutiny of his drug prescription activity.

How the outcome of this case will affect the prescribing activity of doctors who specialize in pain control remains to be seen. However, the United States has an aging population that is living longer. With more people living more years with chronic conditions that cause pain, the "access vs. control" debate over pain relief drugs will continue.

consequence may be the loss of life that can result from the abuse of a prescription drug—whether it is from the physical effects of an overdose or through violence that occurs as a result of the addiction.

When meperidine is used exclusively as a recreational drug, consequences include the very real possibility of overdose or severe interactions with other substances. According to the Partnership for a Drug-Free America, nearly half of all teens believe that the recreational use of prescription drugs is safer than the use of ILLICIT street drugs. About one-third of teens do not realize that narcotic painkillers are addictive.

Unexpected Outcomes

Teens are drawn to the use of prescription drugs for a variety of reasons, including ease of availability, relatively low cost, and a perception that the pills are harmless because they are legally obtainable by prescription. This lack of knowledge about the physical effects of narcotics, as well as the consequences of using them illegally, can result in unexpected and tragic outcomes.

The misuse of meperidine and other opioids affects people who live with chronic pain, because doctors become reluctant to write prescriptions that are needed for adequate pain relief. Members of

illicit: unlawful

the medical community agree that more education is needed by both doctors and patients to help prevent abuse and addiction. They want to ensure that patients truly in need are not denied access to meperidine and other narcotics based on misperceptions and fear. The benefits for individuals and society are great when pain is treated safely and effectively.

The Law

Meperidine is classified as a Schedule II controlled substance, which means that it is strictly regulated by both United States and international laws and agencies. In the United States, the Food and Drug Administration (FDA) and the Drug Enforcement Administration (DEA) control the manufacture and distribution of meperidine. International control is coordinated by the International Narcotic Control Board (INCB).

A Schedule II drug is available by prescription only. It is illegal to write a prescription or an order for meperidine without a valid medical license. Medical doctors, osteopathic doctors, podiatrists, dentists, and veterinarians are the only professionals allowed to legally prescribe meperidine and other Schedule II drugs. Medical professionals who intentionally write multiple prescriptions for patients without a valid medical reason may end up in prison. It is an even more serious crime to write and fill phony prescriptions for profit.

Doctor Shopping and Other Illegal Methods

It is illegal for individuals to obtain prescriptions for meperidine and other opioids by lying about their symptoms. Another dishonest way that people try to get drugs for illegal use is by going to several different doctors within the same time period and receiving prescriptions from each of them. Then they pay cash to buy each prescription at a different pharmacy to avoid being tracked by pharmacy or insurance records. This practice has been given the name "doctor shopping." As of 2004, at least nineteen states had laws against doctor shopping. Prescription Monitoring Programs (PMPs) are used on a state-by-state basis to track this activity.

Sometimes people try to acquire Schedule II drugs illegally by stealing prescription pads from doctors' offices, or by printing up phony prescription forms. Then they use those to write false prescriptions with forged signatures. These tactics are rarely successful over the course of time. Pharmacists often verify the validity of prescriptions for opioids by contacting the doctor listed as the prescribing physician. Bogus prescriptions can be stopped at this point. Pharmacists are also among the first to notice high numbers of Schedule II prescriptions being written by particular doctors. One unintended effect of this kind of monitoring is that many doctors have become reluctant to prescribe enough effective medication for patients who experience chronic pain.

For More Information

Books

Gahlinger, Paul M. *Illegal Drugs: A Complete Guide to Their History, Chemistry, Use and Abuse.* Las Vegas, NV: Sagebrush Press, 2001.

Kuhn, Cynthia, Scott Swartzwelder, and Wilkie Wilson. *Buzzed: The Straight Facts about the Most Used and Abused Drugs from Alcohol to Ecstasy,* 2nd ed. New York: W.W. Norton, 2003.

Mogil, Cindy R. *Swallowing a Bitter Pill: How Prescription and Over-the-Counter Drug Abuse Is Ruining Lives—My Story.* Far Hills, NJ: New Horizon Press, 2001.

Pinsky, Drew, et al. *When Painkillers Become Dangerous: What Everyone Needs to Know about OxyContin and Other Prescription Drugs.* Center City, MN: Hazelden Foundation, 2004.

Youngs, Bettie B., and others. *A Teen's Guide to Living Drug Free.* Deerfield Beach, FL: Health Communications, 2003.

Periodicals

Leinward, Donna. "Prescription Abusers Not Just after a High." *USA Today* (May 25, 2005).

Markon, Jerry. "25-Year Sentence for Pain Doctor." *Washington Post* (April 15, 2005): p. B1.

Weathermon, Ronnie A. "Controlled Substances Diversion: Who Attempts It and How." *U.S. Pharmacist* (December, 1999): p. 2.

Web Sites

"Federal Prosecution of Pain Docs Impedes Pain Treatment." *Our Chronic Pain Mission.* http://www.cpmission.com/main/painpolitics/impedes.html (accessed July 26, 2005).

Gayette, Curt. "In Vicodin's Grip." *MetroTimes: Detroit's Weekly Alternative,* May 22, 2001. http://www.metrotimes.com/editorial/story.asp?id=1824 (accessed July 26, 2005).

"Generation Rx: National Study Reveals New Category of Substance Abuse Emerging: Teens Abusing Rx and OTC Medications Intentionally to Get High" (April 21, 2005). *Partnership for a Drug-Free America.* http://www.drugfree.org/Portal/DrugIssue/Research/Generation_Rx_National_Study_Reveals_New_Category/Teens_Abusing_Rx_and_OTC_Medications (accessed July 26, 2005).

"How Can Mis-using or Abusing Rx Drugs Hurt You?" *Freevibe.com.* http://www.freevibe.com/Drug_Facts/prescription_effects_abuse.asp (accessed July 26, 2005).

"Kids Getting High—and Hooked—on Prescription Drugs." *The Official D.A.R.E. Web site.* http://www.dare.com/parents/Parents_NewsRoom/kidsgettinghigh.asp (accessed July 28, 2005).

Monitoring the Future. http://www.monitoringthefuture.org and http://www.nida.nih.gov/Newsroom/04/2004MTFDrug.pdf (both accessed July 26, 2005).

"National Household Survey on Drug Abuse (NHSDA)." *U.S. Department of Health and Human Services, Substance Abuse and Mental Health Services Administration.* http://oas.samhsa.gov/nhsda.htm (accessed July 28, 2005).

National Institute on Drug Abuse. http://www.nida.nih.gov and http://www.drugabuse.gov (both accessed July 26, 2005).

"Opioids: Beyond the ABCs." *Alberta Alcohol and Drug Abuse Commission.* http://corp.aadac.com/other_drugs/the_basics_about_other_drugs/opioids_beyond_abcs.asp (accessed July 26, 2005).

"Prescription Drugs." *National Institute on Drug Abuse.* http://www.nida.nih.gov/drugpages/prescription.html (accessed July 26, 2005).

Rubinkam, Michael. "Heroin Addicts Clamor for Scarce Medicine." *Associated Press My Way News.* http://apnews.myway.com/article/20050429/D89OO4JG0.html (accessed July 26, 2005).

"Teen Drug Use Declines 2003–2004—But Concerns Remain about Inhalants and Painkillers" (December 21, 2004). *National Institute on Drug Abuse.* http://www.nida.nih.gov/Newsroom/04/NR12-21.html (accessed July 26, 2005).

"Trouble in the Medicine Chest (I): Rx Drug Abuse Growing" (March 7, 2003). *U.S. Department of Health and Human Services and SAMHSA's National Clearinghouse for Alcohol and Drug Information: Prevention Alert.* http://ncadi.samhsa.gov/govpubs/prevalert/v6/4.aspx (accessed July 26, 2005).

See also: Codeine; Designer Drugs; Fentanyl; Heroin; Hydromorphone; Methadone; Morphine; Opium; Oxycodone

Mescaline

What Kind of Drug Is It?

Mescaline is a hallucinogen, which is a substance that produces hallucinations. Such hallucinations cause the user to experience strange sights, sounds, or other perceptions of things that are not actually present. Mescaline is a naturally occurring ALKALOID that is produced by certain types of cactus plants. The best known of these plants is the peyote cactus. The natural ingredients that cause hallucinations in people can also be produced artificially in a laboratory.

For many thousands of years, various Native American groups (in the present United States and Mexico) have consumed peyote in religious rituals. In fact, some native peoples still do. They believe that the hallucinations they experience are visions, or messages from spirits who can help them understand themselves and their place in the world. During the twentieth century, mescaline was studied as a possible treatment for mental illness, but no medical use was found for it.

Some abuse of mescaline as a recreational drug occurred during the last half of the twentieth century, but not in any widespread way. (Recreational users are those who take a drug for the high it produces, not for any medical reason.) Peyote use is not widespread because both natural and artificial forms of it are expensive and hard to find. Much of what may be sold on the street as "mescaline" is actually some other substance that is probably more dangerous than the real thing.

Overview

Mescaline is considered the oldest known hallucinogenic drug. Its strange qualities were most likely discovered accidentally, by ancient people who were experimenting to find out which plants made good food. Mescaline was not a good food. In fact, it usually causes people to have intense stomachaches if they eat it.

The History of an Ancient Plant

Despite causing pain and vomiting, however, mescaline-containing plants rarely cause death. Intense, colorful, often terrifying

Official Drug Name: Mescaline (MES-cuh-leen or MES-cuh-lin), peyote (pay-OH-tee)
Also Known As: Big chief, blue cap, buttons, cactus buttons, cactus head, chief, mesc, mescal, moon, topi
Drug Classifications: Schedule I, hallucinogen

alkaloid: nitrogen-containing substances found in plants

547

The peyote cactus is by far the best-known of the mescaline plants, so much so that the word *peyote* is often used to mean any type of mescaline. Peyote plants grow mainly in Texas and Mexico. *AP/Wide World Photos.*

hallucinations follow consumption, lasting for many hours. These vivid pictures and sounds, which exist only in the user's mind, appear to be completely real to the mescaline user. The people who lived in regions where mescaline-producing plants grew believed that the hallucinations were messages from spirits and gods, so the plants became very important in their culture.

ARCHAEOLOGISTS have discovered evidence suggesting that peyote was used in sacred rituals some 3,000 years ago. Archaeologists in Coahuila, Mexico, found a skeleton with a beaded necklace of dried peyote buttons that dates back 1,000 years. In Peru, a carving of a peyote cactus on a stone tablet dates back to 1300 BCE. One archaeological dig in Shumla Cave in Texas uncovered dried, mescaline-containing plant matter that appeared to date back to 5,000 BCE.

archaeologists: scientists who dig up and study the remains of ancient cultures

The earliest written information about mescaline use comes from Fray Bernardino Sahagun (1499–1590), a Spanish missionary who lived among the Indians of Mexico and studied their culture. He stated that the buttons of the peyote plant were sometimes eaten when fighting was likely, because it took away sensations of hunger, thirst, and fear. Dr. Francisco Hernandez, the personal doctor to King Phillip II of Spain, was the first to describe the peyote plant itself. He noted that in addition to peyote buttons being used for spiritual purposes, the root of the plant could be ground up and applied as a paste for the relief of pain in the joints.

When the Spanish began to take control of Mexico in the 1500s, they tried to stamp out the use of peyote and other mescaline-producing plants. Most Spanish people of that era were devout Catholics and regarded mescaline use as a pagan ritual. Paganism is used to describe non-Christian religions that worship many gods. The Spanish did not accept paganism and believed that those native peoples who used peyote and related plants were calling on evil spirits. By 1720, a law had been passed in Mexico outlawing the use of peyote. Still, followers of the peyote cults continued to conduct their ceremonies in secret.

Nineteenth-Century Uses

As European settlements spread across North America, so did the use of mescaline-producing cacti. The first recorded use of peyote in the United States was in 1760. By the time of the American Civil War (1861–1865), some Native American tribes were very familiar with the plants and had developed rituals around their use. The Kiowa and Comanche Indians drew attention for their peyote ceremonies around the year 1880. They had probably learned about peyote when they carried out raids on the Mescalero Indians of northern Mexico.

The Kiowa and Comanche Indians may have embraced the peyote rituals because such practices seemed to offer them some hope of holding on to their traditional way of life. During this era, the Indians' lifestyle was being drastically changed as the U.S. government began forcing the native peoples on to reservations. Quahadi Comanche chief Quanah Parker (c. 1845-1911) was one of the first people to mix elements of the Christian religion with traditional peyote ceremonies. Parker was the son of a Comanche man and a white woman who had been captured by the Indians as a child.

In 1918, the Native American Church (NAC) was founded, giving an official framework to the ritual use of peyote in religious ceremonies. At the same time, a long debate began about whether

Quanah Parker, chief of the Quahadi Comanches, was one of the first people to mix elements of Christianity with traditional peyote ceremonies. Such practices continue in the NAC. © *Corbis/Bettmann.*

or not it should be legal for certain churches to use substances that are normally illegal. The debate continues to unfold. For Native Americans, the issue is one of religious freedom.

During the late nineteenth century, the Western world began to take a scientific interest in hallucinogenic substances. In 1897, German chemist Arthur Heffter (1859–1925) became the first person to identify mescaline as the essential chemical in peyote that caused hallucinations. It was the first hallucinogenic compound to be synthesized, or removed from its parent plant in that way.

From Native Cultures to Modern Use

Shamans, or medicine men, in native cultures had long used peyote and other mescaline-producing plants to treat a variety of ailments, both physical and spiritual. Since the effects of these substances seemed to create states similar to insanity, Western scientists hoped that they might be somehow useful in treating mental illness. They also thought they might get a better understanding of mental illness if they could learn more about the ways in which hallucinogenic substances alter the brain's activity. For many years, serious research was done on mescaline and other hallucinogens, both natural and human-made. Even as research went on, some states passed laws to make the use of peyote and related substances illegal. In 1927, New Mexico was the first state to do so.

Mescaline was rarely used outside of native cultures until the mid-twentieth century, when British novelist Aldous Huxley (1894–1963) wrote a book called *The Doors of Perception,* which described his personal experiments with peyote. Huxley's book, published in 1953, was popular reading during the 1960s and 1970s, a period when experimentation with drugs was widespread. Timothy Leary (1920–1996), a professor at Harvard University, also undertook many personal experiments with mescaline and LSD (lysergic acid diethylamide), a human-made hallucinogen. Leary's writings further promoted interest in hallucinogens, especially on college campuses. Street use of these substances became more common at that time.

Many people believed that research on hallucinogenic drugs, or PSYCHEDELICS as they were also called, had gone on for long enough, and that no helpful information had been learned. However, the abuse of psychedelics was spreading, with dangerous results. Often users had what were called "bad trips," or experiences that were depressing or terrifying. It was also reported that users might have "flashbacks," or recurrences of their drug experiences even when they were not taking the drug. Organizations concerned with public health and safety warned that heavy use of hallucinogens, including any form of mescaline, could result in damage to blood vessels, convulsions, and permanent brain damage.

Laws Ban Hallucinogens

In 1967, the U.S. government passed a law that made hallucinogens illegal throughout the country. In 1970, the Comprehensive Drug Abuse Prevention and Control Act defined peyote, mescaline, and every other hallucinogen as a Schedule I drug, meaning that they have no known medical use. At that time, legal research on mescaline came to an end. Street use of peyote and other forms of mescaline declined sharply and was virtually nonexistent at the end of the twentieth century. Whether peyote and other hallucinogenic plants can be used legally as part of the religious ceremonies of Native Americans is still hotly debated.

psychedelics: drugs that can cause hallucinations

The Native American Church (NAC)

The Ghost Dance religious movement began in 1869 but quickly died out. It was revived in 1889 by Wovoka (c. 1858–1932), a Piute medicine man, who had a vision. In his dream, Jesus Christ came to help Native Americans save their way of life, which was rapidly being destroyed by white settlers and the U.S. government. The dance was supposed to bring back the dead, hence the name Ghost Dance. Leaders from many tribes were interested in learning about the religious movement. Its rituals included five nights of dancing and intense shaking. Those taking part in the dance would enter a trance-like state. Dancers soon began wearing specially made shirts that they believed would protect them from the white man's bullets.

Representatives of the U.S. government were concerned that the Ghost Dance movement would lead to uprisings and tried to outlaw it. In 1890, in a tragic incident at Wounded Knee, South Dakota, the U.S. Army massacred more than 200 Sioux, including men, women, and children. The Ghost Dance shirts offered no protection against the army's guns. After the incident, the Ghost Dance movement faded.

Forced to live on reservations, many Native Americans experienced poverty and depression. Some turned to alcoholism. In 1918 the Native American Church (NAC) was established in an effort to pull together the scattered remains of the native cultures. Following in the tradition of earlier Native American leaders such as Quanah Parker, John Wilson, and John Rave, the NAC combined Christian beliefs with traditional rituals. The establishment of the NAC was also strongly supported by James Mooney, an anthropologist from the Smithsonian Institution. In 1920 NAC membership was made up of 13,000 members from 30 tribes. By 2005 it had grown to 300,000 members, including some people who are not of Native American ancestry.

Peyote rituals differ from one chapter of the church to another, but they are usually very structured. A typical service might be held in a tepee, constructed over an altar made of clay. Often there is ritual purification and confession of sins, and a period of silence. After the peyote is consumed, there may be a prolonged period of chanting and dancing. Sometimes, this period is so long that the people involved become exhausted when the effects of the peyote wear off. Ceremonies may be held for special occasions or on a monthly basis. A person called the Roadman leads them. The ritual itself is sometimes called the Peyote Road.

What Is It Made Of?

Mescaline-producing plants grow in only a few areas of the world. The word "mescaline" refers to the active ingredient in the plants that causes the hallucinogenic effects. However, it is often used as a name for the plants as a whole, or for the parts of the plants that are eaten, in whatever way they may be prepared. The two main sources of mescaline are both members of the plant family Cactaceae. They are the peyote cactus (*Lophophora williamsii*) and the San Pedro cactus (*Trichocereus pachanoi*). The peyote cactus is by far the best known of the mescaline plants, so much so that the word *peyote* is often used to mean any type of mescaline.

The true peyote cactus is a gray-green or blue-green plant. It grows close to the ground and looks something like a small cushion divided up into sections that are called *podarea*. The podarea are arranged around a center piece that has a woolly look to it, as it is made up of tufted hairs called *trichomes*. Unlike other cacti, it does not have sharp, prickly spines to protect itself.

The peyote cactus grows naturally in an area stretching from southern Texas to southern Mexico. There are a few variations of *Lophophora williamsii,* including *Echinocactus williamsii* and *Lophophora echinata var. diffusa.* A close relative of peyote, the cactus *Lophophora diffusa* grows only in the dry region of Queretaro, Mexico, in the central part of the country. It is yellow-green in color, has a fleshier body than the peyote cactus, and lacks the well-defined podarea.

Slow Growing

The peyote is one of the slowest-growing of all cacti. A plant is not considered mature until it is about thirteen years old. If it reaches the age of thirty, it will still be only about the size of a baseball. The Native Americans call a plant of this size and age "Father Peyote" or "Grandfather Peyote." Usually, a peyote cactus must grow for at least four years before it will produce even one "button," or dime-sized section on its top. It is the button that is cut off and eaten for the hallucinogenic effects. The name of the plant is thought to come from either a Nahuatl word, *pi-youtl,* which means "silk cocoon" or "caterpillar cocoon," or from the Mexican word *piule,* which simply means "hallucinogenic plant."

The San Pedro cactus looks quite different from the peyote. It does have prickly spines, and it grows in tall columns, sometimes reaching as high as twenty feet. It originated in the mountain regions of Peru and Ecuador, but has become widespread, because it is often sold as an ornamental plant. Like the peyote cactus, the San Pedro has some close relatives within its *Trichocereus* family that contain hallucinogenic compounds.

Numbers Declining

Although these PSYCHOACTIVE cacti all contain between forty to sixty alkaloids, or nitrogen-containing compounds, mescaline is the only alkaloid among them that is known to cause hallucinations. The

psychoactive: mind-altering; a psychoactive substance alters the user's mental state or changes one's behavior

The Chihuahuan Desert, mainly in Texas and Mexico, is home to many cacti, including the peyote plant. © *William Manning/Corbis.*

amount of mescaline in a cactus depends on the maturity of the plant. On average, a peyote cactus might contain about 4 percent mescaline. It can be extracted from the plant, and in its pure form, it is crystalline.

Mescaline can also be artificially produced in a laboratory. Pure mescaline, either extracted or manufactured, is extremely rare, however, because it is very expensive to produce. Therefore, almost all mescaline used is in the form of peyote buttons, or material from one of the other mescaline-producing plants. The number of peyote cacti is declining, in part because of the development of roads and buildings in the places where the plants grow naturally.

How Is It Taken?

Usually, dried buttons from the peyote cactus are chewed up and swallowed in order to get the mescaline into the body. Users eat from twelve to thirty of these pods at a time. Sometimes the buttons are brewed in hot water, which is then consumed as a tea. Dried peyote buttons are sometimes ground into a powdered form, which can be put in capsules. According to the Drug Enforcement Administration (DEA), it takes a dose of about 0.3–0.5 grams of mescaline to produce hallucinations. That would be the amount contained in approximately 5 grams of dried peyote. It takes about 0.5 grams of synthetic mescaline to produce hallucinations, but the cost of producing this substance is so high that it would cost between $50 and $100 for each use.

Therefore, mescaline is almost nonexistent in the world of illegal drugs, as there is very little market for it. Authorities report that most tablets or capsules sold as "synthetic mescaline" have a very small amount of real mescaline in them. Usually they have been mixed with another substance, often phencyclidine (PCP), LSD, or ecstasy (MDMA). All of these drugs can be much more dangerous than true mescaline.

Are There Any Medical Reasons for Taking This Substance?

Native peoples believed that physical illness was a reflection of a spiritual problem. Their shamans, or medicine men, treated the body and spirit together in ways that blended spiritual beliefs and practices with herbal remedies. Those who came from the peyote cultures considered peyote to be a powerful medicine. It was used in a variety of ways, from grinding the root to make a paste for sore joints, to using the buttons to help combat depression and alcoholism. The use of alcohol became a serious problem for many Native Americans after their way of life was disrupted by white settlers, who forced them off their lands and on to reservations. The alcohol brought by white settlers was also new to native peoples, so their bodies were unaccustomed and more susceptible to the effects of alcohol.

Western researchers became interested in the possible uses of mescaline as soon as they became aware of it. By the late 1800s, people were already working to find ways that mescaline and other hallucinogens might be useful in understanding and treating insanity. By the 1960s, interest in the possible beneficial uses of mind-altering drugs was at its peak. It was hoped that mescaline, along with human-made hallucinogens such as LSD, might be able to treat depression, autism, obsessive-compulsive behavior, and other mental illnesses. Yet, no

Peyote is a part of religious rituals for some Native Americans. Once consumed in tepees (like those shown here), the practice dates back many years. The hallucinations caused by peyote consumption are said to be visions or messages from spirits who would help users understand themselves and their place in the world. © *Corbis.*

definite use for them was ever found, and all legal research came to a halt in 1970 when the Comprehensive Drug Abuse Prevention and Control Act ruled that such substances have no known use in medicine. Nevertheless, during the 1990s there was some renewed interest in studying the effects of peyote after testimony was given before the U.S. Congress. At that time, advocates of peyote talked about its use in treating alcoholism among the Native American population.

The Huichol and Tarahumara Indians of Mexico still use peyote in religious ceremonies. Here, a group of Tarahumara Indians participates in traditional games and dances. © *Phil Schermeister/Corbis.*

Usage Trends

The use of peyote was well established among the Aztecs and other native peoples in the New World long before the arrival of the first Europeans. Spanish authorities in Mexico outlawed peyote in 1720, but its use continued to be widespread, although the rituals were conducted in secret. Use of peyote extended northward during the 1800s. It increased dramatically when Native Americans were being removed from their traditional lands and resettled on government reservations. Shortly after the start of the twentieth century, the NAC was founded, which incorporated peyote use with Christian and other religious beliefs. It remains active to this day. In modern times, the Huichol and Tarahumara Indians in Mexico still use peyote in traditional ceremonies.

Experimentation and Research on Mescaline

Outside of Native American religious ceremonies, there was little use of mescaline by anyone for many years, except for those involved in research. However, that situation changed during the mid-twentieth century. The writings of novelist Aldous Huxley, Harvard professor Timothy Leary, and anthropologist Carlos Castaneda (c. 1925–1998), all of whom experimented with peyote and related substances, sparked a wider interest in these drugs and the vivid visions they cause. Castaneda wrote several books supposedly describing his experiences with a Mexican medicine man, who introduced him to an otherworldly being called "Mescalito." Mescalito was said to give insight to those seeking his guidance through peyote. Castaneda detailed many strange and terrifying visions, but in his later works, he downplayed the importance of using hallucinogens to gain greater spiritual awareness.

At the height of the drug subculture of the 1960s and 1970s, there was some street use of peyote and other forms of mescaline. However, much of what was sold as mescaline was probably something else since the natural and artificial forms of the drug have always been difficult to obtain and are quite expensive when they are available. Peyote is one of the slowest-growing plants. Plus, its natural habitat is being threatened due to continued development of land for building and cattle grazing. Therefore, it is unlikely to become more plentiful. In Texas, it is cultivated legally and protected under the supervision of Texas legal authorities for use within the NAC.

A report by the DEA revealed how little peyote and mescaline are used as street drugs. From 1980 to 1987, about 19.4 pounds (9 kilograms) of peyote were taken in drug raids. In contrast, 15 million pounds (7 million kilograms) of marijuana were confiscated during the same timeframe. Furthermore, no illegal trafficking of peyote was reported at all. After 1998, mescaline showed up infrequently on government reports, usually being included in a category such as "other hallucinogens," which refers to hallucinogens other than LSD. The "2003 National Survey on Drug Use and Health (NSDUH)" reported that overall hallucinogen use dropped from 4.7 million users in 2002 to 3.9 million users in 2003. The study showed that 1 percent of youths between the ages of twelve and seventeen abused hallucinogens, with .8 percent of adults above the age of twenty-six abusing them.

Effects on the Body

Peyote buttons taste very bitter and unpleasant, as do the teas and powders made from them and other psychoactive cacti. Frequently, the human body's first response to them is intense stomach pain, nausea, and vomiting. Approximately thirty to sixty minutes after the substance is eaten, its effects on the brain begin to occur. Hallucinations are most intense for approximately two hours, but the effects of the drug may last for as long as ten to twelve hours. Mescaline's other effects can include trembling, sweating, dizziness, numbness, high blood pressure, increased heart rate, loss of appetite, sleeplessness, dilated pupils, and anxiety. It can cause contractions of the intestines and the uterus, which could be dangerous for pregnant women taking the drug.

Much of what is known about how hallucinogens, including mescaline, work on the brain was learned during research done on LSD in the 1960s and 1970s. The chemical structure of these types of drugs is similar to that of serotonin, a naturally occurring substance within the body. Serotonin is a NEUROTRANSMITTER, or chemical that passes signals from one nerve cell to another in order to relay messages to the brain. Serotonin is not the only neurotransmitter, but it is especially important because it regulates many of the others.

Playing with the Senses

Hallucinogens seem to disrupt the normal interaction between nerve cells and neurotransmitters within the brain. This causes the sight, smell, sound, and feel of things in the real world to become strangely warped. Emotions may also be wildly exaggerated or out-of-place due to the chemical changes being caused in the brain. Rapid mood swings are common, with users laughing for no apparent reason, only to become terrified the next moment. Emotions may seem to be layered or to come in waves. Someone who has taken a hallucinogen may feel a heightened awareness of all kinds of things, and senses may become confused.

The drug-induced state of any hallucinogen is commonly referred to as a TRIP. Trips can be good or bad. People have frequently reported trips that make them feel happy, stimulated, or more aware of themselves and their place in the world. This is one reason why researchers have thought that psychedelic drugs might have a valid medical use in treating mental and emotional illness.

But not every trip is good. For various reasons, which are not well-understood, people who take hallucinogens may instead

---

Seeing Sounds and Hearing Colors

Users of hallucinogens report that they "see sounds" or "hear colors." This phenomenon of blended sensory experiences is called synesthesia (sinn-ess-THEE-zhuh). Although other hallucinogens may play strange tricks with the appearance of reality, mescaline seems to have the strongest tendency to conjure up vividly colored visions that have little or nothing to do with the user's actual environment.

---

neurotransmitter: a substance that helps spread nerve impulses from one nerve cell to another

trip: an intense and usually very visual experience produced by an hallucinogenic drug

experience a "bad trip." In a bad trip situation, hallucinations can be extremely terrifying and realistic. Feelings of unbearable sadness and anxiety may consume the user. Users may feel completely out of control, that they are going insane, or that they are about to die. They may have false feelings of power and attempt to do things that are dangerous. Or, they may become fearful about the frightening hallucinations they see and then panic, endangering themselves trying to escape their visions.

Is It Really Mescaline?

It is important to realize that anything sold on the street as "mescaline" may in fact be mixed with other drugs or substances. Or, it may be completely made up of some other psychedelic drug or unknown substance. True mescaline is rare. Common additives to false mescaline tablets are LSD and PCP. Sometimes called "angel dust," PCP can cause extreme fear and aggressive behavior, as well as convulsions and coma. These types of side effects would rarely be caused by mescaline without the addition of another drug.

Some drugs are known as mescaline analogs. They are made in a laboratory and are similar in chemical structure to mescaline, but far more dangerous. These include the "designer drugs" MDA and MDMA, or ecstasy. Other dangerous amphetamines and methamphetamines are also classified as mescaline analogs. Any of these manufactured drugs may be added to or sold as genuine mescaline, but they are even more dangerous than the real substance would be. Side effects cannot be predicted or understood when additives are unknown. Plus, there is no way of really knowing what is in a tablet or capsule of something that is sold as "peyote" or "mescaline" on the street.

Lingering Problems in Users

A true overdose of genuine mescaline or peyote is rare, although even a low dose of the substance can leave users feeling very ill. It is not considered as addictive as many drugs are, including heroin and cocaine. If people develop a habit of using drugs like heroin or cocaine, their bodies will go through withdrawal symptoms if they try to stop. That means they will feel very ill because their bodies have developed a physical need for the drug. This is not the case with mescaline, but that does not mean there are no consequences for using it.

When a mescaline trip ends, there is a dip in serotonin activity in the brain. This may lead to a condition called dysphoria, or a general feeling of restlessness, anxiety, and depression. When people use hallucinogens frequently, they will develop a tolerance, meaning that they need larger and larger doses to get the same effect. This tolerance carries over from one psychedelic drug to another. In other words, a heavy user of mescaline would also have a high tolerance to LSD. The body's level of tolerance to the substance will revert to normal levels, however, if use is discontinued.

Psychedelic use can potentially lead to two long-term mental health problems. One is known as hallucinogen-persisting perception disorder (HPPD), more commonly known as flashbacks. In a flashback, the user enters hallucinogenic states even though he or she has not taken a recent dose of the drug. Long-term use of hallucinogens can also lead to a condition called persistent or drug-induced PSYCHOSIS. This occurs when former users fall into long-lasting states similar to psychosis. They may be severely depressed, experience mood swings, and have distorted visions and other hallucinations. These symptoms can go on for years, and may occur in people who have no previous history of mental illness.

Reactions with Other Drugs or Substances

Drug users sometimes combine drugs to obtain different or more intense effects. "Love flipping" or taking a "love trip" is the practice of taking mescaline and ecstasy at the same time. Ecstasy is a mescaline analog, or an artificially produced drug with chemical similarities to mescaline. It has very dangerous side effects, which could be made even more extreme by taking it at the same time as mescaline.

Treatment for Habitual Users

There are no formally recognized treatments for hallucinogen-persisting perception disorder (HPPD) and drug-induced psychosis. People experiencing flashbacks may become confused and fearful about the renewed hallucinations. They often feel they have suffered brain damage and are losing their minds. PSYCHOTHERAPY may help these patients to deal with the episodes. Antidepressants may also be useful for those suffering from HPPD and drug-induced psychosis. Users should consult their doctors to determine the best course of treatment.

Consequences

Mescaline can have serious long-term effects on users. HPPD and drug-induced psychosis can require extended treatment. This can affect job performance and personal relationships. People

psychosis: pronounced sy-KOH-sis; a severe mental disorder that often causes hallucinations and makes it difficult for people to distinguish what is real from what is imagined

psychotherapy: the treatment of emotional problems by a trained therapist using a variety of techniques to improve a patient's outlook on life

Linda and James "Flaming Eagle" Mooney appeared in court to learn whether it is illegal for them to distribute peyote to members of the Native American Church. The case went before the Utah Supreme Court, which ruled in 2004 that the Mooneys were within their legal rights. In mid-2005, the Mooneys were arrested again, this time on federal charges. The debate over religious peyote use continues. *AP/Wide World Photos.*

who had psychological problems before taking mescaline may find those problems become worse after taking the drug. Normal social functioning is certainly made more difficult by the hallucinations, confusion, and strong emotions that users may experience. Anxiety and fear caused by a bad trip can lead to poor judgment and dangerous acts that could endanger the user or other people.

Even if a user does not experience a bad trip or have HPPD or drug-induced psychosis, there are still serious consequences that go along with using mescaline, peyote, and the other psychoactive cacti. This is because they are illegal. The DEA has defined peyote as a Schedule I hallucinogen, meaning it has a high potential for abuse and no medical value. Using any Schedule I substance, including peyote or mescaline, can lead to a long prison sentence. Even members of the NAC can be prosecuted if they use peyote outside their religious ceremonies. Although the federal guidelines refer to the peyote cactus, *L. Williamsii,* the penalties are the same for anyone buying other psychoactive cacti with the intention of extracting or using their active ingredients.

Legal consequences can be even more severe for U.S. citizens if they travel to other countries. Using, buying, selling, or carrying any type of drug, including mescaline or peyote, outside of the United States could result in interrogation and imprisonment for weeks, months, and perhaps even for life. Every country has its own laws and punishments for drug trafficking and use. Some countries make no distinctions between a person carrying a small amount of an illegal substance for personal use and someone acting as a large-scale drug trafficker. In some countries, even the most minor drug offenses are punishable by death.

The Law

The legal history of mescaline and its primary source, peyote, is long and somewhat complicated. The ban on its use for recreational purposes is clear. It is classified as a Schedule I hallucinogen, meaning that there is no medical reason it may be possessed, sold, or used. Doing so may result in severe penalties, including imprisonment and heavy fines. However, peyote is a long-established part of the religious rituals of Native Americans. The founding of the NAC in the early twentieth century gave support to this practice by making peyote use part of an established religion, rather than just a cultural tradition. Declaring peyote use illegal in its religious setting puts the federal drug laws in opposition to First Amendment rights that guarantee freedom to practice one's religion. Because of these conflicts, the legal status of peyote use by Native Americans has changed several times since it first became an issue during the American Civil War era.

Religious Rights and Mescaline Regulations

New Mexico became the first state to outlaw the use of peyote, doing so in the 1920s. This law was changed in 1959 to allow Native Americans to use the substance during their religious ceremonies. Most states had no laws against peyote use or possession even into the 1950s and 1960s. At that time, dried buttons from the peyote cactus were available for purchase through mail-order catalogs. This sort of free marketing of the psychoactive cacti and their components slowed drastically after peyote was declared illegal throughout the

Peyote Law in Individual States

The role of peyote in the ancient religions of Native Americans makes for a confusing legal situation in modern times. Federal law allows the use of peyote in Native American religious ceremonies, but each state government has documented its own interpretation of the law. In Oregon and Arizona, the law exempts use with "sincere religious intent." Colorado, Minnesota, Nevada, and New Mexico require that users must be "members of a bona fide religious organization" in order to be exempt. Idaho, Texas, and Wyoming require that users be members of the NAC. Iowa, Idaho, Kansas, Oklahoma, South Dakota, and Wisconsin state that the peyote must be used "only within an NAC ceremony." Idaho and Texas require that in addition to NAC membership, users must be of Native American descent. In Kansas, the law adds that prisoners are not protected by the exemption, even if they are members of the NAC.

Texas requires people to be at least 25 percent Native American. This situation raises various issues, including the fact that some tribes are not recognized officially by both state and federal authorities. Also, there is a controversy about what percentage of Native American ancestry should be required or if any should be required at all. Such issues remind people of the so-called Jim Crow laws, now struck down, that once determined who was considered to be African American and who was not.

Another controversial issue is whether a non-native person can become a member of the NAC church. Some chapters of the NAC allow non-Native Americans to join, while others do not. Non-Native Americans who join the NAC are not protected from federal law even if state laws would allow them exemption. Both state and federal laws on this topic continue to be challenged, reconsidered, and changed. Cases involving the law and its exemptions often go all the way to the U.S. Supreme Court.

United States in 1967. This decision was strengthened by the Comprehensive Drug Abuse Prevention and Control Act in 1970. The passage of the act identified peyote as a Schedule I hallucinogen. At that point, buying, selling, or using it became a serious crime for anyone except a member of the NAC participating in a legitimate religious ceremony. Even members of the NAC could be held accountable to the law for using peyote in any other setting or distributing it to people outside the church.

In 1978 the American Indian Religious Freedom Act was adopted. It was intended to protect the religious traditions of Native Americans. However, almost from the start, there were many challenges to it. In 1990 the U.S. Supreme Court heard the case *Employment Division v. Smith*. Ultimately, the court ruled that religious use of peyote by Native Americans was not protected by the First Amendment. Many religious groups and civil liberties activists protested this decision.

Eventually, the ruling was contradicted by the Religious Freedom Restoration Act of 1993 and the American Indian Religious Freedom Act Amendments (AIRFA). AIRFA, which was amended again in 1996, protected the rights of American Indians to use peyote in traditional, ceremonial ways in all of the fifty states. It states that the "use, possession, or transportation of peyote by an Indian for bona fide traditional ceremonial purposes in connection with the practice of a traditional Indian religion is lawful, and shall not be prohibited by the United States or any State."

In Texas, where the peyote cactus grows, the state government supervises its CULTIVATION and hires a crew of experienced people, called *peyoteros,* to properly harvest, dry, and distribute the buttons to Native American churches. Many complex questions have come up about this conflict between enforcing drug laws and protecting freedom of religion. The various states continue to try to sort out these complexities, as they make their own laws and decisions about the transportation, possession, and use of peyote.

Penalties for Nonreligious Use

Aside from the exemptions made for members of the NAC, possession of peyote, mescaline, or any other Schedule I substance can result in a prison sentence ranging from one to twenty years, and fines ranging between one thousand to several thousand dollars. Selling peyote or mescaline, or possessing with the intent to sell, can result in fines ranging from $250,000 to several million dollars and prison sentences ranging from five years to life, depending on the circumstances. In Mexico, peyote is illegal even for use in religious ceremonies. In Canada, peyote and mescaline are restricted, and possession or use may lead to prison sentences of up to three years and fines of up to $4,000. Penalties for trafficking the drug are even more severe. The 1971 Convention on Psychotropic Substances declared an international ban on mescaline.

For More Information

Books

Anderson, Edward F. *Peyote: The Divine Cactus.* Tucson, AZ: University of Arizona Press, 1996.

Schaefer, Stacy B., and Peter T. Furst, eds. *People of the Peyote: Huichol Indian History, Religion, and Survival.* Albuquerque: University of New Mexico Press, 1998.

Schultes, Richard Evans. *Plants of the Gods: Their Sacred, Healing and Hallucinogenic Powers.* Rochester, VT: Healing Arts Press, 2001.

cultivation: planting and tending with the intention of harvesting

Periodicals

"A Field Full of Buttons." *Economist* (April 1, 1999).

Halpern, John H. "Hallucinogens and Dissociative Agents Naturally Growing in the United States." *Pharmacology & Therapeutics* 102 (2004): pp. 131-138.

Nelson, Nick. "Medicine Man May Still Face Battle to Get Peyote Back." *Daily Herald* (May 6, 2005).

Nelson, Nick. "Mooneys Arrested for Distribution, Possession of Peyote." *Daily Herald* (June 24, 2005).

Nelson, Nick. "Mooney's Wife Released in Federal Peyote Case." *Daily Herald* (June 29, 2005).

O'Reilly, David. "Interview with Huston Smith." *Philadelphia Inquirer* (June 18, 2000).

Web Sites

"2003 National Survey on Drug Use and Health (NSDUH)." *U.S. Department of Health and Human Services, Office of Applied Studies.* http://www.oas.samhsa.gov (accessed July 27, 2005).

"American Indian Religious Freedom Act Amendments of 1994." *The Center for Regulatory Effectiveness.* http://www.thecre.com/fedlaw/legal22x/aipaamen.htm (accessed July 31, 2005).

"Church's Peyote Use OK'd: High Court Ruling May Clear Founder of Charges." *Deseret News,* June 23, 2004. http://deseretnews.com/dn/view/0,1249,595072326,00.html (accessed July 27, 2005).

"National Institute on Drug Abuse Research Report Series: Hallucinogens and Dissociative Drugs." *National Institute on Drug Abuse.* http://www.drugabuse.gov/ResearchReports/Hallucinogens/Hallucinogens.html (accessed June 27, 2005).

"Peyote." *Partnership for a Drug-Free America.* http://www.drugfree.org/Portal/drug_guide/Peyote (accessed June 27, 2005).

"Peyote & Mescaline." *U.S. Drug Enforcement Administration (DEA).* http://www.usdoj.gov/dea/concern/peyote.html (accessed June 27, 2005).

See also: 2C-B (Nexus); Benzylpiperazine/Trifluoro-methyl-phenylpiperazine; Designer Drugs; Dimethyltryptamine (DMT); Ecstasy (MDMA); Ketamine; LSD (Lysergic Acid Diethylamide); PCP (Phencyclidine); Psilocybin

Methadone

What Kind of Drug Is It?

Methadone is a synthetic drug, meaning that it is made in a laboratory from chemicals. It behaves like an opiate drug in the brain. Opiates are drugs, derived from the opium poppy plant, that tend to decrease restlessness, bring on sleep, and relieve pain. The natural opiates—such as codeine, heroin, morphine, and opium—are known for their painkilling properties, but also for their addictive nature. Such substances encourage abuse because they induce euphoria, or feelings of extreme happiness or enhanced well-being.

Methadone works differently. Its slow onset and long-lasting impact lessen the chances that the user will get high from taking it. At the same time, it blocks the receptors in the brain that are stimulated by opiates, so those using methadone do not get high even if they take heroin or morphine too. (Entries on codeine, heroin, morphine, and opium are also available in this encyclopedia.) Methadone is best known as the medication prescribed to help opiate addicts end the destructive behavior associated with drug addiction.

People with opiate addictions often use drugs such as heroin and morphine more to avoid withdrawal symptoms than to achieve a high. Withdrawal is the process of gradually cutting back on the amount of a substance being taken until use can be discontinued entirely. Indeed, withdrawal from opiates—even prescription drugs such as OxyContin and Vicodin—can be difficult and challenging. Methadone eases all symptoms of opiate withdrawal, including anxiety and insomnia, a sleep disorder. Those who receive methadone treatment from trained, licensed doctors—and who follow the treatment schedule carefully—face little danger of overdose, infectious disease, or organ failure. When used properly, it is a medicine that helps users end their addictions and get on with their lives.

When Methadone Is Abused

When used illegally or improperly, though, methadone is one of the most dangerous drugs on the street. According to the Drug Abuse Warning Network (DAWN), emergency room visits related

Official Drug Name: Methadone; Dolophine
Also Known As: Dolls, dollies, fizzies
Drug Classifications: Schedule II, opioid narcotic

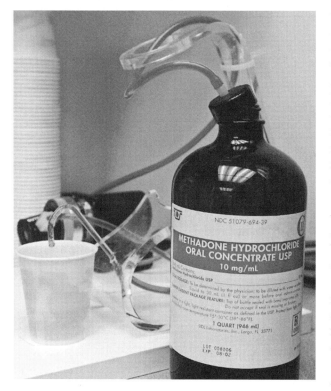

Methadone is dispensed in sugary liquid. *AP/Wide World Photos.*

to methadone overdose tripled between 1997 and 2001. Since then, methadone-related deaths and hospitalizations have continued to rise. Two factors have contributed to the spike in methadone-related emergencies. First, doctors are prescribing the drug more often as a painkiller. In that form, methadone is dispensed by pharmacies as pills and taken into homes. Sometimes it is either used improperly by the patient or sold on the street or to drug dealers.

The second possibility for methadone ER visits involves multi-drug use. Numerous drug deaths have occurred when people combine methadone with other painkillers, opiates, cocaine, tranquilizers, or alcohol. (Separate entries on these drugs are available in this encyclopedia.) The presence of other substances increases the likelihood that methadone will cause COMA, breathing difficulties, and even death.

Since the beginning of the twenty-first century, drug enforcement agents have seized greater quantities of methadone that have been diverted or put into illegal use. Concern over this diversion has led to high-level government meetings and studies on how to keep this powerful pain reliever with many useful qualities out of the wrong hands.

Overview

Naturally occurring opiates are derived from the sticky sap of the opium poppy. Opium products have been used for many thousands of years, both for their pain-controlling properties and for the feelings of intense happiness and well-being they provide. From the ancient Egyptians to the celebrated British poets of the nineteenth century, opiate users have known of the plant's effects—and of its drawbacks. The latter includes addiction, TOLERANCE, and death by overdose. In his book *Illegal Drugs: A Complete Guide to Their History, Chemistry, Use and Abuse,* Paul M. Gahlinger noted that the famous ancient Roman general Hannibal kept a fatal dose of opium in a ring on his finger and actually used it to kill himself in 183 BCE.

coma: a state of unconsciousness from which a person cannot be aroused by noise or other stimuli

tolerance: a condition in which higher and higher doses of a drug are needed to produce the original effect or high experienced

Beginning in the nineteenth century, scientists worked with opium products, trying to isolate the painkilling qualities from the habit-forming qualities. They met with little success. In fact, all natural and synthetic opiate and OPIOID products on the market in the twenty-first century are still known to be addictive. Methadone is no exception. Users develop a dependence, or a physical need for the drug in order to ward off withdrawal symptoms. And they suffer withdrawal symptoms if they do not follow a careful program of specific directions for use.

Usage Grows in the 1940s and 1950s

Methadone was developed in Nazi Germany in 1939 because of wartime shortages of morphine. The German scientists called it Amidon and used it as a painkiller. At the end of World War II (1939–1945), the American pharmaceutical company Eli Lilly began clinical trials of the substance. Lilly called it "methadone." The drug has also been marketed as Dolophine, leading to nicknames such as "dolls" and "dollies." Methadone was found to be an effective, long-lasting painkiller and cough suppressant.

According to a report issued by the Substance Abuse and Mental Health Services Administration (SAMHSA), in 1950 researchers began using methadone to treat the many symptoms of withdrawal associated with heroin dependence. Heroin addicts typically need two to three "FIXES" of the drug each day to ward off the wide range of symptoms that occur when the brain craves opiates. The desperate search to buy the illegal drug leads some addicts into criminal behavior, ranging from theft and burglary to prostitution and drug-dealing. People with opiate addictions feel trapped by their dependency. The desperation is sometimes described as a "monkey on the back."

Treating Addictions with Methadone

In 1964 a group of researchers discovered that heroin addicts could avoid the drug and live more normal lives if they received a daily dose of methadone. The methadone eased

---

Pharmacy Mix-ups

According to the *Knight Ridder/Tribune Business News,* several deaths have occurred in children because *methadone* has a name similar to *methylphenidate,* the generic name for Ritalin. (A separate entry on Ritalin and other methylphenidates is available in this encyclopedia.) In a few cases, children who were prescribed Ritalin to treat attention-deficit/hyperactivity disorder (ADHD) actually received methadone pills instead.

It is important to note that methadone is *never* prescribed for ADHD. Children should never be allowed to take Ritalin without having the tablets checked by a parent to be certain that the tablets are Ritalin, and not methadone. Anyone who has a prescription for Ritalin filled has the right to examine the product at the pharmacy counter and to double-check with the pharmacist that no one preparing the prescription has confused *methylphenidate* with *methadone*. Mistakes can be fatal.

---

opioid: a substance created in a laboratory to mimic the effects of naturally occurring opiates such as heroin and morphine

fixes: a slang term referring to doses of a drug that the user highly craves or desires

withdrawal symptoms and lessened cravings for heroin. Better yet, people taking methadone could not get high on heroin because methadone binds to the same brain receptors that heroin does.

Some problems remained. Methadone is itself an opioid, so it causes dependency too. Its side effects are identical to the natural opiates and include constipation, nausea, drowsiness, dry mouth, and the possibility of breathing problems. Researchers concluded that some people trying to wean themselves off heroin or other opiates by following a methadone treatment plan might have to take methadone for a very long time. The treatment was not foolproof, either. Many addicts returned to drug abuse, sometimes turning to cocaine to get high. Because methadone and cocaine work differently in the brain, methadone treatment does not help cocaine addicts stop using cocaine, nor does it block the effects of cocaine. (An entry on cocaine is available in this encyclopedia.)

Despite these drawbacks, methadone has remained the drug of choice for treatment of opiate dependency since the 1960s. It is not a "perfect cure," but it does provide a way for motivated people to straighten out their lives, hold jobs, and otherwise live more normally. The SAMHSA report stated: "Methadone is a medication valued for its effectiveness in reducing the mortality associated with opioid addiction as well as the various medical and behavioral morbidities associated with addictive disorders." In other words, even the U.S. government believes that methadone, when used properly, saves lives and cuts down on crime.

Methadone Clinics Open

In the late 1960s, the U.S. government began sponsoring methadone clinics in many parts of the country, especially the nation's largest cities. At methadone clinics, people line up to take their daily dose of the drug under the watchful eye of a nurse or other health care worker, and then leave. After a period of months, a patient who has followed the treatment program carefully might be allowed to carry one or two doses home. These doses are called "CARRIES." Most patients use their "carries" as carefully as the doses given to them at the clinics, but some turn the "carries" over to illegal use. In addition, the drug is being prescribed more by doctors. Some patients sell their medications to others. In these ways, some of the drug makes its way on to the street illegally.

carries: doses of methadone given to users to take home for another day

In some of the nation's largest cities, addicts go to clinics daily to receive their dose of methadone. They take it under the watchful eye of a nurse or other health care worker and then leave. *AP/Wide World Photos.*

What Is It Made Of?

Methadone is not derived from the opium poppy plant. It is synthetic, or made from chemicals in a laboratory. Pure methadone is an odorless white powder that dissolves easily in water, juice, or alcohol. Hospitals also have solutions of methadone that can be delivered by injection.

Methadone takes effect slowly and stays in the brain for a period of twenty-four to thirty-six hours. During that time the user—assuming he or she uses no other drugs—will function normally, perhaps feeling a bit sluggish or groggy. Sleep cycles will be normal, but appetite may be lessened. Constipation is a troublesome side effect.

How Is It Taken?

In most clinics, methadone is dispensed in sugary liquids and swallowed by the patient. The drug can also be taken as a biscuit ("diskette") or in pill form. Very rarely, in a hospital or

Methadone Chronology

1939 German scientists develop a synthetic opioid painkiller in response to wartime shortages of morphine. They call the new drug Amidon.

1947 American pharmaceutical company Eli Lilly begins trials of the painkiller. Lilly calls the drug methadone.

1950 Researchers begin using methadone to treat withdrawal symptoms in heroin addicts.

1964 Researchers in Lexington, Kentucky, conclude that a daily dose of methadone allows heroin users to avoid withdrawal symptoms while also being unable to experience a heroin high. The first methadone clinic opens in Lexington.

1970 The U.S. Controlled Substances Act places methadone on its list of Schedule II substances, recognizing that the drug has medical uses but also the potential for misuse and abuse.

2000 Prescriptions for the pill form of methadone rise sharply in response to abuse and illegal use of other opiate/opioid painkillers such as Vicodin and OxyContin.

2003 U.S. trials begin on the drug buprenorphine for use as an alternative to methadone.

clinical setting, the drug is injected into a muscle. Methadone is not commonly used in post-surgical settings because other drugs such as morphine and fentanyl work faster to relieve pain. (Separate entries on morphine and fentanyl are available in this encyclopedia.) Rather, methadone is used for long-lasting pain, such as that resulting from cancer, back injuries, or severe arthritis.

In 2000 the federal government relaxed rules on prescribing methadone in pill form. Doctors who complete an eight-hour training seminar become certified to dispense methadone pills that vary in strength from 20 to 120 milligrams.

The first week of methadone use for chronic pain can be difficult and dangerous. Doctors need to monitor patients carefully because the drug acts slowly on the pain and accumulates in the body. Patients must be watched for tolerance levels so that they are not given deadly doses. They must also be cautioned that methadone is not a "quick fix" for pain, and that taking an extra dose will not make the drug work any faster. Typically, patients will see little or no pain relief from methadone for the first twenty-four to forty-eight hours. After that, methadone works well for chronic pain, provided the user follows the directions and does not mix the medication with other drugs, except on the advice of a doctor.

Illegal Use

People also use methadone illegally as a recreational drug, which is a drug used solely to get high, not to treat a medical condition. People have been known to grind up methadone tablets and snort the powder or inject the drug. This can be extremely dangerous, even in the absence of other drugs or alcohol. Because methadone works so slowly, it does not provide the RUSH of euphoria that the user craves. This may entice the user to take more methadone, eventually leading to a deadly build-up of the drug in the body. It is often hours and sometimes even days before the poisonous effects of methadone become apparent, as the user first slips into a deep sleep, then into a coma, and then stops breathing.

Are There Any Medical Reasons for Taking This Substance?

Methadone is an effective means of taking control of an opiate habit. It lessens the withdrawal symptoms of opiate abuse and helps control—but does not eliminate—cravings for opiates. People driven to desperation in their search for illegal heroin or painkillers can resume a normal lifestyle if they follow a methadone treatment plan. Studies have shown that long-term use of methadone *in the absence of other drugs and alcohol* has no adverse effects on the heart or other internal organs.

Someone who stops using methadone suddenly will suffer the withdrawal symptoms typical of all opiates, including diarrhea, nausea, chills, muscle pains, anxiety, insomnia, sweating, and frequent yawning or sneezing. In order to quit using the drug without these symptoms, it is necessary to lower the dose slowly over a period of months. This allows the body to adjust its brain chemistry gradually. Again, patients must be highly motivated to stay with the program, as even small reductions in dosage can bring a mild onset of withdrawal symptoms.

An epidemic of illegal OxyContin abuse since 2000 has led more doctors to prescribe methadone for chronic pain. Methadone is very effective in this role, but patients must be aware that the full effects of the pain relief may take as much as a week to achieve. During that time, they must be careful to monitor sleep patterns and to be aware of how the drowsiness might affect them while driving or operating machinery. If the painful condition improves, patients must taper their use of methadone gradually to avoid withdrawal symptoms.

rush: a feeling of euphoria or extreme happiness and well-being

In 2004 a group of Russian doctors visited the University Health Center methadone clinic in Vermont to learn more about how to treat heroin addiction with methadone. Heroin use has increased dramatically in Russia in recent years. *AP/Wide World Photos.*

Drugs like methadone are not prescribed on an "as needed" basis. The kind of pain for which methadone is used is a crippling, ongoing, day-and-night pain that may never improve. For extremely sick cancer patients, methadone allows a quality of life that might be impossible otherwise. The drug does not cure the cancer or even slow its progress, but it can help patients manage the pain. The same holds true for other conditions such as chronic back pain and osteoarthritis.

Usage Trends

The amount of methadone dispensed in clinics for the treatment of opiate addiction has remained stable for decades. However, between 1999 and 2002, the number of doctor-generated prescriptions for methadone increased by 331 percent, according to a report by SAMHSA. Pills and biscuits account for almost all of this increase.

Researchers at SAMHSA acknowledged several reasons for the jump in prescriptions for methadone—and a related jump in methadone deaths. First, doctors began prescribing more methadone for pain, believing that its potential for abuse is less than that of oxycodone (OxyContin) and hydrocodone (Vicodin). Second, some doctors began prescribing methadone to patients who are trying to recover from oxycodone or hydrocodone habits. The SAMHSA researchers also suggested that some opiate addicts do not want to be seen visiting a methadone clinic and may be turning to their personal doctors for help in kicking their habits. Getting a prescription from a doctor, and having it filled at the local pharmacy, is far more anonymous than arriving at a clinic every morning. Some communities even fight expensive legal battles to keep methadone clinics out of their neighborhoods.

Methadone on the Streets

The increase in methadone prescriptions has led to an increase of the drug being sold on the street. Seizures of illegal methadone by drug enforcement agents increased 133 percent between 2001 and 2002. Deaths associated with methadone have grown sharply since the early 1990s. SAMHSA used data to show that between 1993 and 2002, methadone-related fatalities jumped 200 percent in the state of Washington. The report declared: "While overdose mortality was declining among [clinic] patients, such fatalities were rising in the overall population." DAWN statistics are quite similar. Between 1994 and 2001, DAWN reported a 230-percent increase in the number of emergency room patients being seen for methadone-related problems or multi-drug problems with methadone in their systems.

According to the "Pulse Check" report in 2004, methadone addicts tend to be "white, middle-socioeconomic males older than 35." Florida, Pennsylvania, Ohio, Indiana, and Texas are among the states with the largest methadone problems. The availability of the drug in these states stems from patients in treatment centers who are saving their doses and selling them on the streets. "Pulse Check" authors noted that the cities of Tampa and St. Petersburg, Florida, in particular, have seen a "dramatic increase in emergency department episodes and deaths involving methadone."

Increased Abuse of Painkillers

The *Join Together* Web site published a survey by Kentucky's *Louisville Courier-Journal* that found 345 fatalities in that state from methadone overdoses between January of 2003 and May of 2004. In Kentucky during that same period, methadone surpassed Oxy-Contin as "the most misused prescription drug in the region," according to the article.

The "2003 National Survey on Drug Use and Health" also determined that illegal use of methadone was on the rise among

Alternative to Methadone

Beginning in the early twenty-first century, the U.S. Food and Drug Administration (FDA) approved trials on a drug called buprenorphine (marketed as Buprenex, Subutex, and Suboxone). A painkiller used in Europe to treat opiate addiction, buprenorphine works the same way as methadone without some of the complications of methadone treatment. The drug has similar effects on the body as methadone but it is not as addicting as other opiate or opioid-like drugs. In its Suboxone form, it contains naloxone, a drug that rids the body of opiates. Scientists are optimistic about the possibilities of Suboxone because grinding it up and snorting or injecting it will simply release the naloxone and cause withdrawal symptoms rather than a high.

teenagers. The survey found that methadone use had increased 25 percent in just one year, part of a general increase in the abuse of prescription painkillers. Overall, methadone is becoming less associated with heroin addicts trying to go straight and more associated with the quiet epidemic of prescription painkiller use and abuse. The epidemic includes men and women of all races, ages, and economic levels.

Effects on the Body

Taken by mouth in pill, biscuit, or liquid form, methadone passes into the digestive system and from there is broken down in the liver. The liver releases the drug into the bloodstream, and it is carried to the brain and spinal cord, where it attaches to opiate receptors.

When no drugs are in the brain, opiate receptors take in ENDORPHINS and ENKEPHALINS, two brain chemicals that regulate feelings of well-being, overall motor coordination, breathing and coughing, and moods. Opiates replace these natural chemicals quickly and in such quantity that the user experiences a rush of pleasurable sensations and a calm drowsiness for hours afterward. This is the "high" that opiate users seek.

No "Rush" with Methadone

When methadone is introduced to the opiate receptors, it does not cause the rush of pleasure that other opiates and painkillers do. Its onset is slower, and it stays in the brain and body longer. Users may feel drowsy and relaxed. Any kind of pain will gradually cease, and it will not return as long as the user takes regular, carefully prescribed doses of the drug. As the dose of methadone leaves the brain and body—generally in about twenty-four to thirty-six hours—the user will begin to feel the discomfort of withdrawal unless a new dose is taken.

In other parts of the body, methadone causes the same symptoms as other opiates and opioids. It inhibits the muscles in the bowels, leading to constipation, and works as a cough suppressant. If taken improperly, it can also affect breathing and lead to asphyxiation—the inability to breathe, which results in death.

endorphins: a group of naturally occurring substances in the body that relieve pain and promote a sense of well-being

enkephalins: pronounced en-KEFF-uh-linz; naturally occurring brain chemicals that produce drowsiness and dull pain

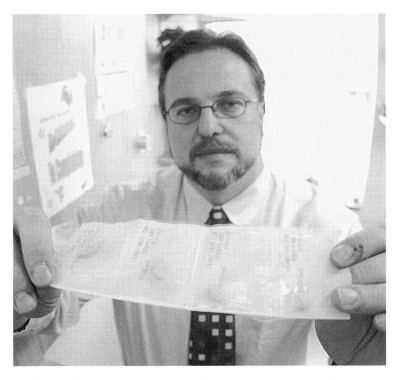

Dr. Warren Bickel displays a sample of buprenorphine, a painkiller used to treat opiate addiction. Buprenorphine works the same way as methadone, but is not believed to pose the risk of an overdose. *Photo by Jordan Silverman/ Getty Images.*

Users may also experience nausea and loss of appetite, dry mouth that can lead to tooth decay and gum disease, and pinpoint pupils leading to sensitivity to light. Methadone may also lessen sexual function and desire.

At the end of methadone treatment, users must taper doses slowly to allow all the bodily systems to return to normal. A sudden end to methadone use brings on diarrhea, anxiety, insomnia, and flu-like symptoms.

Reactions with Other Drugs or Substances

Methadone becomes far more dangerous when combined with other drugs or alcohol. All types of tranquilizers, sedatives, antidepressants, and anti-anxiety drugs will increase the likelihood of breathing problems if taken along with methadone. The drug should not be combined with other painkillers, even over-the-counter medications like acetaminophen (Tylenol) and ibuprofen (Advil), unless supervised by a doctor.

In a 2004 report, the National Drug Intelligence Center revealed that in 65 percent of all emergency room visits related to methadone use, another drug was also present. Frequently the second drug was alcohol. When used together, methadone and alcohol magnify each others' effects. Drinking while taking methadone can lead to very poor motor control, vomiting and breathing problems, coma, and asphyxiation.

Illegal users of methadone sometimes combine it with cocaine as well. Cocaine causes a different sort of high in the brain, one that is unaffected by methadone. Users of cocaine and methadone find themselves in the difficult position of being addicted to two different substances at the same time, with a host of side effects unique to each substance.

Methadone should not be combined with medications that increase metabolism time in the liver. These include medicines for tuberculosis, such as Rifampin, and medicines for seizures and EPILEPSY, including Dilantin. Some antibiotics, and even over-the-counter vitamins, can increase the level of methadone retained in the bloodstream. Methadone decreases the power of medicines prescribed for the human immunodeficiency virus (HIV), the virus that can lead to acquired immunodeficiency syndrome (AIDS). Methadone can worsen nausea, vomiting, and fatigue in patients with AIDS. Since people can be infected with HIV by sharing needles to inject heroin, some ill addicts might not be able to tolerate a methadone plan of treatment.

Treatment for Habitual Users

Habitual use of methadone is encouraged in people trying to kick an opiate habit. This is because proper use of methadone allows addicts to resume a normal life again. Studies from many countries show that heroin addicts who have lost jobs and contact with their families, and have fallen into criminal behavior, can turn their lives around as long as they adhere to a strictly supervised methadone plan. Sometimes recovering addicts take methadone for years. In other cases, the methadone doses are gradually decreased over a period of months until a full recovery is achieved.

However, many addicts who start a methadone treatment program will have difficulties following the plan. Some quit and go back to hard drugs. Others falter here and there, or become dependent on

epilepsy: a disorder involving the misfiring of electrical impulses in the brain, sometimes resulting in seizures and loss of communication

U·X·L Encyclopedia of Drugs & Addictive Substances

Natural Sources of Drugs

Left: Wild ephedra is shown growing in a canyon in Utah. *See* Ephedra, Vol. 3. *(© Scott T. Smith/Corbis)*

Above right: The sap of the opium poppy is used to make a variety of prescription and illegal painkillers. See Codeine, Vol. 2; Heroin, Vol. 3; Morphine, Vol. 4; and Opium, Vol. 5. *(© Vo Trung Dung/Corbis)*

Natural Sources of Drugs

Right: Some Native Americans use the hallucinogenic peyote cactus in religious rituals. *See* Mescaline, Vol. 4. *(AP/Wide World Photos)*

Below left: Tobacco is one of the most widely abused, mind-altering drugs in the world. See Nicotine, Vol. 4. *(© Kevin Fleming/Corbis)*

Natural Sources of Drugs

Top: Marijuana is the most widely used illegal controlled substance in the world. *See* Marijuana, Vol. 4. *(AP/Wide World Photos)*

Middle: Coffee is a major source of caffeine. *See* Caffeine, Vol. 2. *(© Renée Comet/PictureArts/Corbis)*

Bottom: DMT is found in the poisonous venom of the cane toad. *See* Dimethyltryptamine (DMT), Vol. 2. *(© Wayne Lawler; Ecoscene/Corbis)*

Herbal Drugs and Dietary Supplements

Top: Wild echinacea is shown growing near Mount Adams in Washington. *See* Herbal Drugs, Vol. 3. *(© Steve Terrill/Corbis)*

Middle: St. John's Wort is used to treat depression and anxiety. *See* Antidepressants, Vol. 1, and Herbal Drugs, Vol. 3. *(© Clay Perry/Corbis)*

Bottom: The bulking supplement creatine is used by weight lifters, bodybuilders, and other athletes. *See* Creatine, Vol. 2. *(© Najlah Feanny/Corbis)*

Older Illicit Drugs

Top: When snorted, cocaine reaches the brain in less than one minute. *See* Cocaine, Vol. 2. *(Photo by Lezlie Light)*

Middle: Putting tiny amounts of LSD on blotter papers is a common way to take a dose. *See* LSD (Lysergic Acid Diethylamide), Vol. 3. *(Sinclair Stammers/Photo Researchers, Inc.)*

Bottom: Heroin is a Schedule 1 drug, meaning that it has no medical value but a high potential for abuse. *See* Heroin, Vol. 3. *(Garry Watson/Science Photo Library)*

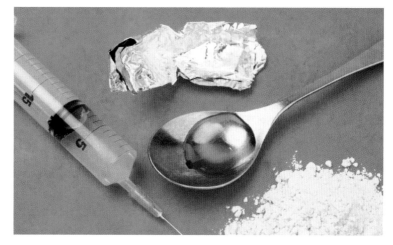

Prescription Drugs

Top row, left: Adderall®, 5 mg. *See* Adderall, Vol. 1.

Top row, middle: Darvocet-N®, 100 mg. *See* Opium, Vol. 5.

Top row, right: Demerol®, 100 mg. *See* Meperidine, Vol. 4.

2nd row, left: Dexedrine®, 5 mg. *See* Dextroamphetamine, Vol. 2.

2nd row, middle: Dilaudid®, 4 mg. *See* Hydromorphone, Vol. 3.

2nd row, right: Halcion®, 0.25 mg. *See* Benzodiazepine, Vol. 1.

3rd row, left: Lasix®, 40 mg. *See* Diuretics, Vol. 2.

3rd row, middle: MS Contin®, 15 mg. *See* Morphine, Vol. 4.

3rd row, right: Nitroglycerin, 6.5 mg. *See* Amyl Nitrite, Vol. 1.

4th row, left: OxyContin®, 40 mg. *See* Oxycodone, Vol. 5.

4th row, middle: Paxil®, 40 mg. *See* Antidepressants, Vol. 1.

4th row, right: Restoril®, 7.5 mg. *See* Benzodiazepine, Vol. 1.

5th row, left: Ritalin®, 20 mg. *See* Ritalin and Other Methylphenidates, Vol. 5.

5th row, middle: Valium®, 5 mg. *See* Tranquilizers, Vol. 5.

5th row, right: Vicodin ES®, 7.5 mg. *See* Meperidine, Vol. 4.

Bottom row, left: Wellbutrin®, 100 mg. *See* Antidepressants, Vol. 1.

Bottom row, middle: Xanax®, 2 mg. *See* Benzodiazepine, Vol. 1.

Bottom row, right: Xenical®, 120 mg. *See* Diet Pills, Vol. 2.

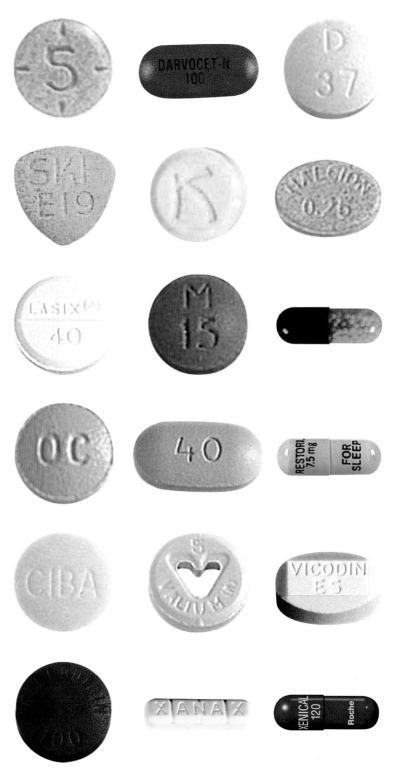

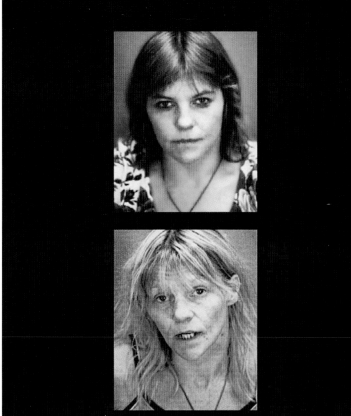

DON'T LET DRUG DEALERS CHANGE
THE FACE OF YOUR NEIGHBOURHO(
Call Crimestoppers anonymously on 0800 555 111.

SNIFFING MARKERS CAN DAMAGE YOUR BRAIN.

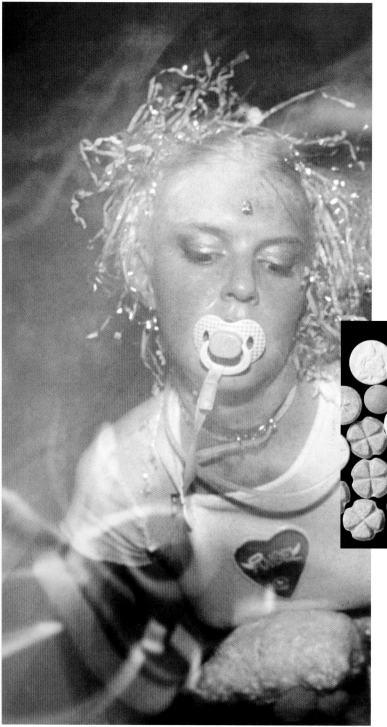

The Rave Culture

Left: A young rave dancer swirls light sticks and sucks on a pacifier. *See* 2C-B (Nexus) and Amyl Nitrite, Vol. 1; Designer Drugs, Vol. 2; Ecstasy (MDMA), GBL, GHB, and Ketamine, Vol. 3; Methamphetamine, Vol. 4; and PCP (Phencyclidine) and PMA and PMMA, Vol. 5. *(© Scott Houston/Corbis)*

Below right: Ecstasy pills come in various shapes and sizes with symbols, words, and characters stamped on them. See Ecstasy (MDMA), Vol. 3, and PMA and PMMA, Vol. 5. *(© Scott Houston/ Corbis)*

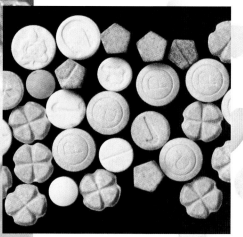

Ann Livingston, the director of the Vancouver Area Network of Drug Users, leans against a poster seeking volunteers to participate in an opiate study in 2005. The controversial program is designed to help hard-to-treat heroin addicts in Vancouver, British Columbia, Canada. Under the 12-month program, half of the participants are given prescription-grade heroin while the other half are treated with methadone. *Photo by Jeff Vinnick/Getty Images.*

another drug such as cocaine. Some combine methadone with other brain-altering drugs or alcohol. This greatly complicates the treatment process.

One researcher in a nationally published report by SAMHSA likened opiate addition to illnesses such as diabetes and extreme obesity. People with diabetes know that they have to manage their weight and watch what they eat. Some do, others do not. The ones who follow doctors' orders live longer than the ones who ignore the advice and carry on with their habits. The same holds true for obesity. People must be highly motivated to lose weight. Some are,

In the News

How many ways can methadone kill? Newspapers reveal personal stories of tragic deaths.

- In 1999, an eight-year-old boy died following a mix-up in his prescription, having taken methadone instead of Ritalin (methylphenidate). It was one of six documented cases of confusion over the similar names for the two drugs.
- In 2001, an eight-year user of prescription methadone, a father with a young child, died in Ontario, Canada, after doctors refused to place him on a liver-transplant list. The man died of liver failure unrelated to his methadone use. A physician admitted that the victim was discriminated against because he used methadone.
- In 2002, a Fort Lauderdale, Florida, woman died in her home at age forty-one of a multiple-drug overdose, including prescribed methadone. She was being treated for an intensely painful back deformity.
- In 2002, a two-year-old boy died of methadone overdose in Sheffield, England, after drinking the sweetened liquid containing methadone that his mother had brought home from a clinic. His mother was high on heroin at the time.
- In 2002, a fifteen-year-old Toronto girl lapsed into a coma and stopped breathing many hours after drinking a beverage laced with methadone. Someone had spiked her drink without her knowledge.
- In 2004, a Colorado State University student died a month before his twenty-first birthday from a combination of alcohol and methadone. He collapsed on a street near the campus.

some are not. The ones who make a commitment to change often live longer than the ones who do not change their lifestyles. Drug addicts are also suffering from a disease, and their willingness to fight the disease influences their ability to overcome it.

Most doctors realize that simply dispensing methadone tablets to people with a drug addiction will not end the cycle of abuse. Opiate addicts must also undergo talk therapy with counselors who are trained to offer strategies for combating drug use. Self-help groups such as Narcotics Anonymous can be helpful but might not be enough for those requiring methadone therapy. Most methadone clinics combine drug treatment with personal counseling.

Self-Healing on the Street

Studies are being conducted of methadone abuse on the streets to see how the drug is used recreationally. Some researchers suggest that ILLICIT methadone is used less for the high it produces and more as a self-treatment for withdrawal symptoms when other opiates are not available. Methadone is not a safe recreational drug. It is

illicit: unlawful

habit-forming. Anyone using it for any reason should be under the close supervision of a doctor.

Consequences

When used properly, methadone can literally save lives. Heroin users expose themselves to many deadly diseases, including HIV and hepatitis (a liver disease), when they share dirty needles. Heroin users are also prone to commit crimes or indulge in risky behavior. By stopping heroin use, the cycle of the desperate pursuit of the next "fix" ends. A thirty-one-year-old recovering heroin addict, quoted in the *York Daily Record,* said he rode a bus two hours each way from his home every day for his methadone treatments. Admitting he had been jailed "at least ten times," the man said that methadone "gives me the ability to get on with my day." While methadone treatment for drug abuse is not easy, quick, or always successful, it does offer hope to people who are harming themselves and others.

As a prescription painkiller, methadone use must be monitored very carefully for the potential of poisonous build-up in the body. Doctors prescribing it for pain need to be quite knowledgeable about how to adjust the doses and how to monitor patients for overdose. Patients must be aware that they need to take the medicine *exactly as prescribed* or face possibly fatal consequences. Doctors must be particularly careful when patients are taking any other medications, either prescription or over-the-counter drugs. When used as a prescription painkiller, methadone is typically a drug of last resort.

Any use of methadone with other drugs and alcohol in a recreational setting can be fatal. Failure to store the medicine properly can lead to poisoning in children. Crushing methadone pills and snorting or injecting them for recreational use can cause death, sometimes many hours or even a day or two after use. Methadone overdose generally causes the user to fall asleep, and the sleep then deepens into a coma that ends when the user's breathing stops.

Methadone is a habit-forming drug. Community leaders often fight against having methadone clinics in their neighborhoods because the clinics attract drug abusers who may have committed criminal acts. Anyone considering experimentation with methadone should keep in mind that those who really *need* the drug have very difficult lives with extremely challenging mental or physical illnesses.

The Law

Methadone is a Schedule II controlled substance, meaning that the U.S. government finds it to have some medical uses but also a high potential for abuse and addiction. Penalties for possession and sale of illegal methadone vary from state to state and can be quite harsh, since the drug carries so many potential dangers. Even a first conviction for possession or sale of illicit methadone can carry jail time. Second and third offenses can result in a lifetime in prison.

In 2000 the FDA relaxed some of the restrictions on the legal prescription of methadone. Still, doctors who prescribe the drug must attend training sessions to learn about methadone's profile, how to prescribe the drug safely, and how to monitor patients for life-threatening side effects. Doctors who finish the training are issued a special license to prescribe methadone. Needless to say, any doctor or pharmacist who issues methadone without the proper documentation can face prosecution as a criminal.

Methadone's dangerous side effects, its history as a substance used to help addicts, and its long-lasting effects on the body have all combined to bring its uses—both legal and illegal—under greater scrutiny.

For More Information

Books

Clayman, Charles B., ed. *The American Medical Association Encyclopedia of Medicine.* New York: Random House, 1989.

Gahlinger, Paul M. *Illegal Drugs: A Complete Guide to Their History, Chemistry, Use and Abuse.* Las Vegas, NV: Sagebrush Press, 2001.

Smith, D., and Richard Seymour. *Clinician's Guide to Substance Abuse.* New York: McGraw-Hill, 2000.

Periodicals

Babb, J. J. "Colorado State U. Student's Death Result of Alcohol, Methadone." *America's Intelligence Wire* (January 18, 2005).

"Cocaine Abuse by Methadone Patients Is a Growing Problem." *The Addiction Letter* (March, 1995): p. 1.

Dalrymple, Theodore. "An Official License to Kill." *New Statesman* (March 3, 2003): p. 30.

"Florida's Prescription Drug Deaths Now Exceed Those from Cocaine, Heroin." *South Florida Sun Sentinel* (November 13, 2002).

Gebhart, Fred. "Methadone-Related Deaths on the Rise, Report State Boards." *Drug Topics* (October 11, 2004): p. 65.

Hawaleshka, Danylo. "Too Many Deaths: As Ontario's Methadone Program for Drug Addicts Expands, So Do Fatalities." *Maclean's* (February 25, 2002): p. 44.

Henle, Mark. "Dartmouth College: New Hampshire Methadone Clinic Stymied by Zoning." *America's Intelligence Wire* (May 10, 2004).

Higgins, Michael. "Deerfield, Ill.-Based Walgreens Admits Giving Methadone to Brain-Damaged Boy." *Knight Ridder/Tribune Business News* (October 8, 2003).

Kinross, Ian. "Methadone Clients Denied Life-Saving Liver Transplants." *Journal of Addiction and Mental Health* (March-April, 2001): p. 3.

Patterson, Karen. "Beyond Methadone: New Hope for Heroin Addicts Comes in Tablet Form." *Dallas Morning News* (January 11, 2003).

Randerson, James. "Painkiller Linked to Rise in Overdose Deaths." *New Scientist* (March 6, 2004): p. 14.

Sadovsky, Richard. "Public Health Issue: Methadone Maintenance Therapy." *American Family Physician* (July 15, 2000): p. 428.

Schulte, Fred, and Nancy McVicar. "Rx for Death: Patients in Pain Overdosing in Alarming Numbers." *South Florida Sun-Sentinel* (May 12, 2002).

Smith, Sharon. "York County, Pa., Heroin Addicts Make Daily Trek for Methadone." *York Daily Record* (November 7, 2003).

Wainwright, Martin. "Boy, 2, Died from Mother's Methadone." *Europe Intelligence Wire* (October 8, 2002).

Wilson, Clare. "Fixed Up: When Nothing Else Works, Heroin Addicts Should Be Prescribed the Drug They Crave." *New Scientist* (March 30, 2002): p. 34.

Web Sites

"2003 National Survey on Drug Use and Health (NSDUH)." *Substance Abuse and Mental Health Services Administration (SAMHSA)*. http://www.drugabusestatistics.samhsa.gov (accessed July 29, 2005).

"The DAWN Report: Trends in Drug-Related Emergency Department Visits, 1994-2001 At a Glance" (June, 2003). *Drug Abuse Warning Network: Office of Applied Studies, Substance Abuse and Mental Health Services Administration*. http://dawninfo.samhsa.gov/old_dawn/pubs_94_02/shortreports/files/TDR_EDvisits_glance_1994_2001.pdf (accessed July 31, 2005).

"Information Bulletin: Methadone Abuse Increasing" (September, 2004). *National Drug Intelligence Center*. http://www.usdoj.gov/ndic/pubs6/6292/6292t.htm (accessed July 28, 2005).

"Methadone" (April, 2000). *Executive Office of the President, Office of National Drug Control Policy (ONDCP)*. http://www.whitehousedrugpolicy.gov/publications/factsht/methadone/index.html (accessed July 28, 2005).

"Methadone Abuse Surpasses OxyContin in Kentucky." *Join Together.* http://www.jointogether.org/sa/news/summaries/reader/0,1854,570886,00.html (accessed July 28, 2005).

"Methadone-Associated Mortality: Report of a National Assessment." *Substance Abuse and Mental Health Services Administration.* http://dpt.samhsa.gov/reports/methodone_mortality-03.htm (accessed July 31, 2005).

"Pulse Check: Drug Markets and Chronic Users in 25 of America's Largest Cities" (January, 2004). *Executive Office of the President, Office of National Drug Control Policy.* http://www.whitehousedrugpolicy.gov/publications/drugfact/pulsechk/january04/january2004.pdf (accessed July 28, 2005).

See also: Cocaine; Codeine; Fentanyl; Hydromorphone; Morphine; Opium; Oxycodone; Ritalin and Other Methylphenidates

Methamphetamine

What Kind of Drug Is It?

Methamphetamine, commonly referred to as "meth," is a synthetic, or laboratory-made, stimulant. Stimulants increase alertness, endurance, and feelings of well-being in the user. Examples of other stimulant drugs include cocaine and caffeine. (Entries on both of these drugs are available in this encyclopedia.) Methamphetamine is considered an especially powerful and addictive substance—far more addictive even than cocaine—because of its powerful effect on the brain.

Methamphetamine was developed by a Japanese chemist in 1919 from amphetamine, another laboratory-made drug. Amphetamine increases energy, reduces appetite, and helps keep users awake. (An entry on amphetamines is also available in this encyclopedia.) The first amphetamine had been made by a German chemist in the late 1880s, but it was not used for medical purposes until decades later. In its earliest form, amphetamine was found to be an effective treatment for asthma (AZ-muh), a lung disorder that interferes with normal breathing. Because of its similar ability to unclog breathing passages, methamphetamine was originally used as a nasal decongestant.

As of 2005, the medical use of methamphetamine was extremely limited. However, illicit, or unlawful, use was quite high worldwide. Like other amphetamines, methamphetamine boosts energy levels and produces an intense rush or high in the user. These properties have made it popular with recreational drug users—those who use a drug solely to get high, not to treat a medical condition. The dangers of methamphetamine lie in its strength and its high potential for addiction. Few people can "try" methamphetamine once without wanting more. Experts in the medical, behavioral, and law enforcement fields considered meth abuse one of the most serious social threats of the early twenty-first century.

Overview

Methamphetamine is a highly addictive stimulant drug. It is closely related to amphetamine but has a longer lasting and more TOXIC effect on individuals who abuse it. Because of its potentially harmful side effects, methamphetamine is only prescribed by doctors when other

Official Drug Name: Methamphetamine (METH-am-FETT-uh-meen), methamphetamine hydrochloride (Desoxyn [des-OK-sinn]); deoxyephedrine (dee-OK-see-ih-FEH-drinn; Methedrine)

Also Known As: Batu, chalk, crank, crystal, crystal meth, glass, ice, meth, poor man's cocaine, shabu, speed, tina, trash, ya ba, zip

Drug Classifications: Schedule II, stimulant

toxic: harmful, poisonous, or capable of causing death

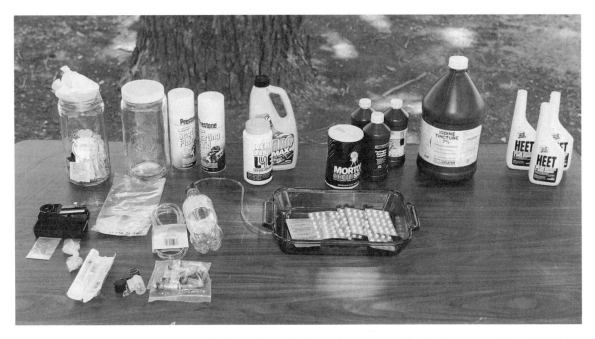

Methamphetamine is made from ingredients that are readily available in homes and stores. (Some of the products used are displayed here.) Many of the chemicals used to make meth carry warning labels noting that they are toxic or harmful if consumed. *AP/Wide World Photos.*

medications have failed to help their patients. Methamphetamine has been used with some success in individuals with attention-deficit/hyperactivity disorder (ADHD). Children and adults who have been diagnosed with ADHD are typically impulsive, somewhat edgy, and have difficulty focusing and controlling their actions. These symptoms often interfere with their ability to function socially and academically. Methamphetamine is also approved for use in treating obesity as well as narcolepsy, a rare sleep disorder characterized by daytime tiredness and sudden attacks of sleep.

What is of great concern to drug-control authorities, however, is the increasingly widespread abuse of methamphetamine. During the 1990s and early 2000s, the illegal manufacture and distribution of the drug increased dramatically in the United States. According to the 2004 "National Synthetic Drugs Action Plan" prepared by the U.S. Office of National Drug Control Policy (ONDCP), the bulk of the methamphetamine sold in the United States is produced illegally in California. "Most of the large super labs in California are run by organizations with ties to Mexico," noted the authors of the "Action Plan." However, record numbers of smaller, independent labs began popping up throughout the American Midwest beginning in 2003. Authorities considered the eastward movement of the methamphetamine problem and the "dramatic increase" in these Midwestern labs to be "particularly troubling."

The illegal use of methamphetamine had reached epidemic proportions in the United States as of 2005. According to the "2003 National Survey on Drug Use and Health (NSDUH)," 12.3 million Americans age twelve and older—more than 5 percent of the U.S. population— have tried methamphetamine at least once in their lives. The majority of users that year were between the ages of eighteen and thirty-four, and more than half of the new users were under eighteen.

Homemade Meth

Methamphetamine can be manufactured or "cooked" in home laboratories. *MSNBC.com* special reporter Jon Bonné noted in the online article "Meth's Deadly Buzz" that the drug "is easily manufactured domestically with common household items such as batteries and cold medicine." Meth "cooks" are usually untrained, and the chemicals they use are highly flammable, meaning they are capable of catching fire and burning quickly. This increases the likelihood of accidental explosions in meth labs. Despite the risks, drug traffickers set up their operations in small spaces such as bathrooms, sheds, basements, crawl spaces, motel rooms, and even suitcases. The business has become something of a family tradition in some cases, with parents passing recipes and production tips down to their children.

In order to avoid being caught, some meth cooks set up their equipment in mobile labs. These labs might be assembled in car trunks, vans, travel trailers, motor homes, and even trucks. But because meth production has a great potential for explosions, especially among inexperienced cooks, the mobile labs become toxic time bombs that present a very real threat to police and motorists. In addition to explosions, mobile labs have been known to leak hazardous materials, resulting in road closures while the cleanup work is being done. In many cases, both mobile and non-mobile labs have to be disassembled by hazardous materials (hazmat) crews or law enforcement officers dressed in protective gear.

Abusing Meth Equals Quick Addiction

Methamphetamine produces feelings of euphoria, which is a state of extreme happiness and enhanced well-being. It also increases energy by raising the levels of two NEUROTRANSMITTERS in the brain: 1) dopamine (DOPE-uh-meen), which is a combination

neurotransmitters: substances that help spread nerve impulses from one nerve cell to another

Narcotics task force agents are shown combing through the various chemicals used to make methamphetamine found on a truck in Kentucky. Some people make meth in vans, trucks, or trailers so they can move from place to place in order to dodge police. Moving meth labs contain toxic ingredients that can explode, causing injuries to motorists, highway closures, and thousands of dollars in damages and cleanup costs.

AP/ Wide World Photos.

of carbon, hydrogen, nitrogen, and oxygen; and 2) norepinephrine (nor-epp-ih-NEFF-run), which is a natural stimulant. The drug causes excessive amounts of these chemicals to be released, resulting in a spike, or sudden increase, in their concentration in the brain.

Methamphetamine's effect on dopamine levels can help treat patients with ADHD and narcolepsy. Dopamine plays a key role in regulating attention. It acts on the part of the brain

Children of Users Suffer Neglect

The growing abuse of methamphetamine has had an enormous impact on users' children. As of 2005, the child welfare issue was particularly problematic in rural areas of the United States. Oklahoma and Kentucky seem to have been hit especially hard. The number of neglected children in these areas has skyrocketed as more and more parents have begun using, making, and selling methamphetamine at home.

According to Kate Zernike in a July 2005 *New York Times* article, the problem is compounded by the fact that these rural areas lack the kind of social services needed to help youths who have been raised in a drug-using environment. Under such circumstances, children are forced to fend for themselves because their parents are often either high or sleeping off the effects of their last binge. When parents are arrested for their drug activity, their underage kids are typically placed in foster homes.

"Many of these neglected children struggle with emotional, developmental and abandonment issues," noted Zernike. "It has become harder to attract and keep foster parents because the children of methamphetamine arrive with so many behavioral problems; they may not get into their beds at night because they are so used to sleeping on the floor, and they may resist toilet training because they are used to wearing dirty diapers."

responsible for filtering incoming information, making choices, and deciding when and how to act. However, in users who do not have ADHD or narcolepsy, methamphetamine's effect on dopamine increases alertness, brings on a sense of happiness and contentment, and creates an urge for more and more of the drug. That is what makes it so dangerous. As Julia Sommerfeld explained in the article "Beating an Addiction to Meth" on *MSNBC.com*: "While high levels of dopamine in the brain usually cause feelings of pleasure, too much can produce aggressiveness, irritability, and schizophrenic-like behavior." Schizophrenic behavior refers to exhibiting the symptoms of schizophrenia, a severe mental disease characterized by a withdrawal from reality and other intellectual and emotional disturbances.

Methamphetamine addiction can occur easily. Users who want to lose weight take methamphetamine to decrease their appetites. Others might try it for the burst of energy it provides to cram for exams or work extra hours. But the effects of the drug are so intense that occasional users or even first-timers often find themselves craving more. *KCI: The Anti-Meth Site* posts stories of users who have been drawn into the world of addiction. Their accounts illustrate the drug's destructive effects.

"The Meth Epidemic in America"

In July of 2005, a report titled "The Meth Epidemic in America" was released by the National Association of Counties (NACo). Five hundred counties from forty-five states participated in the survey. About 87 percent of responding law enforcement agencies reported increases in meth-related arrests since 2002. In addition, 40 percent of child welfare officials surveyed reported an increase in children needing out-of-home placements due to methamphetamine-related activities.

NACo president Angelo D. Kyle wrote in his executive summary of the survey: "The methamphetamine epidemic in the United States, which began in the West and is moving East, is having a devastating effect on our country. The increasingly widespread production, distribution and use of meth are now affecting urban, suburban and rural communities nationwide."

Impact on the Environment

The illegal manufacture of methamphetamine takes its toll on the environment as well. Statistics from "The Meth Epidemic in America" indicate that for every pound of methamphetamine produced, five to seven pounds of toxic waste are created. The solid wastes are usually dumped down household drains, in yards, or on back roads. The accompanying poisonous gas is released into the air. Chemicals from large-scale methamphetamine laboratory dump sites have killed livestock, contaminated streams, and destroyed trees and vegetation.

According to the ONDCP: "The cleanup operation following the discovery of a dump or . . . laboratory site is typically an extremely expensive endeavor." California spent nearly $5 million cleaning up meth sites in 2002, and costs are on the rise. As meth makers refine their skills and upgrade their labs, larger amounts of the drug can be produced at a single site. More meth means more TOXINS, which translates into more expensive cleanup operations. "Some labs are now able to produce 100 pounds or more of methamphetamine per production cycle," notes the ONDCP report. "[T]his increased productivity leaves behind increased amounts of toxic waste." The effect of these chemicals on the nation's water supply—and all the people who drink from it—remains to be seen.

What Is It Made Of?

Methamphetamine is closely related to amphetamine but has longer lasting and more toxic effects on the user's system. Meth is a white, odorless powder that dissolves easily in water or alcohol. Production of the drug begins with common

toxins: poisonous substances

Meth makers concoct various devices to create the drug, including those resembling old moonshine (illegal alcohol) stills of years past. Drug makers use abandoned houses, trailers, barns, vans, motel rooms, and other hidden places to make the drug. *AP/Wide World Photos.*

chemicals, including EPHEDRINE or PSEUDOEPHEDRINE. Ephedrine-containing pills and powders were banned by the U.S. Food and Drug Administration (FDA) in 2004. However, as of mid-2005, illicit supplies were still available through the Internet. Pseudoephedrine is a key ingredient in cold medicines and asthma drugs. (An entry on over-the-counter drugs is available in this encyclopedia.)

ephedrine: pronounced ih-FEH-drinn; a chemical substance that eases breathing problems

pseudoephedrine: pronounced SUE-doh-ih-FEH-drinn; a chemical similar to ephedrine that is used to relieve nasal congestion

Methamphetamine is relatively easy to produce in homemade laboratories. Various newspaper accounts note that meth cooks routinely brew small batches of the drug in their home labs using household goods that they purchased legally in stores. Many use recipes they find on the Internet posted by amateur chemists. As such, the strength and toxicity of each batch can vary considerably. By 2005, more and more Americans were expressing their concern over the ease with which these meth ingredients could be purchased. As a result, lawmakers began to push for crackdowns on the sale of ephedrine and greater restrictions on the sale of pseudoephedrine-containing medicines.

How Is It Taken?

Methamphetamine is swallowed, snorted, injected, smoked, absorbed through the gums, or inserted through the anus.

Legal Form

The prescription form of methamphetamine (Desoxyn) comes in the form of a white tablet. Each tablet contains 5 milligrams of methamphetamine HYDROCHLORIDE. Its chemical formula is $C_{10}H_{15}NHCl$.

Illegal Forms

Illegally produced methamphetamine tablets often contain large amounts of caffeine. The tablets are sweet, brightly colored, and about the size of a pencil eraser. These pills are called ya ba, the Thai term for "crazy drug." Ya ba is especially popular in the Southeast Asian countries of Thailand, Burma, and Laos. It first appeared in the United States in 1999, with use centered in the Southeast Asian communities of California. In a September 2002 article for the *North County Times,* Louise Chu explained, "Ya ba has become a vague label for any type of meth in pill form, although it specifically refers to the brand produced in Southeast Asia."

The powdered form of methamphetamine is much more common. Users absorb it through mucous membranes in a variety of ways—snorted up the nose, rubbed onto the gums, wrapped in a cigarette paper and swallowed, or even wrapped and inserted into the anus. The powder dissolves quickly and is sometimes added to coffee or alcoholic drinks.

hydrochloride: a chemical compound composed of the elements hydrogen and chlorine, often in the form of a crystallized salt

Liquefied methamphetamine is made by adding water to the powdered form of the drug. As a liquid, it can be injected directly into a user's vein or muscle.

Drug smugglers will try just about anything to get their product into the United States. This U.S. Customs photo shows the drug ya ba, a form of methamphetamine, concealed in a shipment of dead bugs.
AP/ Wide World Photos.

Chunks of methamphetamine hydrochloride look like clear crystals and are often referred to as "ice." A common way to smoke ice is in a glass pipe with a bulb on one end. According to G. C. Luna in a 2001 article posted on the *SciELO Public Health* Web site, "some methamphetamine users break off the tops of light bulbs, put the drug into the glass bulb, heat the underside of the bulb, and inhale the contents."

A quarter of a gram of methamphetamine costs anywhere from twenty to sixty dollars on the BLACK MARKET. Meth users are willing to spend the money to purchase such a small amount of the drug because a long-lasting high can be achieved with very small quantities.

black market: the illegal sale or trade of goods; drug dealers are said to carry out their business on the "black market"

Was Hitler a User?

During World War II (1939–1945), methamphetamine was one of several stimulant drugs given to soldiers to fight off battle fatigue. Some experts suspect that Nazi dictator Adolf Hitler (1889–1945) used methamphetamine regularly from the mid-1930s until the end of the war, when he committed suicide in an underground bunker. According to the 2005 History Channel television documentary *High Hitler,* "In 1938 the king of Italy told his foreign minister that Hitler was being injected [with] narcotics and stimulants. Hitler's valet said that every morning before he got out of bed he had an injection that made him immediately alert and fresh for the day."

Hitler also had symptoms such as tremors, shuffling, and poor eyesight. It is unknown if some of these symptoms were caused by a neurological disorder such as Parkinson's disease, or by a drug habit. It is well documented, however, that Hitler's personal physician, Dr. Theodor Morell, provided him with a variety of daily medications. As noted in "High Hitler," Morell admitted in his diary that he supplied Hitler with a substance called "vitamultin" in both pill and injectable form. Many experts are convinced that Germany's leader was taking methamphetamine. Historians believe that Hitler's drug abuse affected his judgment and may have influenced his decision-making abilities during the war.

Are There Any Medical Reasons for Taking This Substance?

In the United States, methamphetamine is approved for use in treating certain medical conditions. It is used medically to manage the symptoms of ADHD and narcolepsy. It can also be used as a short-term treatment for obesity.

Usage Trends

Methamphetamine was developed in the early twentieth century from amphetamine. Its stimulating effects on the brain and body quickly led to its abuse as a recreational drug.

Methamphetamine in the Second Half of the Twentieth Century

By the 1960s, the availability of injectable methamphetamine had increased, and the rate of addiction grew substantially. In 1970 the U.S. government passed the Controlled Substances Act (CSA), which classified methamphetamine as a Schedule II substance. This meant that it is approved for medical use with a prescription but nevertheless possesses a high potential for abuse. This legislation severely restricted the legal production of methamphetamine. With these restrictions, however, came a huge jump in the number of illegal labs that were manufacturing the drug. In the 1980s, a smokeable form of methamphetamine, known as ice or crank, came into widespread use.

Methamphetamine TRAFFICKING and abuse has been on the rise in the United States and throughout the world since the 1990s. Various sources, including the ONDCP's "Action Plan," have found that the methamphetamine problem is spreading from the western United States to the Midwest and the South. Much of the illegal supply is made and distributed by Mexican drug trafficking organizations. By the early 2000s, meth was being distributed by Mexican traffickers through networks that had been established earlier for cocaine, heroin, and marijuana sales. (Entries on these three drugs are also available in this encyclopedia.) According to the Drug Enforcement Administration's "Statistics: DEA Drug Seizures," more than 118 million doses of methamphetamine were seized in 2002. In addition, the agency's National Clandestine Laboratory Database reported that some 7,000 meth labs were destroyed in 2004. The states of Iowa, Missouri, and Tennessee reported the highest number of meth lab incidents that year.

Is There Such a Thing as a Meth User Profile?

Most methamphetamine users report that they began taking the drug as an experiment. They wanted to have more energy and experience a powerful high. In the late 1990s, meth use in the United States was highest among white, male, blue-collar workers on the West Coast. As of 2005, the user profile had broadened to include diverse groups in all regions of the country. The authors of the 2005 study "The Meth Epidemic in America" noted that more high school- and college-aged students were taking the drug. Use had grown enormously among individuals in their twenties and thirties. There is no longer a definition of a "typical meth user." Use is high among the employed and the unemployed, white-collar workers and blue-collar workers, men and women. Though typically associated with whites, use is spreading among Hispanics and Native Americans as well.

Other groups showing increased use of methamphetamine include homeless and runaway youths, individuals who attend RAVES, and homosexuals. The gay community is at special risk because of the "party and play" trend developing in homosexual circles. As reported by David J. L. Jefferson in a February 2005 *Newsweek* article, "party and play" refers to using methamphetamine and then having sex—often without a condom. There is growing concern that this type of abuse

trafficking: making, selling, or distributing a controlled drug

raves: wild overnight dance parties that typically involve huge crowds of people, loud techno music, and illegal drug use will lead to an increase in the spread of acquired immunodeficiency syndrome (AIDS). Jefferson noted that when comparing nonusers and users of methamphetamine, the users were twice as likely to engage in unprotected sex and four times as likely to be HIV positive (carrying the human immunodeficiency virus, which can lead to AIDS).

Teen Use in the United States

The results of the Monitoring the Future (MTF) study were released to the public on December 21, 2004. An annual survey on adolescent drug use and attitudes, it is conducted by the University of Michigan (U of M) with funding from the National Institute on Drug Abuse (NIDA). According to the report, the percentage of eighth, tenth, and twelfth graders who had used methamphetamine in a one-year period decreased over the previous five years. In 1999, some 3.2 percent of eighth graders used methamphetamine at least once during the year, compared to 1.5 percent of eighth graders in 2004. Tenth-grader use in a one-year period decreased from 4.6 to 3 percent, and senior use of methamphetamine dropped from 4.7 to 3.4 percent.

The DAWN Reports

The Drug Abuse Warning Network (DAWN) keeps track of drug-related emergency department (ED) visits throughout the United States. Prior to 2003, statistics on methamphetamine and other amphetamines were grouped together in DAWN reports. The report titled "Amphetamine and Methamphetamine Emergency Department Visits, 1995-2002" showed a rise in the number of ED mentions related to these drugs over the seven-year span. Between 1995 and 2002, methamphetamine and amphetamine ED visits rose from 25,245 to 38,961—an increase of 54 percent. The latest DAWN figures available as of mid-2005 were from the last two quarters of 2003. During that six-month period, methamphetamine use alone accounted for more than 25,000 drug abuse-related ED visits. An additional 18,129 visits were attributed to other amphetamine use. Most of the patients were white males between the ages of eighteen and thirty-four.

Meth Use High Worldwide

Methamphetamine abuse is a global problem. The CBC-TV documentary series *The Fifth Estate* ran an episode called "Dark Crystal" in March of 2005 that reported on the meth problem in Canada. The number of illegal labs shut down by Canadian authorities in 2003 was nearly ten times higher than the number

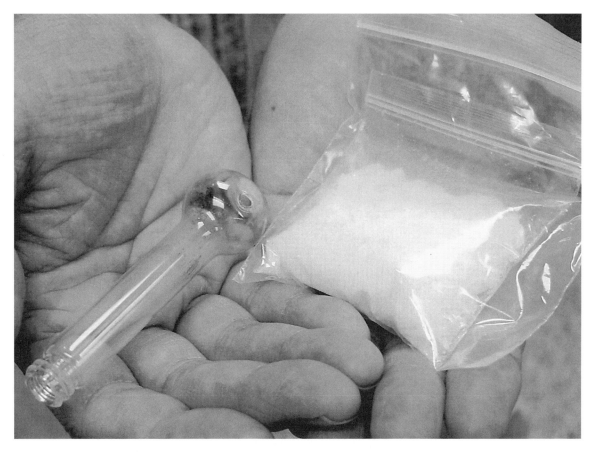

A one-ounce bag of crystal meth, also known as "ice," is shown here by police in Hawaii. It was seized during a raid on a home located on the same street as the police department. *AP/Wide World Photos.*

shut down in 1998. In addition, methamphetamine-related deaths rose from three in the year 2000 to thirty-three in the year 2004. Most of the deaths resulted from overdoses or car crashes involving a driver high on meth.

According to the 1998 United Nations fact sheet "Amphetamine-Type Stimulants: A Problem Requiring Priority Attention," in Japan nearly 90 percent of all drug-law violations involved methamphetamine. High rates of abuse have also been a problem in Thailand, the Philippines, and Korea since the 1990s. The World Health Organization's "Management of Substance Abuse" report states that "a major epidemic of methamphetamine use . . . appears to be spreading across the entire Asia Pacific region."

Effects on the Body

When snorted or taken orally, one "hit" of methamphetamine can produce a high that lasts for about twelve hours. In general, the faster the meth is absorbed into the body, the more intense the pleasurable feelings experienced by the user. Injecting and smoking methamphetamine deliver a "rush" that cannot be achieved by snorting powder or swallowing pills, which slows the absorption process. Most addicts inject liquid methamphetamine or smoke crystal meth because the rush is what they're seeking.

Injecting methamphetamine is the most dangerous method of use. When methamphetamine is dissolved in water, dust, germs, and other materials can get into the liquid. The syringe used to inject the drug into the veins may be dirty as well. Any contaminants in the liquid or on the needle will be injected directly into the bloodstream. Users who inject methamphetamine run the risk of contracting both HIV and HEPATITIS A from sharing needles. The injections can also cause sores at the injection sites.

Methamphetamine is an extremely dangerous and addictive drug. It increases heart and breathing rates, blood pressure, and body temperature. Other effects include NAUSEA, diarrhea, increased talka-tiveness, and a tendency to engage in repetitive actions. When the drug is injected, the initial rush leads some individuals to report feeling invincible, as if they can take on the world. Throughout the high that follows, users frequently appear more self-assured, "pumped up," and sexually aroused. They also may become extremely aggressive. As time passes, however, the surge of energy begins to fade. At that point, users are said to be crashing. They typically experience: 1) dehydration—an abnormally low amount of fluid in the body; 2) anxiety—feelings of being extremely overwhelmed, restless, fearful, and worried; 3) tiredness; and 4) depression—feelings of hopelessness, loss of pleasure, self-blame, and sometimes suicidal thoughts.

In severe cases, a mental disorder known as methamphetamine psychosis (sy-KOH-sis) develops. Symptoms of psychosis include paranoia, or abnormal feelings of suspicion and fear; hallucinations, or visions or other perceptions of things that are not really present; and uncontrolled anxiety that may lead to rage and violent behavior. And the hallucinations are not only visual. Users may hear voices. They have also been known to tear their skin apart in search of imaginary "crank bugs" that they think they feel crawling all over their bodies.

hepatitis A: inflammation of the liver caused by a virus

nausea: upset stomach, sometimes with vomiting

A Nasty Cycle

Because methamphetamine users know what to expect when they crash, their main goal is to avoid coming down by getting high again. This process is referred to as "bingeing." Bingers may continue the drug-taking cycle for so long that they end up staying awake for days. But all meth users eventually reach a point where no amount of the drug will sustain their high. Users in this phase, which is known as "tweaking," become extremely frustrated, irritable, and likely to be involved in a serious fight or accident.

Over time, heavy methamphetamine use takes an extreme toll on the user's body—both inside and outside. A noticeable loss of weight and a tendency to sweat makes them appear ill. They may also develop body odor; yellowing, decay, or loss of teeth; and chalky pale skin. The internal effects of methamphetamine can include an irregular heartbeat, high blood pressure, and possible STROKE. Dangerously high body temperatures, convulsions, and even death may occur if a user overdoses. Methamphetamine abuse during pregnancy can lead to premature delivery and harm to the baby.

What Meth Does to the Brain

Research conducted by Dr. Nora D. Volkow and published in the March 2001 issue of the *American Journal of Psychiatry* indicates that methamphetamine impairs the brain's ability to resist repeated use of the drug. Volkow's research shows that methamphetamine users have fewer dopamine RECEPTORS in their brains than nonusers. With continued abuse, the reward center in the brains of meth addicts will not respond to any stimuli—except more meth. In the 2001 Brookhaven National Laboratory article "Methamphetamine Delivers 'One-Two' Punch to the Brain," Volkow noted that such research "may help explain why drug addicts lose control and take drugs compulsively."

In another study headed by Volkow and published in the December 2001 issue of the *Journal of Neuroscience,* users with damaged dopamine receptors were reexamined after a period of abstinence from the drug. The participants in the study were longtime abusers of methamphetamine, reporting at least two years of continued use for at least five days per week. Changes in their brains were measured in two ways: 1) using brain-imaging techniques, and 2) using their scores on tests of various physical and intellectual abilities.

In the April 2002 edition of "NIDA Notes," Patrick Zickler summarized the results of this second study. Heavy methamphetamine abusers who managed to remain drug-free "for at least nine months showed substantial recovery from damage to the dopamine transporters but not from impairments in motor skills and memory." In other words, the pictures of the recovered addicts' brains looked more like the brains of non-meth users, but their physical and intellectual performance remained low. Zickler quoted Volkow as

stroke: a loss of feeling, consciousness, or movement caused by the breaking or blocking of a blood vessel in the brain

receptors: groups of cells that receive stimuli

Number of methamphetamine lab seizures* in the United States, 2000 and 2004

State	2000	2004	Change (+/−)	State	2000	2004	Change (+/−)
Alabama	84	378	+294	Montana	28	64	+36
Alaska	26	57	+31	Nebraska	36	200	+164
Arizona	384	95	−289	Nevada	283	79	−204
Arkansas	243	743	+500	New Hampshire	1	2	+1
California	2,198	673	−1,525	New Jersey	N/A	N/A	N/A
Colorado	142	223	+81	New Mexico	50	118	+68
Connecticut	N/A	N/A	N/A	New York	2	28	+26
Delaware	1	3	+2	North Carolina	14	317	+303
Florida	15	277	+262	North Dakota	34	217	+183
Georgia	54	233	+179	Ohio	29	211	+182
Hawaii	5	7	+2	Oklahoma	399	652	+253
Idaho	127	43	−84	Oregon	351	420	+69
Illinois	127	926	+799	Pennsylvania	8	106	+98
Indiana	363	1,002	+639	Rhode Island	1	N/A	N/A
Iowa	283	1,300	+1,017	South Carolina	4	154	+150
Kansas	641	538	−103	South Dakota	7	31	+24
Kentucky	104	562	+458	Tennessee	249	1,259	+1,010
Louisiana	15	113	+98	Texas	429	434	+5
Maine	2	3	+1	Utah	209	67	−142
Maryland	N/A	1	N/A	Vermont	N/A	1	N/A
Massachusetts	N/A	1	N/A	Virginia	1	73	+72
Michigan	21	282	+261	Washington	944	743	−201
Minnesota	123	165	+42	West Virginia	3	145	+142
Mississippi	126	244	+118	Wisconsin	26	74	+48
Missouri	889	2,707	+1,818	Wyoming	12	21	+9

*Includes all meth incidents, including labs, "dumpsites" or "chemical and glassware" seizures.
Notes: In 2000 California had the most incidents (2,198); in 2004, it was Missouri (2,707). The 2000 figures are based on results submitted by 45 states; 47 states participated in 2004. N/A means that the state did not supply results data.

SOURCE: Compiled by Thomson Gale staff from data reported in "Maps of Methamphetamine Lab Seizures," *National Clandestine Laboratory Database*, U.S. Drug Enforcement Administration (DEA), U.S. Department of Justice, Alexandria, VA [Online] http://www.usdoj.gov/dea/concern/map_lab_seizures.html [accessed May 25, 2005].

saying that the changes in the brains of heavy methamphetamine abusers "are roughly equivalent to 40 years of aging." Furthermore, people who use meth may run a greater risk of developing Parkinson's disease as they age. The bottom line is that methamphetamine abuse can cause lasting brain damage.

Reactions with Other Drugs or Substances

Various drugs and substances cause dangerous health effects when taken with meth.

- The use of other stimulants along with methamphetamine has an additive effect, which can damage the heart.
- Methamphetamine mixed with over-the-counter cold medicines can cause a dangerous rise in blood pressure.

- To decrease the negative feelings experienced during tweaking, an abuser often self-medicates with a DEPRESSANT such as alcohol. But alcohol only masks the effects of methamphetamine, causing the user to crave another "hit."
- Methamphetamines taken in combination with antidepressant drugs may pose life-threatening health risks.

Treatment for Habitual Users

Methamphetamine users experience extreme psychological withdrawal when they stop using the drug. People suffering from psychological withdrawal feel that they need to keep taking the drug because they can't function without it. Sommerfeld quoted drug researcher Douglas Anglin of the University of California at Los Angeles as saying, "There's not severe physical withdrawal with methamphetamine, but rather a feeling of ANHEDONIA ... that can last for months and which leads to a lot of relapse at six months." Withdrawal from methamphetamine is characterized by drug cravings, depression, an inability to sleep, and an increased appetite. Users in this stage may become suicidal.

Rehab: Difficult but Possible

Methamphetamine addicts often resist any form of treatment or intervention, according to Luna. They feel that they'll be able to quit on their own when they're ready. Among addicts who do seek help, the treatment process is typically lengthy. It can continue for months or even more than a year after the user has quit the drug. Antidepressant medications may be used to help battle the depression that can accompany withdrawal.

However, drug therapy usually is most helpful when combined with COGNITIVE BEHAVIORAL THERAPY (CBT). According to the *Drug-Rehabs.org* Web site, the most effective treatment for methamphetamine addiction consists of behavioral interventions such as individual and group counseling. These treatments help addicts establish a new circle of non-using friends and improve their coping skills to deal with everyday stressors.

NIDA Fights Against Meth Abuse

NIDA is pursuing research on drugs that could help with the treatment of methamphetamine addiction. Dr. Nora D. Volkow, the head of NIDA, appeared before the U.S. Senate to talk about methamphetamine abuse in 2005. She stated: "To further speed

depressant: a substance that slows down the activity of an organism or one of its parts

anhedonia: pronounced ann-heh-DOE-nee-uh; the inability to experience pleasure from normally enjoyable life events

cognitive behavioral therapy (CBT): a type of therapy that helps people recognize and change negative patterns of thinking and behavior

Oregon Takes Action

To combat the illegal production of methamphetamine in Oregon, the state's lawmakers moved to make various over-the-counter (OTC) medications available only by prescription. Through such actions, occurring in mid-2005, Oregon became the first state in the nation to pass legislation to reclassify OTC cold and allergy products containing pseudoephedrine as prescription drugs. The bill was signed into law and made effective starting in mid-2006. The news was met with enthusiasm by some citizens and concern from others.

Meth is one of the biggest drugs of abuse in Oregon. As such, lawmakers looked for ways to make it more difficult for meth cooks to obtain the ingredients needed to make it. While the bill passed by a large margin in both Oregon's House and Senate, some citizens believe that the new law will create a hardship for the state's citizens who do not have health insurance or can't afford to go to a doctor. Plus, others contend that they are being punished because of the illegal actions of a few criminals. Cold and allergy drug makers also have concerns about the new law, claiming that it will drive up the price of the once-inexpensive OTC drugs.

Those favoring the bill point out that pseudoephedrine-free cold and allergy products are beginning to enter the market. In addition, doctors will be able to phone in prescriptions of the drug, so a visit to one's physician may not be necessary. Whether the measure will curb illegal meth production in Oregon will be studied by various lawmakers, police officers, and other researchers in the years ahead.

medication development efforts, NIDA has ... established the Methamphetamine Clinical Trials Group (MCTG) to conduct clinical (human) trials of medications for [methamphetamine addiction] in geographic areas in which ... abuse is particularly high, including San Diego, Kansas City, Des Moines, Costa Mesa, San Antonio, Los Angeles, and Honolulu." Among the drugs being tested are medicines used to treat high blood pressure, an anti-nausea drug, several antidepressants, and an anti-epilepsy drug. (Epilepsy is a disorder involving the misfiring of electrical impulses in the brain, sometimes resulting in seizures and loss of consciousness.) In addition, NIDA is funding research on a substance to treat meth overdoses.

Consequences

The consequences of illicit methamphetamine use include lowered productivity among addicted workers, increased health care costs, higher accident and death rates, and more crime and violence.

Crime and Meth

The increase in methamphetamine abuse by Americans has led to a surge in methamphetamine-related crimes, including theft, domestic violence, and child neglect. In 2001, Luna reported that there were "more persons incarcerated in the United States for drug-related 'crimes' than in any other country in the world." According to "The Meth Epidemic in America," law enforcement agencies in the Southwest reported a 96-percent increase in methamphetamine-related arrests between 2002 and 2005. The Northwest saw a 90-percent increase. "With the growth of this drug from the rural areas of the western and northwestern regions of this country and its slow but continuing spread to the east, local law enforcement officials see it as their number one drug problem," the report concluded.

The ONDCP's "Action Plan" refers to "drug-endangered children" as "the darkest side of the entire methamphetamine problem." In 2003 alone, more than 3,500 children in the United States were involved in meth lab incidents. The authors of the plan noted that "forty-one of these children were reported injured and one child was killed by explosions or fires" at illegal lab sites.

In the Pacific Northwest, lawmakers have stepped up legislation to combat the meth problem there. They aim to reduce the number of meth labs and the sale of the drug. But, they also have other issues to contend with regarding the use of methamphetamines. In 2005, police in several communities reported that a few teens had exchanged sex for meth. Law enforcement officials also announced that meth addicts had begun to support their habit by stealing metal and selling it for scrap at recycling centers. The addicts use the money to buy more meth. Thieves had stolen metal from irrigation systems, roadways, bridges, and even a historic train. They had removed guardrails on various back roads, particularly those in heavily forested areas. The guardrails protect drivers from going over the edge of bridges or driving off the edge of mountainous roads. Police in many communities participate on meth task forces to find ways to combat the problems of meth-related crime and abuse. Students, parents, and teachers also work to educate the public about the dangers of meth.

"The Faces of Meth"

In Multnomah County, Oregon, Sheriff's Deputy Bret King noticed some differences when looking at a batch of mug shots taken of repeat meth offenders. What he saw was shocking. When looking at images taken just a few years apart, King discovered just

DON'T LET DRUG DEALERS CHANGE
THE FACE OF YOUR NEIGHBOURHOOD.
Call Crimestoppers anonymously on 0800 555 111.

METROPOLITAN POLICE   Working for a safer London

Meth is known to alter people's appearance drastically in just a few years. In the top picture, a woman is shown at age 36. The bottom picture shows the same woman after four years of methamphetamine abuse at age 40.
© Handout/Reuters/Corbis.

how much meth abuse had changed people's appearances. Some users looked like they had aged ten to fifteen years in just a couple of years. In order to educate people about the meth problem and its devastating effects, King put together a presentation called "The Faces of Meth." In creating the program, he interviewed meth users to learn what advice they would give to young people who might be tempted to try meth. According to "The Faces of Meth" Web site, in his presentation, King wanted "to be honest with kids, let them hear directly from the inmates." The program is presented in schools and on the Internet.

AIDS Risk

A connection has been established between methamphetamine use and AIDS. In the *MSNBC.com* article "Hooked in the Haight: Life, Death, or Prison," Jon Bonné quoted San Francisco-based meth abuse counselor Michael Siever. "If you're at a party where a lot of people are injecting, when you put your needle down, someone else may pick it up." Sharing used needles greatly increases the risk of transmitting HIV (the human immunodeficiency virus, which leads to AIDS). Meth's reputation for lowering INHIBITIONS and enhancing sexual pleasure often leads users to engage in unprotected sex— another major reason for the spread of HIV and other sexually transmitted diseases.

The Law

Methamphetamine is a Schedule II drug under the Controlled Substances Act (CSA) of 1970. The CSA established five schedules, or lists, of controlled medications and substances. Substances in Schedule I have the highest potential for abuse, while those in Schedule V have the lowest abuse potential. A Schedule II substance is approved for medical use with a prescription but nevertheless has a high potential for abuse.

Unless obtained by prescription, the possession, use, or distribution of methamphetamine is prohibited in the United States. Each of these offenses carries a maximum ten years in prison and $10,000 fine. Repeat offenders receive much harsher jail sentences and fines of up to several million dollars.

Pseudoephedrine Measures

To fight the illegal manufacture of methamphetamine, some of the chemicals used in its production are included in the Comprehensive Methamphetamine Control Act of 1996 (MCA). The MCA increased penalties for the trafficking and manufacturing of methamphetamine along with the chemicals used to produce the drug. Illegal labs can produce about 1.5 pounds (0.68 kilograms) of meth from 2.2 pounds (1 kilogram) of ephedrine. Pseudoephedrine,

inhibitions: inner thoughts that keep people from engaging in certain activities

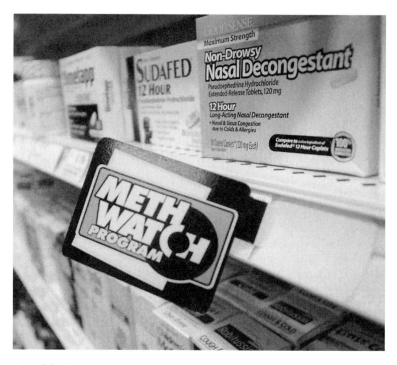

One of the ingredients used in the production of methamphetamine can be found in over-the-counter cold and allergy medicines. In an effort to curb meth production, some pharmacies began limiting the sales of such OTC drugs as part of a "Meth Watch Program." *AP/Wide World Photos.*

a substance found in cold medicines, can be used for the same purpose. Stores that sell pseudoephedrine are required to report to authorities any large-volume sales of the chemical.

By mid-2005, about thirty states had either passed or were considering passing laws that would limit the sale of pseudoephedrine. Some retailers have voluntarily moved these "over-the-counter" medicines "behind-the-counter" to the pharmacy area. There, the products are locked up and distributed only in limited amounts to customers showing picture identification. Federal and state laws restricting the sale of pseudoephedrine-based cold medicines are leading drug companies to reformulate their products with a substance called phenylephrine (FENN-uhl-EFF-reen or FENN-uhl-EFF-rin). Phenylephrine has been used in the past as an ingredient in eye drops and decongestants. It cannot be converted to methamphetamine in a home laboratory. As of mid-2005, cold products that contain phenylephrine were being sold in Europe.

For More Information

Books

Clayton, Lawrence. *Designer Drugs.* New York: Rosen Publishing Group, 1998.

McDowell, D., and Henry Spitz. *Substance Abuse: From Principles to Practice.* Philadelphia: Taylor & Francis, 1999.

Olive, M. Foster. *Designer Drugs.* Philadelphia: Chelsea House, 2004.

Pennell, S., and others. *Meth Matters: Report on Methamphetamine Users in Five Western Cities.* Washington, DC: U.S. Department of Justice, 1999.

Weatherly, Myra. *Ecstasy and Other Designer Drug Dangers.* Berkeley Heights, NJ: Enslow Publishers, 2000.

Periodicals

Jefferson, David J. L. "Party, Play—and Pay." *Newsweek* (February 28, 2005): p. 38.

Klee, Hilary. "The Love of Speed." *Journal of Drug Issues* (Winter, 1998): pp. 33-55.

Kowalski, Kathiann. "Stimulants: Fast Track to Disaster." *Current Health 2* (February 1, 2001).

Mapes, Jeff. "House Votes to Restrict Meth Ingredient." *Oregonian* (July 21, 2005): pp: A1, A5.

Mapes, Jeff. "Lawmakers Score Pills to Cook Up Support for Prescription Bill." *Oregonian* (July 20, 2005): pp: A1, A7.

Murray, John B. "Psychophysiological Aspects of Amphetamine-Methamphetamine Abuse." *Journal of Psychology* (March, 1998): pp. 227-237.

Snell, Marilyn Berlin. "Welcome to Meth Country." *Sierra Magazine* (January/February, 2001).

Volkow, Nora D., and others. "Association of Dopamine Transporter Reduction with Psychomotor Impairment in Methamphetamine Abusers." *American Journal of Psychiatry* (March, 2001): pp. 377-382.

Volkow, Nora D., Linda Chang, and others. "Loss of Dopamine Transporters in Methamphetamine Abusers Recovers with Protracted Abstinence." *Journal of Neuroscience* (December 1, 2001): pp. 9414-9418.

Zernike, Kate. "A Drug Scourge Creates Its Own Form of Orphan." *New York Times* (July 11, 2005): p. A1.

Web Sites

"2003 National Survey on Drug Use and Health (NSDUH)." *U.S. Department of Health and Human Services, Substance Abuse and Mental Health Services Administration (SAMHSA).* http://www.oas.samhsa.gov/nhsda.htm (accessed August 5, 2005).

"Amphetamine-Type Stimulants: A Problem Requiring Priority Attention" (Fact Sheet No. 3, June 8-10, 1998). *United Nations International Drug Control Programme: U.N. General Assembly, Special Session on the World Drug Problem.* http://www.un.org/ga/20special/presskit/themes/ats-3.htm (accessed August 5, 2005).

Bonné, Jon. "Hooked in the Haight: Life, Death, or Prison." *MSNBC.com,* February, 2001. http://msnbc.msn.com/id/3071769 (accessed August 5, 2005).

Bonné, Jon. "Meth's Deadly Buzz." *MSNBC.com,* February, 2001. http://msnbc.msn.com/id/3071772 (accessed August 5, 2005).

"Brain Shows Ability to Recover from Some Methamphetamine Damage" (December 1, 2001). *Brookhaven National Laboratory.* http://www.bnl.gov/bnlweb/pubaf/pr/2001/bnlpr120101b.htm (accessed August 5, 2005).

"Children Suffer from Parental Meth Addiction." *MSNBC.com,* March 30, 2005. http://msnbc.msn.com/id/7297846/ (accessed August 5, 2005).

Chu, Louise. "Sweeping into California Communities." *North County Times,* September 21, 2002. http://www.nctimes.com/articles/2002/09/22/export18876.txt (accessed August 5, 2005).

"The DAWN Report: Amphetamine and Methamphetamine Emergency Department Visits, 1995-2002" (July, 2004). *Drug Abuse Warning Network: U.S. Department of Health and Human Services, Substance Abuse and Mental Health Services Administration (SAMHSA).* http://dawninfo.samhsa.gov/old_dawn/pubs_94_02/shortreports/files/DAWN_tdr_amphetamine.pdf (accessed August 5, 2005).

"Drug Abuse Warning Network, 2003: Interim National Estimates of Drug-Related Emergency Department Visits" (December, 2004). *U.S. Department of Health and Human Services, Substance Abuse and Mental Health Services Administration (SAMHSA).* http://dawninfo.samhsa.gov/files/DAWN_ED_Interim2003.pdf (accessed August 5, 2005).

"Drug Firms Rushing to Change Cold Medicines." *MSNBC.com,* June 22, 2005. http://msnbc.msn.com/id/8322753 (accessed August 5, 2005).

"Drug Intelligence Brief: Club Drugs: An Update" (September, 2001). *U.S. Department of Justice, Drug Enforcement Administration (DEA).* http://www.usdoj.gov/dea/pubs/intel/01026 (accessed August 5, 2005).

"Drugs of Abuse: Uses and Effects Chart" (June, 2004). *U.S. Department of Justice, Drug Enforcement Administration (DEA).* http://www.usdoj.gov/dea/pubs/abuse/chart.htm (accessed August 5, 2005).

"The Faces of Meth." *Multnomah County Sheriff's Office.* http://www.facesofmeth.us/ (accessed August 10, 2005).

Hargreaves, Guy. "Clandestine Drug Labs: Chemical Time Bombs." *FBI Law Enforcement Bulletin,* April, 2000. http://www.fbi.gov/publications/leb/2000/apr00leb.pdf (accessed August 5, 2005).

"Indepth: Go-Pills, Bombs & Friendly Fire." *CBC News*, November 17, 2004. http://www.cbc.ca/news/background/friendlyfire/gopills.html (accessed August 5, 2005).

Kyle, Angelo D., and Bill Hansell. "The Meth Epidemic in America" (July 5, 2005). *National Association of Counties (NACo)*. http://www.naco.org/Content/ContentGroups/Publications1/Press_Releases/Documents/NACo-MethSurvey.pdf (accessed August 5, 2005).

Luna, G. C. "Use and Abuse of Amphetamine-Type Stimulants in the United States of America." *SciELO Public Health Web site* (2001). http://www.scielosp.org/pdf/rpsp/v9n2/4306.pdf (accessed August 6, 2005).

"Management of Substance Abuse." *World Health Organization*. http://www.who.int/substance_abuse/facts/psychoactives/en/ (accessed August 6, 2005).

"Maps of Methamphetamine Lab Seizures" (from National Clandestine Laboratory Database [January 1, 1999, to December 31, 2004]). *U.S. Department of Justice, Drug Enforcement Administration (DEA)*. http://www.usdoj.gov/dea/concern/map_lab_seizures.html (accessed August 6, 2005).

Mathias, Robert. "NIDA Notes: Rate and Duration of Drug Activity Play Major Roles in Drug Abuse, Addiction, and Treatment" (March/April 1997). *National Institutes of Health, National Institute on Drug Abuse (NIDA)*. http://www.drugabuse.gov/NIDA_Notes/NNVol12N2/NIDASupport.html (accessed August 6, 2005).

"Meth Addiction." *Drug-Rehabs.org*. http://www.drug-rehabs.org/faqs/FAQ-meth.php (accessed August 6, 2005).

"Methamphetamine Abuse: Stories and Letters." *KCI: The Anti-Meth Site*. http://www.kci.org/meth_info/links.htm (accessed August 6, 2005).

"Methamphetamine Delivers 'One-Two' Punch to the Brain" (December 1, 2001). *Brookhaven National Laboratory*. http://www.bnl.gov/bnlweb/pubaf/pr/2001/bnlpr120101a.htm (accessed August 6, 2005).

"Mind over Matter: Teaching Guide—Methamphetamines." *NIDA for Teens: The Science behind Drug Abuse*. http://teens.drugabuse.gov/mom/tg_meth1.asp (accessed August 6, 2005).

Monitoring the Future. http://www.monitoringthefuture.org/ and http://www.nida.nih.gov/Newsroom/04/2004MTFDrug.pdf (both accessed August 6, 2005).

"Myths about Meth." *Methamphetamine Awareness Project*. http://www.methawarenessproject.org/cgi-bin/display.cgi?page=myths (accessed August 6, 2005).

National Institute on Drug Abuse (NIDA). http://www.nida.nih.gov/ and http://www.drugabuse.gov (both accessed August 6, 2005).

"National Synthetic Drugs Action Plan" (May 23, 2004). *Executive Office of the President, Office of National Drug Control Policy (ONDCP)*. http://www.whitehousedrugpolicy.gov/publications/national_synth_drugs (accessed August 6, 2005).

"An Overview of Club Drugs: Drug Intelligence Brief" (February, 2000). *U.S. Department of Justice, Drug Enforcement Administration (DEA), Intelligence Division.* http://www.usdoj.gov/dea/pubs/intel/20005intellbrief.pdf (accessed August 6, 2005).

"Pulse Check: Drug Markets and Chronic Users in 25 of America's Largest Cities" (January, 2004). *Executive Office of the President, Office of National Drug Control Policy (ONDCP).* http://www.whitehousedrugpolicy.gov/publications/drugfact/pulsechk/january04/january2004.pdf (accessed August, 2005).

"Researchers Document Brain Damage, Reduction in Motor and Cognitive Function from Methamphetamine Abuse" (March 1, 2001). *Brookhaven National Laboratory.* http://www.bnl.gov/bnlweb/pubaf/pr/2001/bnlpr030101.htm (accessed August 6, 2005).

"Selected Intelligence Brief: Methamphetamine Myths." *U.S. Department of Justice, Drug Enforcement Administration (DEA), Office of Forensic Sciences, Microgram Bulletin,* February, 2005. http://www.usdoj.gov/dea/programs/forensicsci/microgram/mg0205/mg0205.html (accessed August 6, 2005).

Sommerfeld, Julia. "Beating an Addiction to Meth." *MSNBC.com,* February 2001. http://msnbc.msn.com/id/3076519 (accessed August 6, 2005).

"Statistics: DEA Drug Seizures" (1986-2002). *U.S. Department of Justice, Drug Enforcement Administration (DEA).* http://www.usdoj.gov/dea/statisticsp.html (accessed August 6, 2005).

Volkow, Nora D. "Methamphetamine Abuse: Testimony before the Senate Subcommittee on Labor, Health and Human Services, Education, and Related Agencies—Committee on Appropriations" (April 21, 2005). *National Institutes of Health, National Institute on Drug Abuse (NIDA).* http://www.drugabuse.gov/Testimony/4-21-05Testimony.html (accessed August 6, 2005).

Zickler, Patrick. "NIDA Notes: Methamphetamine Abuse Linked to Impaired Cognitive and Motor Skills Despite Recovery of Dopamine Transporters" (April 2002). *National Institutes of Health, National Institute on Drug Abuse (NIDA).* http://www.drugabuse.gov/NIDA_Notes/NNVol17N1/Methamphetamine.html (accessed August 6, 2005).

Other

"Dark Crystal." *The Fifth Estate.* CBC-TV, March 23, 2005. http://www.cbc.ca/fifth/darkcrystal/canada.html (accessed August 6, 2005).

"High Hitler." *The History Channel,* 2005. http://www.thehistorychannel.co.uk/site/tv_guide/full_details/People/programme_2603.php (accessed August 6, 2005).

See also: Adderall; Amphetamines; Cocaine; Dextroamphetamine; Ephedra; Herbal Drugs, Over-the-Counter Drugs; Ritalin and Other Methylphenidates

Methaqualone

What Kind of Drug Is It?

Methaqualone (meth-a-KWAY-lone) is a highly addictive, illegal, SYNTHETIC drug. It was once widely prescribed as a treatment for insomnia, a sleep disorder, and anxiety, a condition characterized by feelings of fear, worry, restlessness, and panic. Methaqualone is probably best known by its former brand names, Quaalude and Mandrax. It was a legal substance from the 1960s until the early 1980s. Shortly after its introduction as a prescription drug in 1965, however, its popularity as a recreational drug skyrocketed among college students and pop-culture figures in music, film, and television. Recreational drugs are those used solely to get high, not for any medical reason.

By the early 1970s, the U.S. government reclassified the prescription status of methaqualone in an attempt to limit its availability. By then, though, imitations of the drug were flooding the market. During the 1970s, the illegal use of methaqualone grew steadily, reaching a peak in the early 1980s. The drug was popular at discos, where people went to socialize and dance. Soon doctors realized the problems associated with the drug and stopped prescribing Quaaludes. Several states then outlawed the sale of methaqualone.

In 1984, the government finally reclassified methaqualone as a Schedule I controlled substance. This is the designation given to a drug that is highly addictive and has no current medical use in the United States. It is illegal to manufacture, use, or possess a Schedule I drug. Within just two years of this action, the use of methaqualone dropped dramatically in the United States. By 1988, the drug was illegal in almost every country throughout the world.

Overview

Methaqualone was first manufactured in 1955 by scientists in India who were trying to find a cure for malaria, a serious tropical disease spread by mosquitoes. The drug was found to have properties that made it useful as a sleep aid and a sedative to help calm anxiety. Sedatives help people relax, relieving nervousness and restlessness. Doctors and scientists believed this new drug was non-addictive.

Official Drug Name: Methaqualone (meth-a-KWAY-lone)
Also Known As: 714s, buttons, disco biscuits, love drug, ludes, mandies, mandrakes, Mandrax, Quaalude, quads, quay
Drug Classifications: Schedule I, depressant

synthetic: made in a laboratory

611

Quaaludes were popular at many discos in the 1970s, including Studio 54 in New York. The widespread use of the drug in such nightclubs gave it the nickname "disco biscuit." © *Bettmann/Corbis.*

It was soon on the market in Japan and Europe as a "safe" alternative to the highly addictive BARBITURATES that had previously been the only choice for effective treatment of insomnia.

Methaqualone was approved for use in the United States in 1965 by the Food and Drug Administration (FDA). It had been sold for several years in other countries under names such as Mandrax, Malsed, Malsedin, and Renoval. Doctors were glad to have a new prescription drug available to help patients deal with anxiety and sleeplessness. In the United States, the new drug was marketed under names such as Sopor, Parest, Optimil, and the most famous of all, Quaalude. Although the drug was available by prescription only, it

barbiturates: pronounced bar-BIH-chuh-rits; drugs that act as depressants and are used as sedatives or sleeping pills; also referred to as "downers"

was originally classified as a Schedule V drug, which meant that it was considered a very safe drug without any serious risk of addiction or harmful side effects.

Highly Abused in the 1960s and 1970s

Methaqualone was a big part of the "sex, love, drugs, and rock 'n' roll" culture of the 1960s and 1970s on both sides of the Atlantic Ocean. In the United Kingdom, the most popular version of methaqualone was combined with an ANTIHISTAMINE and sold as Mandrax. Its slang names included "mandies" and "mandrakes." In the United States, the drug was referred to as "quaaludes," "ludes," or the "love drug." By the late 1960s, the Quaalude brand of methaqualone was wildly popular with students who used the drug as an antidote to the stresses of college life. They also believed, in error, that the drug was an aphrodisiac—a substance that would increase sexual desire and performance. The drug also became popular at nightclubs during the disco dancing craze.

The Quiet Interlude

Quaalude was a brand name created to remind American consumers of the benefits of a popular over-the-counter product called Maalox, which was sold by the same company. Maalox was named for its ingredients—*ma*gnesium and *al*uminum hydr*ox*ides. In the 1960s it was the best-known product of the William H. Rorer pharmaceutical company. Then (and now), Maalox was a product people took to relieve digestive problems and stomach distress. The company decided to use the "aa" of Maalox in the name of their new "feel-better" drug Quaalude. The new drug was marketed as a prescription-only sleeping pill. The intent was to plant the idea that just as Maalox could provide relief for an upset stomach, Quaalude could provide a "quiet interlude" of relief for sleepless nights.

In 1973, the U.S. government reclassified methaqualone from a Schedule V to a Schedule II controlled substance. This is the category given to highly addictive drugs that nonetheless have a particular medical use. It means that doctors can still prescribe the drug for patient use, but there are numerous restrictions on how the drug may be prescribed. One of the requirements is that a patient be examined by a physician before a prescription is written. In addition, Schedule II prescriptions cannot be renewed by phone. They must be rewritten by a doctor each time a patient runs out of the drug. This reclassification of the drug was an attempt to restrict its availability.

By this time, however, two things had happened that made it almost impossible for the government to control access to methaqualone. First, prescriptions were readily available through so-called "stress clinics" that were set up in several states. These were not full-service doctors' offices, but were designed specifically to dispense prescriptions for anti-anxiety medications such as Quaalude. Because minimal physical exams were provided, and because the drug was legally available by prescription, it was difficult for law enforcement agencies to close down such clinics.

antihistamine: a drug that blocks *histamine,* a chemical that causes nasal congestion related to allergies

In addition, the world market was flooded with imitation methaqualone pills. During the peak of methaqualone use in the United States, approximately one billion counterfeit pills entered the country every year. Consequently, cracking down on the legal prescription process did little to slow the tide of demand for—or supply of—the drug.

No Longer Available Legally

By the early 1980s, as the medical world realized that methaqualone was too dangerous and addictive for most people, many doctors stopped prescribing the drug in any form. In 1984, nine states, including Florida, Georgia, and Illinois, banned the sale of the drug. The last U.S. company still manufacturing methaqualone stopped making and selling it on January 31, 1984. Within months, the drug was reclassified yet again by federal authorities. By order of Congress, methaqualone became a Schedule I controlled substance in August 1984. This made it illegal for any use.

Outlawing the manufacture, sale, or possession of methaqualone resulted in a dramatic drop in its use. According to the National Narcotics Intelligence Consumers Committee, U.S. emergency room visits related to methaqualone overdoses dropped from 2,764 in 1982 to only 163 in 1988.

Another reason for the drop in methaqualone abuse was the end of the disco dance era. In the late 1980s and early 1990s, young adults began attending raves—all-night dance parties that usually involve huge crowds of people, loud techno music, and illegal drug use. Raves brought new drugs onto the dance scene and the once-popular disco drug methaqualone was replaced by other more trendy and readily available drugs, such as ecstasy. In the twenty-first century, methaqualone is no longer monitored as a domestic drug of abuse in the United States.

Methaqualone Survives in South Africa

By 1988, methaqualone was illegal in most countries of the world as well. As of 2005, the drug was still in use in South Africa. Mandrax, which contains both methaqualone and an antihistamine, became the most popular illegal, synthetic drug used in South Africa. The chemicals used to produce methaqualone are made in southern Asia. Since the exportation of these chemicals is not well monitored or regulated, illegal drug manufacturers can buy the chemicals and produce methaqualone anywhere. Labs producing methaqualone have been found in several African countries, including Kenya, Mozambique, Swaziland, Tanzania, Zambia, and South Africa.

Methaqualone abuse is no longer a major problem in the United States. However, it has become the most popular illegal synthetic drug in South Africa. As depicted here, a man smokes Mandrax from a broken beer bottle near Cape Town, South Africa. *Photo by Per-Anders Pettersson/Getty Images.*

South Africa was both the largest producer and the largest consumer of the drug in the world in the early twenty-first century.

What Is It Made Of?

Methaqualone is a drug synthesized from several other chemicals. The key ingredients include compounds such as anthranilic acid, N-acetyl-anthranilic acid, and N-acetyl-o-toluidine. The formal name for methaqualone is 2-methyl-3-O-tolyl-4(3H)quinazolinone, and its chemical formula is $C_{16}H_{14}N_2O$.

Illegal drug makers sometimes use a variety of "filler" substances, including talcum powder and heroin, when manufacturing counterfeit methaqualone pills. No inspection process is available to ensure or measure the purity of the finished product because the substance is illegal.

White Pipe

"White pipe" is a blend of Mandrax, cannabis (marijuana), and tobacco that is unique to South Africa. Although Mandrax is manufactured as a pill to be taken orally, South African users prefer it crushed and smoked as part of this drug combination.

How Is It Taken?

When it was legal, methaqualone was made in tablets (solid pills) and capsules (water-soluble casings filled with a powdery form of the drug). The legal form of the drug was available in various strengths. In the United States, the most prescribed strengths of Quaalude were 150-milligram and 300-milligram pills.

Just as counterfeit versions of methaqualone were produced throughout the world and sold in the United States until the early 1980s, imitations were still being manufactured in 2005 in places such as India and South Africa. The tablets are designed to look like the original pharmaceutical versions, right down to the manufacturer's markings. Illegal forms of methaqualone are also produced in powder and capsule forms. In South Africa, the drug is also mixed with marijuana and smoked.

During the 1970s, one of the most popular ways to take methaqualone was with wine. Called "'luding out," this practice was widespread on college campuses. Taking methaqualone with alcohol was also quite popular—and particularly dangerous, since alcohol increases the DEPRESSANT effect of the drug. This can interfere with the normal breathing process and lead to accidental overdose.

Are There Any Medical Reasons for Taking This Substance?

Methaqualone was originally thought to be safe and nonaddictive as a sleep aid. Once its addictive and dangerous properties were discovered, the medical community and the government determined that the negative effects outweighed any benefits. Thus, there is no current medical use for the drug.

Usage Trends

When methaqualone was introduced in the United States in the 1960s, it was a drug that could be taken by anyone with a doctor's prescription. This meant that the abuse of the drug easily crossed lines of culture, race, and economic status. It was neither an expensive drug accessible only to the wealthy, nor a budget-class drug associated only with low-income users. It did become a drug of

depressant: a substance that slows down the activity of an organism or one of its parts

choice on the rock music scene, which made it appeal to mainstream American teens. Its reputation as a love-enhancing substance popularized the drug on college campuses.

Major Drop in Use during the 1980s

Illegal use of the brand drug Quaalude was widespread on college campuses in the 1970s. Its use rose dramatically between 1978 and 1981, but dropped very quickly after the drug was made illegal in the mid-1980s. In 1981, according to the National Institute of Drug Abuse (NIDA) and the University of Michigan, 10.4 percent of college students said they had tried methaqualone at least once in their lifetimes, and 6.5 percent of college students reported having used it without a prescription at least once in the previous year. In the 1989 survey, which was done five years after the drug was reclassified as a Schedule I substance, only 0.2 percent of college students said they had used methaqualone during the previous year.

A similar reduction in use took place among American high school students, according to the Monitoring the Future survey. This annual study follows drug use patterns of secondary school students in the United States. In 1981, 8 percent of American twelfth-graders surveyed reported use of methaqualone during the previous twelve months, as compared to 0.5 percent and 0.6 percent, respectively, in 1991 and 2003.

Effects on the Body

Methaqualone is a depressant that has both physical and psychological effects on users. It lowers the levels of chemicals called NEUROTRANSMITTERS in the brain and nervous system. When neurotransmitters are decreased, blood pressure drops and the breathing and pulse rates slow. The user enters a state of deep relaxation. These properties explain why methaqualone was originally thought to be a useful drug to treat sleeplessness and anxiety.

Methaqualone reaches its peak levels in the bloodstream within one or two hours after being taken. Its effects generally last from four to eight hours. Regular users of methaqualone build up a physical tolerance to the drug, which means they need more of it each time to achieve the same physical and psychological effects. As a user takes more of the drug to experience a particular response, the nervous system can be overwhelmed and shut down, leading to coma and death.

Methaqualone's effects are intensified with the use of other substances, including alcohol. The average lethal dose of methaqualone

neurotransmitters: substances that help spread nerve impulses from one nerve cell to another

Ludes and Pop Culture

In the late 1960s and 1970s, methaqualone's reputation grew to mythic proportions in the media. America's Quaalude craze was seen in the popular, and less-popular, music of the time. Syd Barrett (1946–), founding member and original guitarist and vocalist of Pink Floyd, was asked to leave the band shortly after appearing on stage heavily sedated and sporting a mixture of crushed Mandrax and hair gel on his head. Fee Waybill (1950–) of the lesser-known The Tubes regularly performed as alter-ego Quay Lude in the band's glam rock opera, "White Punks on Dope."

In the song "Flakes" (1979), musician and songwriter Frank Zappa (1940–1993) took a jab at Bob Dylan (1941–) and the folksinger's alleged frequent use of Mandrax. In the song, Zappa sings in the style of Dylan and asks, "Want to buy some Mandies, Bob?" Zappa, who was staunchly anti-drug, referred to Quaaludes in one interview as a way of creating stupid behavior in people.

Methaqualone overdose claimed a number of celebrity lives during the era. In 1972, Billy Murcia (1951–1972), drummer for the New York Dolls, overdosed on methaqualone during a concert and subsequently choked to death. In 1975, Anissa Jones (1958–1975), former child star of the television show *Family Affair,* died of an overdose of barbiturates and Quaaludes. While under the influence of Quaaludes, comedian Freddie Prinze Sr. (1954–1977) died of an accidental, self-inflicted gunshot wound to the head. Other methaqualone users who died in the 1970s in drug-related circumstances include legendary guitarist Jimi Hendrix (1942–1970), Rolling Stone Brian Jones (1943–1969), and the king of rock and roll Elvis Presley (1935–1977).

used alone is between 8 and 20 grams, depending on the size and tolerance level of the user. However, death and coma can result at much lower dosages in the presence of alcohol, which also functions as a depressant on the body.

"Feeling No Pain" Can Be Dangerous

Common side effects of methaqualone include diarrhea, stomach cramps, nausea and vomiting, headache, chills or sweating, irregular heartbeat, skin rash and itching, fatigue, slurred speech, and seizures. Methaqualone affects muscle movement and coordination and can produce a "pins and needles" sensation called paresthesia (pah-russ-THEE-zhuh), usually in the face and fingers. Under the influence of heavy doses of methaqualone, users have a heightened pain threshold, which means they do not feel pain as readily as they would otherwise. The consequence is that they can hurt themselves without noticing any pain. Because their thought processes are also slowed down, they cannot respond quickly enough to avoid serious injury.

Musician and singer Frank Zappa (right) was highly anti-drug. In his song called "Flakes," off his 1979 album *Sheik Yerbouti* (left), he took a jab at folksinger Bob Dylan's alleged frequent use of Mandrax. In the song, Zappa asks "Want to buy some Mandies, Bob?" © *Neal Preston/Corbis.*

Methaqualone can also cause a condition called ATAXIA, in which muscles twitch and move uncontrollably. Users experiencing ataxia are sometimes called "wallbangers." They appear to have lost control of their bodies and may repeatedly run into things because they cannot feel any pain. Driving or operating heavy machinery is especially dangerous for anyone who is under the influence of methaqualone because of ataxia and the slowed reflexes that accompany the sedative effect of the drug.

In the early 1980s, emergency rooms across the country reported increased numbers of trauma victims whose injuries were related to automobile crashes caused by users of methaqualone, often in conjunction with alcohol. According to Paul M. Gahlinger in *Illegal Drugs: A Complete Guide to Their History, Chemistry, Use and Abuse,* in Broward County, Florida, 82 percent of drunk drivers apprehended in 1980 also had methaqualone in their systems.

ataxia: pronounced uh-TAKS-ee-uh; loss of control of muscle coordination

Dependence and Addiction

Methaqualone also has significant mental effects on users. When it was considered safe, one of its benefits was thought to be its ability to reduce anxiety. Before long, it became clear that users were becoming psychologically addicted to the drug. Common symptoms of PSYCHOLOGICAL DEPENDENCE on methaqualone are memory loss, learning and judgment problems, difficulty focusing on work or school tasks, and a preoccupation with getting more of the drug.

Reactions with Other Drugs or Substances

The sedative effects of methaqualone are increased significantly when the drug is combined with other depressant substances such as alcohol or marijuana. The combination can result in coma or death. In addition, unknown substances in illegally produced methaqualone can cause unexpected, damaging side effects. Some of the ingredients that might be used to make methaqualone pills include talcum powder, flour, baking soda, heroin, decongestants, pain relievers, and laxatives. Impurities may also enter the drug during the illegal manufacturing process.

Treatment for Habitual Users

When a person suddenly stops taking a drug like methaqualone, the body overreacts to the loss of the substance. For example, if the heart rate is slowed by a drug, when that drug is abruptly discontinued, the heart rate will accelerate rapidly and unevenly. Such body changes can cause withdrawal symptoms, which include a range of extremely uncomfortable and sometimes life-threatening physical symptoms. These symptoms last until the user has undergone DETOXIFICATION. Due to the intensity of methaqualone withdrawal, inpatient treatment is highly recommended.

In the case of methaqualone, seven to ten days is considered the average detox time for someone who has become dependent on the drug. Withdrawal symptoms will begin at approximately twelve to twenty-four hours after the last dose is taken. They peak twenty-four to forty-eight hours later. Symptoms typically include nausea, vomiting, tremors, an irregular heartbeat, heavy sweating, anxiety and PANIC ATTACKS, insomnia, confusion, convulsions, and seizures. Methaqualone detoxification should always take place in a hospital or rehab setting, under the supervision of healthcare professionals, so that withdrawal symptoms can be treated properly.

psychological dependence: the belief that a person needs to take a certain substance in order to function

detoxification: often abbreviated as detox; a difficult process by which substance abusers stop taking those substances and rid their bodies of the toxins that accumulated during the time they consumed such substances

panic attacks: unexpected episodes of severe anxiety that can cause physical symptoms such as shortness of breath, dizziness, sweating, and shaking

During medically supervised withdrawal, doctors may prescribe a substitute sedative to ease the initial symptoms. Antidepressant medication may also be prescribed for individuals experiencing anxiety or sleep disorders.

Consequences

The consequences of methaqualone use are not just physical and psychological. Social and legal consequences accompany the use of an illegal controlled substance such as methaqualone. As with users of other highly addictive substances, methaqualone abusers quickly become focused on when and where to get the next dose of the drug. Relationships with friends and family often break down when drug use becomes the most important aspect of a person's daily life. Financial consequences result from spending money on drugs as well as from the job loss that frequently accompanies drug addiction.

Use of an illegal drug usually leads to legal consequences, as well. A Schedule I drug like methaqualone is illegal to make, sell, take, or even have in one's possession. Conviction on any level will carry heavy fines and possible jail time as well. Convictions often result in the suspension of a user's driver's license, whether or not jail time is

Early drug education is one way to help students learn about the dangers of certain drugs and ultimately avoid the pain of addiction. Here, a police officer talks with elementary school children in their classroom. © *James Marshall/Corbis.*

also required. Criminal drug charges may also limit employment and education options. For example, federal law requires that applicants for student college loans reveal whether or not they have ever been convicted of a drug offense. Having a conviction on one's record will result in either temporary or permanent ineligibility for federal financial aid for college.

The Law

Possession of methaqualone is a federal offense in the United States. Even if the amount of the drug is small, the fine for a first offense may be as much as $10,000. The fine amount is set according to the offender's income, financial assets, and circumstances of the case. A first offense for "personal use" possession typically does not

While under the influence of Quaaludes, comedian Freddie Prinze Sr. died of an accidental, self-inflicted gunshot wound to the head in 1977. His son, Freddie Prinze Jr., also an actor, paid tribute to his father in 2004 when the late comedian received a star on the Hollywood Walk of Fame. © Fred Prouser/ Reuters/Corbis.

result in jail time. However, the offender must pay the fine, stay out of trouble, and pass drug tests as administered.

This is not the case for someone who is convicted of transporting or selling methaqualone. A first-time offender faces as many as twenty years in prison and a $1 million fine. If the case also carries a charge of causing death or serious injury to another person, the sentence is automatically set at between twenty years and life.

For More Information

Books

Gahlinger, Paul M. *Illegal Drugs: A Complete Guide to Their History, Chemistry, Use and Abuse.* Las Vegas, NV: Sagebrush Press, 2001.

Kuhn, Cynthia, Scott Swartzwelder, and Wilkie Wilson. *Buzzed: The Straight Facts about the Most Used and Abused Drugs from Alcohol to Ecstasy,* 2nd ed. New York: W.W. Norton Company, 2003.

Ziemer, Maryann. *Quaaludes.* Berkeley Heights, NJ: Enslow Publishers, 1997.

Web Sites

"Background Information: Methaqualone." *South African Police Service.* http://www.saps.gov.za/drugs/drugs/bground.htm (accessed July 29, 2005).

"Fact Sheet: Cannabis and Mandrax Use in South Africa." *SA HealthInfo.* http://www.sahealthinfo.org/admodule/cannabis.htm (accessed July 29, 2005).

"Glutethimide and Methaqualone." *U.S. Department of Justice, Drug Enforcement Administration.* http://www.usdoj.gov/dea/concern/glutethimide.html (accessed July 29, 2005).

"Methaqualone Timeline." *The Vaults of Erowid.* http://www.erowid.org/chemicals/methaqualone/methaqualone_timeline.php (accessed July 29, 2005).

Monitoring the Future. http://www.monitoringthefuture.org/ and http://www.nida.nih.gov/Newsroom/04/2004MTFDrug.pdf (both accessed July 31, 2005).

See also: Barbiturates; Rohypnol; Tranquilizers

Morphine

Official Drug Name: Morphine sulfate, morphine hydrochloride (for injection); Duramorph (spinal injection); MS Contin, Oramorph, Kadian, MSIR (pill and tablet forms); Roxanol (liquid for oral use)

Also Known As: M, Miss Emma, monkey, morph, white stuff

Drug Classifications: Schedule II, opiate

opiate: any drug derived from the opium poppy or synthetically produced to mimic the effects of the opium poppy; opiates tend to decrease restlessness, bring on sleep, and relieve pain

What Kind of Drug Is It?

Morphine is a natural product of the opium poppy plant. Of the many mind-altering compounds in the opium poppy, morphine is the strongest. The drug has many important medical uses, all having to do with pain control. It is never used to treat emotional or psychological problems.

For many people recovering from painful surgery—and for even more people facing the daily agony of end-stage cancer—morphine can dramatically improve their quality of life. The drug, called an OPIATE, has been used for pain relief for many years, in many different cultures worldwide.

When prescribed for a patient by a physician, morphine can help speed recovery from operations, ease the pain and trauma of childbirth, and give dying people relief from incurable pain. When used illegally as a recreational drug solely to get high, morphine is highly addictive with many unpleasant side effects. When purchased on the street, it is usually found in the form of heroin, a substance that turns to morphine in the brain. (An entry on heroin is available in this encyclopedia.)

Whether used legally or illegally, morphine is a very dangerous drug. Overdoses can cause fatal breathing problems. Even those who use it for pain relief can develop a dependence or physical need for the drug. Doctors tend to be very conservative when they prescribe it for pain because they are aware of its risks and drawbacks. Since the beginning of the twenty-first century, patients' rights groups have urged the medical community to use morphine more freely to control pain. They believe that patients in severe pain would be more likely to contemplate or commit suicide if they were unable to use the drug.

Overview

Morphine is derived from a flowering poppy called *Papaver somniferum.* This plant can grow in many environments, but it thrives in a soil that contains some sand and loam, in higher elevations with cooler temperatures. Opium poppies were first grown by people

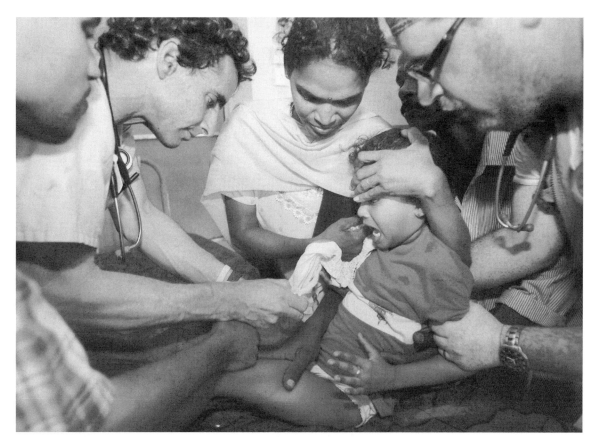

An American doctor and paramedic with the International Medical Corps are shown treating a young tsunami victim with an injection of morphine in Sri Lanka in 2005. The little girl was brought into the makeshift hospital after suffering a broken pelvis during the tsunami tragedy.
Photo by Paula Bronstein/Getty Images.

6,000 years ago in the area that is now Iran and Iraq. A manuscript from the ancient Egyptian city of Thebes, dating to 1552 BCE, mentions opium as a cure for more than 700 illnesses.

From Plant to Drug

Although the leaves and stems of the opium poppy plant also contain opiates, it is the sticky sap in the bulbs that has the most strength. The bulbs begin to ripen after the flower petals fall. As the bulbs ripen, skilled farmers cut them, and the sap flows out. Once collected, the sap is dissolved in boiling water. The twigs and other plant material float to the surface, and the boiled opium is strained.

It is then cooked a second time, this time to remove the water. Once the water has evaporated as steam, what remains is a putty-like substance called "smoking opium." After this simple process, users sometimes smoke or eat the opium to get high.

More commonly, though, the cooked opium goes through another chemical process. Again it is boiled, this time with lime. The lime converts the opium from a non-water soluble morphine ALKALOID into the water-soluble calcium morphenate. Ammonium chloride is added to the solution, and this causes the morphine to settle to the bottom of the cooking pot. The solution is poured through a straining cloth, and what remains is chunks of morphine that are dried in the sun. Legally, these morphine "bricks" are processed into prescription painkillers. Illegally, they are smuggled into laboratories and turned into heroin.

Addictive Effects

None of this chemistry was known to opium farmers in the era prior to modern medicine. In the Middle Ages (c. 500–c. 1500), opium was mixed with wine or other alcohol and called "laudanum." Crude opium was also smoked, particularly after the introduction of pipes from the Americas after Columbus (1451–1506) reached the New World in 1492. When opium smoking became widespread in Asia—and particularly in China—the destructive and habit-forming effects of the drug began to be revealed.

In 1803 German chemist Friedrich Sertürner (1783–1841) experimented with opium and isolated morphine for the first time. He named his discovery after the Greek god Morpheus, who is often depicted in ancient statues sleeping among opium poppies. Within thirty years of Sertürner's discovery, it was possible to buy medicines with morphine from any store that sold remedies. Both morphine and opium cost less than alcohol, and the substances were abused by famous and common people alike. The users of morphine and opium-laced medicines were aware of the dangers. As early as 1821 author Thomas de Quincy wrote *Confessions of an English Opium Eater,* describing his personal experiences of addiction and drug-induced mental breakdown.

Morphine, a painkiller that can be dissolved in water, came to the forefront in 1848, when an inventor perfected the hypodermic needle. This allowed the substance to be injected right into a vein, producing pain relief (and EUPHORIA) in minutes. Surgeons welcomed this new tool, since it enabled them to perform pain-free operations. But the medical community quickly learned that morphine was habit-forming. In his book *Illegal Drugs: A Complete Guide to Their History, Chemistry,*

alkaloid: nitrogen-containing substances found in plants

euphoria: pronounced yu-FOR-ee-yuh; a state of extreme happiness and enhanced well-being; the opposite of dysphoria

Soldiers who needed to have an arm or leg amputated during the American Civil War were given morphine. Addiction to the drug was so common among returning veterans that it was called "the soldiers' disease." Here, a physician prepares to amputate a soldier's leg at Gettysburg, Pennsylvania, in 1863. *AP/Wide World Photos.*

Use and Abuse, Paul M. Gahlinger estimates that 400,000 soldiers became addicted to morphine during the American Civil War (1861–1865). Morphine addiction was so common among returning veterans that it was called "the soldiers' disease."

Discovery of Heroin

Doctors and chemists continued to experiment with morphine, hoping to create a product that would be less habit-forming but would still control pain. Codeine was isolated in

1832. It was not as strong as morphine but was used in cough formulas and diarrhea medications. Soon it was found to be addictive as well. Another experiment on the morphine compound occurred in 1874, when British chemist Alder Wright created diacetylmorphine (DIE-uh-SEE-tuhl-MOR-feen), marketed as heroin.

With the introduction of heroin, morphine users and opium smokers hoped they had found a cure for their addictions. Many tried heroin to wean themselves off the other substances. In doing so, they traded a bad addiction for an even worse one. By that time, over-the-counter medicines containing codeine, morphine, heroin, and cannabis (marijuana) could be bought for problems as varied as toothaches, headaches, and fussy babies. (Entries for codeine and marijuana are available in this encyclopedia.) At that time, people did not realize the dangers of using such products.

Dealing with the Growing Abuse

China had long struggled with large numbers of opium addicts. As Chinese immigrants came to the United States to work, some brought the habit with them. By the late 1800s, almost every major city in the United States had at least 1 opium "den"; New York had more than 300. Opium dens were darkly lit establishments where people went to smoke opium. Many dens had beds, boards, or sofas upon which people could recline while experiencing the effects of the drug.

On February 1, 1909, China and the United States led a meeting called the International Opium Commission. Eleven other countries participated. Three years later, a convention in the Netherlands produced the first international agreement on the regulation of NARCOTICS—especially opium and heroin. Gahlinger wrote: "This began a process whereby the United States took a global leadership in controlling the international narcotics trade, even while its own domestic use of addictive drugs was rampant. One hundred years later, this situation has not changed."

The Harrison Narcotics Act of 1914 made it illegal to sell medicines containing heroin, morphine, or opium without labels warning of the presence of the drug in the product. In 1926 heroin was made completely illegal. Morphine remained legal but only when prescribed by a doctor.

The twentieth century was marked by enormous progress in surgery, medications, and treatments of all sorts of diseases. Scientists

narcotics: a painkiller that may become habit-forming; in a broader sense, any illegally purchased drug

Two morphine addicts from the 1880s are depicted here. The woman on the right is already experiencing the effects of the drug while the woman on the left is giving herself a shot of the painkiller. *Photo by Three Lions/Getty Images.*

developed SYNTHETIC painkillers based on the properties of morphine, such as oxycodone and fentanyl. However, they made no progress in removing the habit-forming effects of the substances. (Entries on oxycodone and fentanyl are available in this encyclopedia.) Morphine is still widely used in hospital settings and is prescribed as pills and liquids. It is also available in a pump implanted in the body, for use in the most stubborn, ongoing, and incurable pain. Except in the case of surgery, doctors use morphine as a drug of "last resort," after all other painkillers have failed. It is most often used when a patient is dying. At the last stage of life, the fact that morphine is addictive is no longer significant.

synthetic: made in a laboratory

Morphine is a natural product of the opium poppy plant. Much of the opium sold illegally throughout the world is grown in Afghanistan. As shown here, Afghan police destroy a poppy crop in 2005. *AP/Wide World Photos.*

What Is It Made Of?

Morphine is an alkaloid, the chemical class to which many drugs belong. It is also an organic product, meaning that it is derived from a plant. The process of extracting morphine from opium is so simple that farmers can do it alongside their fields, with few other tools than cooking pots, lime (an ingredient in fertilizers), and ammonium chloride (also found in fertilizers). In its basic form, the morphine alkaloid is not soluble in water. Once it has been treated with lime and ammonium chloride, however, it becomes the water-soluble compound calcium morphenate. Further treatments produce morphine sulfate, morphine hydrochloride, and morphine. All of these are used in medicines.

After having gone through chemical processing, morphine salts appear as a bitter white powder. Some people take this powder by mouth, while others snort it or dissolve it in water and inject it. Morphine products are not as fat soluble as heroin. A highly fat-soluble drug like heroin enters the bloodstream quicker and moves to the brain faster, no matter how it is taken. As such, morphine products do not work as quickly to produce the intense high that is experienced with heroin use. Injected morphine does work quickly, in about five to ten minutes, whereas heroin works almost immediately.

The vast majority of legal morphine is converted to codeine, a milder painkiller and cough suppressant used in great quantities worldwide. The remainder of legal morphine is processed as a painkiller. More than 1,000 tons of morphine are produced *legally* every year, from poppies grown on government-regulated farms in India, Turkey, and the Australian province of Tasmania. Illegal opium production is widespread in the highlands of Burma, Laos, Vietnam, Thailand, Pakistan, Afghanistan, Colombia, Mexico, and Lebanon.

How Is It Taken?

Prescription morphine comes in many forms. As morphine sulfate and morphine hydrochloride, it is a liquid injected into veins. As Duramorph, it is a liquid injected into the fluid surrounding the spine. This type of injection is called an epidural. Duramorph is used in childbirth and some forms of surgery that can be performed while a patient is awake. Morphine pills of various strengths are also available and are prescribed for cancer pain, back pain, recovery from surgical procedures, and occasionally migraine headaches. The drug can also be found in rectal SUPPOSITORIES. The latter form of morphine is usually given to people suffering from nausea. A liquid form of morphine is available for oral use among patients who have difficulty swallowing pills.

Some patients use morphine pumps. These come in two forms. Either the patient is hooked up to a needle (IV) and can press a button to increase the flow of morphine through the needle, or a morphine dispenser is implanted under the skin, releasing a set dose of the medicine at hourly intervals. The pumps are usually programmed so that a patient cannot receive too much morphine and overdose. Too much morphine can lead to death by stopping a patient's breathing.

Morphine is usually sold illegally on the street in its pill forms. Users crush the pills and snort, smoke, or inject them.

suppositories: medicines that are delivered through the anus

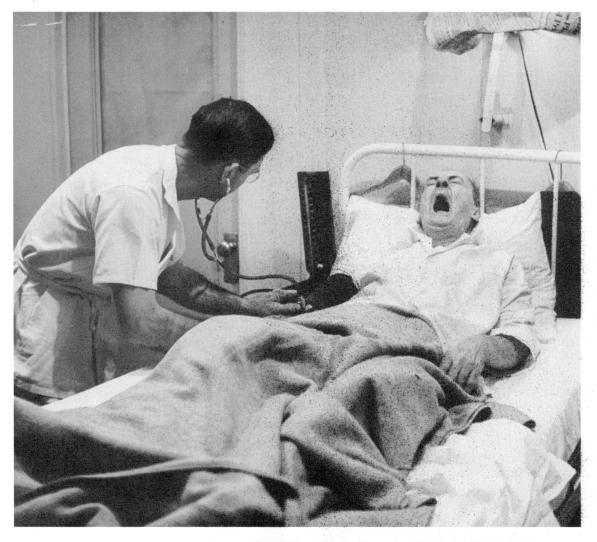

A man addicted to morphine is shown in a hospital setting in the late 1940s. He yawns and gasps for air as he experiences severe withdrawal from the drug. *Photo by Ralph Morse/Time Life Pictures/Getty Images.*

Are There Any Medical Reasons for Taking This Substance?

Morphine is used most often to ease the pain of dying from cancer. Cancer causes tumors (abnormal growths) in just about any organ in the body, from the brain to the limbs. These tumors can cause intense pain that never goes away. Morphine does *not* shrink tumors. Rather, it causes the brain not to respond to the pain that the tumor causes. Patients know they are in pain, but they feel more comfortable. Their anxieties are also eased by the relaxing components of the morphine.

Newspapers and magazines report cases of end-stage cancer patients who, with high doses of morphine, are able to take care of themselves around the home, do tasks such as gardening and attending family functions, and even work on projects they want to finish before death. HOSPICE workers who try to make dying patients as comfortable as possible report a greater sense of calm and less trauma for the patient and family when morphine is used to sedate and control pain.

Recovery from surgery without morphine would be a terrible ordeal for many patients. Even though the drug is often used only for the first few days, it greatly eases the pain and trauma the patient feels after a procedure. Used in this way it does not promote addiction. As the body recovers, doctors reduce the doses of the painkiller, eventually switching to over-the-counter products such as aspirin, acetaminophen, or ibuprofen.

Morphine's Not for All Patients, Though

For chronic, or ongoing, conditions such as back pain and migraine headache, morphine is never used as the first drug for treatment. Typically the drug is only prescribed for people who have used other opiate or opioid painkillers, or other prescription drugs, with disappointing results. Morphine's side effects—TOLERANCE, constipation, nausea, drowsiness, and dizziness—make it a drug of last resort for people in pain.

Some people suffer pain that does not respond to morphine. This kind of pain, known as nerve damage, is particularly frustrating both for patients and their doctors. If nerves are damaged, they cannot read the chemical message morphine sends them.

Doctors who prescribe morphine must be certified to do so by the U.S. Drug Enforcement Administration (DEA). Morphine prescriptions require extra paperwork to determine how much medicine each patient receives and whether or not the doctor is

---

Terri Schiavo

One of morphine's main uses is in end-of-life situations where doctors try to control pain and suffering. In March of 2005, after a long legal battle, Terri Schiavo—who was diagnosed with severe brain damage and no hope of recovery—was removed from the feeding tube that had kept her alive for fifteen years. As she perished from starvation and dehydration, doctors administered morphine to ease any suffering she might have felt. Terri Schiavo died on March 31, 2005.

---

hospice: a special clinic for dying patients where emphasis is placed on comfort and emotional support

tolerance: a condition in which higher and higher doses of a drug are needed to produce the original effect or high experienced

Sniffer dogs are used by custom officials to search planes, cars, trucks, ships, and trains for illegal substances. These trained dogs are able to detect cocaine, marijuana, heroin, methamphetamine, and morphine-based drugs, among others. © *Houston Scott/Corbis SYGMA.*

over-prescribing it. In response, doctors tend to *under-prescribe* morphine for two reasons. First, doctors do not want to be seen as dispensing drugs without good reason. Second, doctors do not want to take the chance that a dose they deem safe for a patient might actually lead to a fatal overdose.

Usage Trends

Morphine enters the illegal market in two ways. Most of it is transformed into heroin in illegal laboratories in Asia, Mexico, and South America and smuggled into the United States. The rest is diverted from its legal use through theft from pharmacies or through "doctor shopping" for prescriptions. An illegal practice, doctor shopping occurs when an individual continually switches physicians so that he or she can get enough of a prescription drug to feed an addiction. This makes it difficult for physicians to track whether the patient has already been prescribed the same drug by another physician. Additionally, some morphine fatalities can be tied to people legally taking the drug, but taking it in higher doses than recommended, or combining it with other painkillers, alcohol, or cocaine.

People of all ages and income levels abuse prescription painkillers, sometimes with fatal results. Users often start taking the prescription drug for a painful condition and wind up abusing it for the mental effects. It is difficult to determine the number of deaths caused by morphine every year because heroin shows up as morphine on drug tests. Sometimes the cause of death is simply listed as "opiate overdose," and this could also include codeine or other prescription painkillers.

According to the "2003 National Survey on Drug Use and Health (NSDUH)," an estimated 119,000 teenagers between twelve and eighteen had tried heroin at least once. If given a drug test, these teenagers would test positive for morphine. Emergency room mentions of pure morphine are much lower than those for heroin, OxyContin, and Vicodin. The strength of morphine, the difficulties doctors face prescribing it, and the close watch kept on supplies in hospitals and pharmacies tend to keep illegal supplies low. Plus, the higher purity of illegal heroin makes that drug more attractive for abuse.

Effects on the Body

Morphine floods a group of receptors in the brain and spinal column that take in ENDORPHINS and ENKEPHALINS. Biologists think that endorphins and enkephalins work together naturally to dull pain or to ease anxiety when someone is hurt or close to death. Morphine replaces these natural molecules, and in a much greater quantity than the body can supply. Pain signals surging from an injury or a cancerous tumor cannot relay their messages to the brain because morphine has blocked the receptors that register the pain, while rewarding the receptors that enhance pleasure. Patients may still hurt, but the pain will not bother them as much, and they will be able to concentrate on other aspects of life.

Not Typically Abused for a High

Morphine is not as fat soluble as heroin, so even when injected it does not produce the instant rush of pleasure that

endorphins: a group of naturally occurring substances in the body that relieve pain and promote a sense of well-being

enkephalins: pronounced en-KEFF-uh-linz; naturally occurring brain chemicals that produce drowsiness and dull pain

makes heroin attractive as an abused drug. Nevertheless, morphine does induce a dreamy state of happiness, drowsiness, and relief from anxiety that can last from four to six hours, depending on the dose and the way it was administered. Most people taking morphine for pain learn to live with the drowsiness and confusion. Some opt to live with the pain instead so that their senses are not dulled by the drug. Usually patients will work closely with their doctors to monitor doses so that a balance can be achieved.

Scientists are finding that patients in pain can become tolerant to very high doses of morphine—doses that, if taken recreationally, would kill a person outright. Tolerance, or needing higher doses of a drug to achieve the same results, is a standard side effect of opiate use.

All opiates produce similar side effects in the body. Morphine users will typically develop constipation because the drug slows muscle movement in the bowels. Breathing may be slowed as well. The drug can affect coordination—users must adjust to the medicine before driving or operating machinery. Other side effects include nausea and vomiting, loss of appetite, loss of sexual function, and pinpoint pupils. Some people develop a mild allergic reaction in the skin that causes itching or prickling.

Even when used as directed, morphine can cause WITHDRAWAL symptoms if a dose is missed or the medication is stopped suddenly. These symptoms include sneezing, runny nose, muscle aches, insomnia and anxiety, diarrhea, muscle twitching, sweaty and clammy skin, and goose bumps.

Reactions with Other Drugs or Substances

Because morphine can slow breathing and reaction time, it is much more dangerous when taken with alcohol, tranquilizers, SEDATIVES, anti-anxiety medications, antidepressants, or even over-the-counter allergy medicines. Doctors must also monitor patients who take the pill form of morphine for reactions with other medicines metabolized in the liver, including medicines for tuberculosis, such as Rifampin, and medicines for seizures and epilepsy, including Dilantin. Some antibiotics can increase the level of morphine retained in the bloodstream.

Cancer patients on CHEMOTHERAPY may have difficulty taking morphine because the drug can upset the stomach. These patients sometimes experience relief by using rectal suppositories or by using

withdrawal: the process of gradually cutting back on the amount of a drug being taken until it is discontinued entirely; also the accompanying physiological effects of terminating use of an addictive drug

sedatives: a drug used to treat anxiety and calm people down

chemotherapy: a treatment for cancer that causes nausea, vomiting, and other side effects

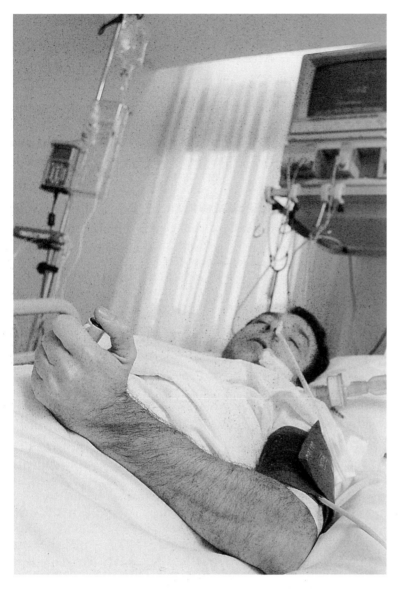

In cases of severe pain, some patients are allowed to self-administer their morphine using a pump. This permits them to take the drug for pain when they need it. Using a programmed pump with doses determined by a doctor, a patient presses a button to release a shot of morphine. The pump is designed to prevent an overdose. *AJ Photos/Hop Americain/Photo Researchers, Inc.*

pumps that bypass the stomach. However, doctors must evaluate the loss of appetite that results when morphine and chemotherapy are combined.

Some drug abusers combine morphine and cocaine. This can be particularly deadly, especially in terms of addiction. The two drugs work differently in the brain, causing high levels of disorientation, and both are habit-forming. Addicts who use opiates and cocaine at the same time find it hard to free themselves completely of both drugs.

Treatment for Habitual Users

Morphine use can lead to addiction. Even after years of not using the drug, opiate users can still crave the drug because they remember how they felt when they were taking it. Withdrawal from morphine and other opiates is a difficult task that lasts three to five days, if the user quits "cold turkey." More commonly, addicts seek treatment with methadone or buprenorphine, medications that will curb the withdrawal symptoms and block the effects of morphine in the brain. (An entry on methadone is available in this encyclopedia.) A morphine overdose that has caused breathing to stop can be treated with naloxone (Narcan), a drug that quickly rids the body of opiates. However, many opiate deaths occur in private settings. The user stops breathing, and no one is present to call for emergency care.

Health professionals advise anyone wishing to end morphine dependency to work closely with doctors and a psychiatrist or other therapist. If the dependency was brought about by morphine's use as a painkiller, a doctor may taper the dose so that the patient gradually becomes free of the drug. If the dependency comes from recreational use, the addict must learn strategies to live free of the drug's influence, often including finding new friends and staying away from the people and places associated with the drug use. Doctors and nurses who take opiates recreationally often lose their jobs—jobs they had trained for over many years.

Narcotics Anonymous (NA) is a self-help group that allows recovering addicts to meet and obtain assistance from other people who have lived through drug abuse. The nonprofit organization has a telephone helpline and group meetings in most cities and towns in the United States. Opiate dependency is one of the toughest addictions to beat, and the support of a group of peers is extremely helpful during moments of CRAVING, anxiety, or depression.

craving: an overwhelming urge to do something, such as take an illegal drug

Morphine Chronology

4000 BCE Opium poppies are cultivated in the Fertile Crescent (now Iran and Iraq) by the ancient cultures of Mesopotamia.

1552 BCE An ancient Egyptian papyrus text from the city of Thebes lists 700 uses for opium.

600-900 CE Arabic traders introduce opium to China.

1524 Swiss doctor Paracelsus mixes opium with alcohol and names the product laudanum.

1803 German scientist Friedrich Sertürner isolates morphine as the most active ingredient in the opium poppy.

1848 The hypodermic needle is invented, allowing for quicker delivery of morphine to the brain.

1861–1865 An estimated 400,000 soldiers return home from the American Civil War with addictions to morphine.

1874 British chemist Alder Wright uses morphine to create diacetylmorphine (heroin), in an effort to produce a less addictive painkiller.

1914 The Harrison Narcotics Act ends over-the-counter purchases of medicines that do not have a full list of ingredients on the label.

1970 The Controlled Substances Act names morphine as a Schedule II controlled substance, recognizing its uses in pain relief and surgical settings.

1974 The first hospice facility opens in the United States.

2005 Terri Schiavo receives injections of morphine as her feeding tube is removed and she is allowed to die, after spending fifteen years in what doctors called a persistent vegetative state.

Consequences

One of the most serious consequences of a heroin or morphine addiction is the long-term profile a person creates for his or her future health care. Doctors are reluctant to prescribe powerful painkillers to people who have no history of drug abuse. They are much less likely to prescribe these drugs to people who have abused opiates in the past.

Advocates for the terminally ill point to another consequence of recreational opiate use. Some people in pain view prescription painkillers as dangerous and addictive, products that will make them crazy, or make them sleep all the time, or turn them into criminals. Such people suffer needlessly because of the negative perception attached to opiates. Doctors feel this too. They feel they are being monitored by the government and their jobs may be in jeopardy if they prescribe too much pain medication. As a consequence, they under-prescribe, even for dying patients. The bottom line: Many people suffer pain because other people abuse painkillers.

The Law

The Controlled Substances Act of 1970 placed morphine on the Schedule II list of controlled substances. This means that the U.S. government deems morphine to be a drug with medicinal uses that also carries the potential for abuse and addiction. Doctors who wish to prescribe morphine must register with the U.S. Drug Enforcement Administration (DEA). Morphine prescriptions are not like the typical slips of paper issued for most prescription drugs. They are more complicated and must be filed with the DEA, where records are kept on each doctor and how much morphine he or she prescribes. If the DEA determines that a doctor is prescribing too much morphine, that doctor can face criminal prosecution and possible jail time.

Illegal possession or sale of morphine, or any Schedule II drug, carries serious penalties, even on a first offense. Anyone caught with the drug can expect fines of as much as $10,000, mandatory drug testing, loss of driver's license, loss of federal government college financial aid, and a permanent criminal record. Judges often order opiate abusers into DETOXIFICATION clinics. Second offenses almost always carry jail time and very heavy fines.

Because morphine is so habit-forming, its use can lead to other sorts of crime. People craving the drug are more likely to rob homes in search of cash or valuables. They are more likely to break into pharmacies or to commit armed robbery. They may resort to prostitution to pay for their habits, making themselves vulnerable to the human immunodeficiency virus (HIV) and other sexually transmitted diseases. An arrest for any of these offenses will result in jail time, where the addict will receive little treatment as he or she faces drug withdrawal.

For More Information

Books

Arsenault, Kathy. *In the Arms of Morpheus: The Tragic History of Laudanum, Morphine, and Patent Medicines.* Somerville, MA: Firefly Press, 2002.

Gahlinger, Paul M. *Illegal Drugs: A Complete Guide to Their History, Chemistry, Use and Abuse.* Las Vegas, NV: Sagebrush Press, 2001.

Hodgson, Barbara. *Opium: A Portrait of the Heavenly Doom.* San Francisco, CA: Chronicle Books, 1999.

Periodicals

"Beware of Morphine Overdoses." *Drug Topics* (October 20, 2003): p. 8.

Girsh, Faye. "Death with Dignity: Choices and Challenges." *USA Today Magazine* (March, 2000): p. 62.

detoxification: often abbreviated as detox; a difficult process by which substance abusers stop taking those substances and rid their bodies of the toxins that accumulated during the time they consumed such substances

Harvey, Kay. "As Her Condition Deteriorates, Gwen Frazier Faces the Loss of Her Independence." *St. Paul Pioneer Press* (April 28, 2000).

Hopkinson, Tom. "Morphine Produced in the Human Brain." *Chemistry and Industry* (October 4, 2004): p. 8.

Hurley, Mary Lou. "New Drug for Postop Pain Is Now Available." *RN* (October, 2004): p. 76.

McAlpin, John P. "Pakistani Paramilitary Troops Seize Morphine, Weapons Near Afghan Border." *America's Intelligence Wire* (August 13, 2004).

"Nine Days in June: Drugs Claim Two Sports Stars—and 147 Others." *Life* (January, 1987): p. 83.

O'Neill, Terry. "Morphine, Murder and Mercy: New Painkilling Guidelines Clarify Issues Surrounding Treatment of the Terminally Ill." *The Report* (October 21, 2002): p. 42.

Ostrom, Carol M. "Oregon Doctors Concerned with Improving Quality at the End of Life." *Seattle Times* (May 14, 2000).

Rauch, Sharon. "Living, Dying with Pain." *Knight Ridder/Tribune News Service* (February 20, 2002).

"Schiavo Denied Communion as Parents' Legal Battle Reaches Desperate Point." *Detroit Free Press* (March 27, 2005).

Shnayerson, Michael. "The Widow on the Hill." *Vanity Fair* (May, 2003): p. 122.

Web Sites

"2003 National Survey on Drug Use and Health (NSDUH)." *Substance Abuse and Mental Health Services Administration (SAMHSA).* http://www.drugabusestatistics.samhsa.gov (accessed July 30, 2005).

"Husband Seeks Autopsy on Terri Schiavo." *CNN.com,* March 29, 2005. http://www.cnn.com/2005/LAW/03/28/schiavo/ (accessed July 31, 2005).

"Morphine." *U.S. Drug Enforcement Administration.* http://www.usdoj.gov/dea (accessed July 30, 2005).

See also: Cocaine; Codeine; Fentanyl; Heroin; Hydromorphone; Methadone; Opium; Oxycodone

Nicotine

Official Drug Name: Nicotine (beta-pyridyl-alpha-N-methylpyrrolidine), tobacco

Also Known As: Bidis (BEE-deez), chew, chewing tobacco, cigars, cigarettes, coffin nails, fags, kreteks, snuff, spit, smokes

Drug Classifications: Not scheduled, illegal for purchase by persons under eighteen years of age; stimulant

psychoactive: mind-altering; a psychoactive substance alters the user's mental state or changes one's behavior

cancer: out-of-control cell growth leading to tumors in the body's organs or tissues

What Kind of Drug Is It?

Nicotine is the ingredient in tobacco that causes changes to the brain and behavior. Tobacco, a broad-leafed plant that originated in the Americas, is one of the most widely abused PSYCHOACTIVE, or mind-altering, substances in the world. In the United States alone, one in four men and one in five women smoke cigarettes, cigars, pipes, or use oral products such as chewing tobacco or snuff. In other parts of the world the percentage of users is even higher.

Nicotine use typically begins among Americans between the ages of eleven and eighteen—an age group too young to buy the product legally. Young users soon discover that nicotine is habit-forming, that all the ways of taking it pose great health risks, and that it can lead to troubles on the job and sometimes an early death.

Movies and tobacco advertisements present nicotine use as a glamorous, rebellious, adult activity. And adults can smoke legally. What the advertisements do not note, however, is the fact that one-third of all smokers live below the poverty level; that the more educated a person is, the less likely he or she is to use tobacco; and that an estimated one billion people will die from tobacco-related illnesses worldwide in the twenty-first century. Tobacco use is one of the leading causes of preventable death. Its link to CANCER, emphysema and asthma (lung disorders), and depression (a mood disorder), has been clearly established. Smokers can expect to live seven to ten years *less* than people who do not use tobacco products.

Popularity Decreases

At the height of tobacco's popularity in the United States in the 1960s, more than half of all adult men and about one in three adult women smoked cigarettes. People smoked in movie theaters and on buses and planes. They smoked at their desks in office buildings and in their beds at night. Famous film and television stars promoted certain brands of cigarettes in commercials and on billboards. Even in those times, however, people knew that smoking could ruin their health.

Nicotine occurs naturally in the leaves of the tobacco plant. For many farmers in the southern United States, tobacco plants are their livelihood.
© Kevin Fleming/Corbis.

A half-century later, in the early 2000s, smokers can find it difficult to get a job if they reveal a tobacco habit. Smoking is not permitted on planes, in theaters, in many office buildings, or on public transportation. Many cities have enacted bans on smoking in restaurants and bars.

Studies have proven that SECONDHAND SMOKE, or "passive" smoke, can cause many health problems for the nonsmoker. Pregnant women who smoke endanger the health of their unborn babies. Most Americans are less tolerant of smoking than they used to be. Yet, the "2003 National Survey on Drug Use and Health (NSDUH)" reported that 40 percent of young adults age eighteen to twenty-five admitted to smoking cigarettes at least once in their lives.

No country that has learned to use tobacco has ever given it up. Nicotine addiction, a physical dependence on the drug due

secondhand smoke: the smoke exhaled from a cigarette user and breathed in by someone nearby

Secondhand smoke can cause many health problems for the non-smoker. In an attempt to protect employees from secondhand smoke, the owners of a casino in Atlantic City, New Jersey, installed devices, called air curtains, on the gambling tables. *AP/Wide World Photos.*

to repeated drug use, continues to be a global public health issue. It is one of the leading causes of preventable illness in adults. The U.S. government keeps a watchful eye on tobacco companies to ensure they do not target cigarette advertisements to teens for several reasons. First, teens are not allowed to smoke legally. Second, adults over the age of twenty-five rarely—if ever—begin smoking after never having smoked before.

Overview

The first European to record seeing tobacco use was the explorer Christopher Columbus (1451–1506), in 1492. On his initial voyage to the New World, Columbus wrote in his diary that the native peoples he encountered "drank" smoke from the burning leaves of a certain plant. Even without understanding their language, Columbus could see that the people he met highly valued their tobacco.

Use Originated in the Americas

Archaeologists are not sure where or when tobacco use began in the Americas. More than sixty varieties of tobacco grew all over North and South America. Even the garden flower known as the petunia is related to tobacco. The earliest documented use of tobacco among Native Americans occurred with the Mayan culture, a civilization from Central America that peaked about 2,000 years ago. A carving on a Mayan temple shows an elaborately dressed man smoking a long-stemmed pipe. Other historians of ancient America believe that pipe smoking may have begun in North America and spread south. Whatever the case, by 1000 CE, most Native American cultures used tobacco in religious and political rituals. The plant did not grow in Europe.

Columbus and his crew were baffled and disturbed by the sight of people smoking tobacco. Nevertheless, they collected specimens of the plant, as well as pipes, and took them back to Spain. As the Spanish and Portuguese began to explore and settle the Americas, they began "drinking smoke" themselves. Sailors who moved between Europe and America were among the first to discover that once they began smoking tobacco, they could not stop.

By 1535, Spanish colonists in the New World were planting tobacco for their own use. At around the same time, farmers in Europe began to cultivate the plant. In 1559, the French ambassador to Portugal, Jean Nicot (1530–1600), became interested in tobacco. He thought it might be useful as a medicine. He introduced powdered tobacco—*snuff*—at the French court and made the substance fashionable. It is from his name, "Nicot," that the word *nicotine* is derived.

Tobacco in the American Colonies

Tobacco was one of the first crops planted when English colonists arrived in Jamestown, Virginia. Ships filled with tobacco sailed from America to Europe, where the tobacco was traded for items the colonists could not make or buy in the New World, including tea, furniture, and high-quality cloth. In some parts of America, tobacco could be used instead of money. The need for new fields to grow tobacco—a plant that uses up the rich nutrients in the ground—pushed settlers westward, into territories occupied by Native Americans. By the time the Declaration of Independence was signed in 1776, tobacco smoking was common in America. Every tavern kept a supply of clay pipes for use by visitors. When smokers were finished with their pipes, they broke off the part of the stems their lips had touched and passed the pipe to a new user.

Tobacco plants are hung up to dry out in barns and other buildings. Once dried, the plants are prepared for use in cigarettes, cigars, and chewing tobacco. © Kevin Fleming/Corbis.

By the nineteenth century, different classes of people used tobacco in different ways. The upper classes tended to "take snuff," inhaling powdered tobacco through the nose. The middle classes preferred pipes, and the lower classes held wads of tobacco between their gums and teeth, a practice known as "chewing." Within 300 years of its discovery by Columbus, tobacco had spread to all parts of the world. Many cultures considered it a beneficial medicine. The Native Americans had wrapped shredded tobacco in larger leaves, and "cigars" became popular by the turn of the twentieth century. "Cigarettes" were invented by people who gathered the shredded cigar tobacco that had gone to waste and wrapped it in small papers to smoke it.

The popularity of cigarettes skyrocketed during World War I (1914–1918), because they were easy to transport into battle. Many young soldiers brought the cigarette habit home with them, and factories stood ready to create the product on assembly lines. By the

1920s, whole industries built on tobacco advertised in print, on billboards, and through movies and radio. Women were encouraged to smoke, and they took up the habit as well. The "Jazz Era" generation was the first to embrace tobacco in great numbers. The era's great athletes smoked when not on the playing field and chewed tobacco during games. During the Great Depression (1929–1941), U.S. President Franklin Delano Roosevelt (1882–1945) was sometimes photographed with a cigarette, in a holder, in his mouth.

Tobacco-Related Illness Begin to Surface

Americans who had been young in the 1920s were entering their sixties by the 1960s. At that time, tobacco use began to show its downside. Even as new generations became hooked on nicotine, older Americans suffered increasing numbers of lung, throat, and mouth cancers. Others died of emphysema, a disorder that affects the lungs' ability to process oxygen. In 1961 the Surgeon General of the United States requested a report on the effects of tobacco use on health. Facing opposition from tobacco companies—who claimed to have done their own research—a panel of experts met to study the problem.

In 1964 the panel submitted a report to the Surgeon General that linked tobacco use to lung cancer, mouth and throat cancer, heart attacks, STROKES, emphysema, and other diseases of the stomach and liver. The report, to no one's surprise, declared that nicotine was habit-forming. At the time the report was issued, 40 percent of adult Americans used some form of tobacco.

By the late 1960s, nonprofit groups from many sectors were uniting to stop tobacco use in the United States. Groups such as the American Heart Association, the American Lung Association, and the American Cancer Society launched advertisements to counter the popular characters featured in cigarette ads, including Joe Camel and the Marlboro Man. Perhaps just as effective for younger people was the personal experience of a loved one—a parent, a grandparent, or an older sibling—suffering the ill effects of tobacco use. Smoking declined among the American public as a result.

The terms PASSIVE SMOKING and "secondhand smoke" had not been invented in the 1960s. However, by the 1990s people had become aware that tobacco smoke posed a threat not only to the smoker, but also to those exposed to the smoldering cigarette or cigar, and the exhaled smoke. Private companies began to ban smoking in office buildings, and a whole series of laws followed, banning smoking in public transportation, on airplanes, in health care facilities, and in government buildings. People who had once puffed at their desks were forced to smoke on their breaks, huddled outside in all

strokes: loss of feeling, consciousness, or movement caused by the breaking or blocking of blood vessels in the brain

passive smoking: inhaling smoke from someone else's burning cigarette

sorts of weather. At the same time, states began to levy higher taxes on cigarettes to help pay for Medicaid and other social welfare programs.

Tighter Laws Cut Down on Nicotine Abuse

On November 16, 1998, forty-seven states and the District of Columbia came to an out-of-court settlement with four major American tobacco companies. (The other three states had previously come to agreements.) The states had sued the tobacco companies for the costs of providing health care to poor people suffering from tobacco-related illnesses. The cigarette companies agreed to pay the states $206 billion for health care. The companies also agreed not to market their product to adolescents through advertisements or promotional items. They further agreed to fund a program to discourage teenage smoking. One consequence of this settlement: The average price of a pack of cigarettes rose fifty cents in one year, from $2.20 in 1998 to $2.70 in 1999. By 2005, cigarettes were selling for about $4.00 per pack. For heavy smokers, many of them poor already, this was a difficult increase to manage.

Despite the successes made in the anti-tobacco campaign, smoking still appealed to youth who wanted to rebel against authority. In fact, by suggesting that tobacco was something that only adults should use just made it more popular with rebellious youth who wanted to seem hip and mature. Smoking was also glamorized in various movies as something that cool people do. As of the early twenty-first century, a large number of teens still take up smoking. The National Center for Chronic Disease Prevention and Health Promotion estimates that about 4,000 people under the age of eighteen begin smoking each day in the United States.

More recently, the healthcare industry has focused on smoking in films. "Product placement" is very important in movies. When a character in a film uses a particular food or beverage product, sales of that product often climb. In 2005 the American Medical Association recommended that the film industry adopt a policy that would automatically give an "R" rating to any movie in which a character uses tobacco. (People under seventeen are not supposed to be admitted to "R" rated movies without a parent or adult.) Whether the film industry will honor that request is uncertain.

What Is It Made Of?

Nicotine is a poisonous ALKALOID that occurs naturally in the leaves of the tobacco plant. While still in the leaves of the plant, it is a colorless liquid. Sixty milligrams of nicotine, about the amount

alkaloid: a nitrogen-containing substance found in plants

Philadelphia Phillies outfielder Lenny Dykstra is shown as he begins chewing a large wad of tobacco in 1990. He later appeared in a public service announcement telling teens to aspire to play like him, not chew tobacco like him. *Jonathan Daniel/Allsport USA.*

a bottle cap would hold, can kill a human being. It is used as a pesticide to kill insects on plants and internal parasites in animals.

The chemical formula for nicotine is $C_{10}H_{14}N_2$. The average cigarette contains 8 to 10 milligrams of nicotine, but much of this is lost in the process of burning. Typically, a smoker receives about 1 milligram of nicotine per cigarette. A pinch of chewing tobacco contains between 4.5 and 6.5 milligrams of nicotine. Since chewing tobacco enters the body more slowly than smoked tobacco, more of the dose is absorbed, but over a longer period of time.

In addition to nicotine, a smoking leaf of tobacco releases more than 4,000 different chemicals. Four hundred of these are known to be poisonous, and forty-three have been shown to cause cancer. A lit cigarette releases, among other things, CARBON MONOXIDE, ammonia, hydrogen cyanide, benzene, formaldehyde, acetone, methanol, and vinyl chloride. Tobacco companies add other ingredients to cigarettes as well, including menthol. Menthol numbs the throat to the irritating effects of the smoke. It also widens the pathways in the lungs, allowing more smoke to penetrate the tissues.

When smoke is exhaled from the lungs, a substance called tar remains in the body. As its name suggests, tar is a sticky residue that clings to lung tissue. Tar contains cancer-causing compounds. Receiving nicotine through the mouth by chewing reduces some of the dangerous chemicals from tar, but it also exposes the tissues in the mouth to cancer-causing agents and compounds that cause tooth decay and gum disease. The same compounds in tar simply cling to the mouth tissues and are absorbed by the gums, cheeks, and throat.

How Is It Taken?

Nicotine is taken in several ways. The most common and quick-acting manner is smoking. The user lights a cigarette, draws the smoke into the lungs, and exhales it. The effects of the nicotine can be felt within ten seconds, and they usually last between fifteen minutes and an hour.

People who smoke cigars and pipes generally "puff" them and do not inhale the smoke into the lungs. Even so, the soft tissues in the mouth absorb the nicotine and send it through the bloodstream to the brain. Smoking pipes or cigars is, indeed, habit-forming. Puffing is just another way to deliver nicotine to the brain.

Tobacco Statistics

Did you know that....
- As of 2005, tobacco use was considered to be the leading preventable cause of death in the United States. Nearly 500,000 deaths are related to tobacco use each year.
- The Centers for Disease Control and Prevention estimates that smoking takes 5.6 million years of potential life away each year in the United States.
- In the United States each day, some 4,000 people under age 18 smoke their first cigarette.
- Most adult smokers started using tobacco before their 18th birthday—nearly 80 percent of them, in fact.

carbon monoxide: a poisonous gas with no odor; carbon monoxide is released when cigarettes burn

The presence of the smoke in the mouth and throat can lead to cancers in those body parts, and to cancer of the esophagus, the tube leading into the stomach.

With chewing tobacco, the user takes a wad of moist tobacco and presses it between the cheek and the gum. As the mouth fills with saliva, the user must spit, because swallowing tobacco-laced saliva could be deadly and certainly causes stomach upset. Users of chewing tobacco generally keep a wad in the mouth for about thirty minutes, during which time about 2 milligrams of nicotine enter the bloodstream through the cheek and gum tissue.

Few people snort snuff anymore, but it was once a popular way to use nicotine. Snuff, finely-ground tobacco, was snorted up the nose and usually removed by sneezing. A "pinch of snuff" was thought to ward off colds and other infectious diseases.

Are There Any Medical Reasons for Taking This Substance?

Some small studies have been performed to see if nicotine patches help reduce memory loss in ALZHEIMER'S DISEASE patients and muscle tremors in PARKINSON'S DISEASE patients. Since nicotine is so highly addictive, however, its valid medical uses are considered very minimal.

The only acceptable medical use for nicotine is to help people overcome addiction to nicotine. "Nicotine delivery systems" include skin patches, gum, inhalers, and nasal sprays. Tobacco users trying to quit the habit can curb nicotine's WITHDRAWAL symptoms with these products. The products become very dangerous if a person smokes while using them. In that case, nicotine overdose is possible. Although some nicotine replacement products are available over the counter, most encourage nicotine addicts to seek the advice and counsel of a medical doctor while attempting to curb nicotine use.

Usage Trends

The *American Heart Association* Web site posts data on patterns of tobacco use among adults age eighteen and older in the United States. As of 2002, 25.2 percent of white American men and 20.7 percent of white American women used tobacco. In 2002, 27 percent of African American men and 18.5 percent of African American women used tobacco. Hispanic/Latino men reported 23.2 percent usage, and Hispanic/Latino women, 12.5 percent. Asian Americans were the least likely to use tobacco, with 21.3 percent of men and 6.9 of women reporting usage. The population most likely to use

Alzheimer's disease: a brain disease that usually strikes older individuals and results in memory loss, impaired thinking, and personality changes; symptoms worsen over time

Parkinson's disease: an incurable nervous disorder that worsens with time and occurs most often after the age of fifty; it is generally caused by a loss of dopamine-producing brain cells; symptoms include overall weakness, partial paralysis of the face, trembling hands, and a slowed, shuffling walk

withdrawal: the process of gradually cutting back on the amount of a drug being taken until it is discontinued entirely; also the accompanying physiological effects of terminating use of an addictive drug

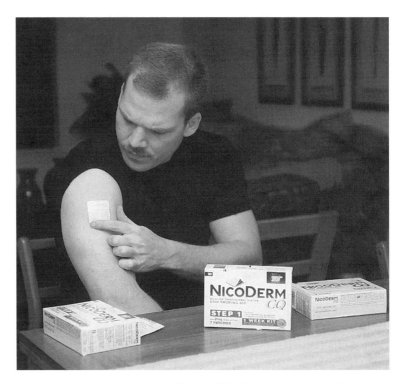

Some chronic tobacco users seek to end their addiction to the drug by using nicotine patches. Such therapies can be habit-forming, too. Patch users must take care not to exceed the recommended dose on the label.
Photograph by Robert J. Huffman/Field Mark Publications.

tobacco, according to the American Heart Association data, is Native Americans/Alaskan Natives, who reported that 32 percent of adult men and 36.9 percent of adult women were tobacco users. The numbers add up to 47.5 million adult American users.

What the Surveys Say

The 2003 NSDUH found 70.8 million tobacco users in the United States, factoring in anyone over the age of twelve who had ever tried tobacco. Of these, the NSDUH characterized 35.7 million as nicotine addicts. This number includes Americans age twelve and older. The NSDUH data on teenage nicotine use does not break down by race or ethnic origin, reporting simply that 12.5 percent of girls age twelve to eighteen use tobacco, along with 11.9 percent of boys. These rates are down from previous years.

Incidents of tobacco use seem to peak between the ages of eighteen and twenty-five, when, according to the NSDUH, 40.8 percent of people report at least one experience with the product. The data clearly show that most Americans begin using tobacco products between the ages of twelve and twenty-five. It is this "target audience" that the anti-smoking campaigns seek to educate about the health dangers of tobacco. According to various anti-smoking organizations, it is this same group that smoking advertisements target.

Although the number of young smokers remains high, data from the 2004 Monitoring the Future (MTF) study show a slow but steady drop in the percentage of eighth-, tenth-, and twelfth-grade students who smoke cigarettes. Back in 1996, 21 percent of eighth graders, 30.4 percent of tenth graders, and 34 percent of twelfth graders had smoked during the month prior to the survey. Eight years later, in 2004, the figures had fallen to 9.2 percent of eighth graders, 16 percent of tenth graders, and 25 percent of twelfth graders reporting past-month cigarette usage. Teens who said they smoked more than a half a pack of cigarettes daily fell significantly over the eight-year span as well. In addition, according to MTF survey authors, "the perception of harm from smoking one or more packs per day increased significantly among eighth- and tenth-graders from 2003 to 2004."

Charley, the Addicted Chimp

According to *First Coast News* in April of 2005, Charley, a resident of the Bloemfontein Zoo in South Africa, picked up a smoking habit after finding a pack of cigarettes thrown into his cage. Helpful zoo visitors lit his cigarettes for him. Charley learned to hide his cigarettes from the zookeepers, who would take them from him. The zoo staff feared he had become addicted. They posted signs asking visitors not to give Charley any more tobacco for fear that it was damaging his health.

Ties to Social Problems?

The various surveys show another fact as well. According to the American Heart Association, people with a high school education or less are three times more likely to be smokers than those with a college education. The prevalence of cigarette smoking is highest among people living below the poverty level, with one in three reporting tobacco use.

A study of more than 4,000 students in Oregon and California linked early smoking with problem behaviors. Kids who start smoking around age twelve are considered "early smokers." In an article published in the *Journal of Adolescent Health,* Phyllis L. Ellickson and her coauthors reached the following conclusion: "Compared with nonsmokers, early smokers were at least three times more likely by grade twelve to regularly use tobacco and marijuana, use hard drugs, [and] drop out of school." In addition, these adolescents were "at higher risk for low academic achievement and behavioral problems at school."

Effects on the Body

Nicotine is the addictive compound in tobacco. When it enters the bloodstream, either through the lungs, the skin inside the mouth, or the nasal passages, it moves to the brain. There it binds with ACETYLCHOLINE receptors, triggering the release of other NEUROTRANSMITTERS and hormones. Basically, nicotine causes two sensations: stimulation in the thought processes, and general relaxation in the user.

The *Need* for a Cigarette

The quick-acting nicotine increases the amount of DOPAMINE in the brain. This causes pleasure and relaxation of muscles. At the same time, it enhances NOREPINEPHRINE and acetylcholine levels, increasing mental stimulation and suppressing appetite. Nicotine also enhances memory and promotes a feeling of well-being. In other words, the drug stimulates the brain's reward system, making the user "feel good."

When people say that cigarettes help them to concentrate, they are not exaggerating. Nicotine does have that effect. However, the effect wears off quickly unless another dose of nicotine enters the brain. Likewise, nicotine does cause a feeling of relaxation, but this too passes quickly, leading to a craving for more of the drug. Many behaviors are related to the addicting qualities of nicotine. The user, taking a puff on a cigarette, might just feel more relaxed because withdrawal symptoms have been held at bay for another hour.

A Dangerous Habit

Nicotine causes a release of EPINEPHRINE, leading to a faster heartbeat, higher blood pressure, quickened breathing, and higher blood sugar. So while the user may feel relaxed, the body is actually working harder to pump blood and take in oxygen. Over a long period of time, this strain on the heart and elevated blood pressure can lead to heart attack and stroke. The drug also complicates the chemistry of the blood, causing blood vessels to become smaller and blood cells to stick together in clots. This can increase the risk of organ damage and stroke. Over time, nicotine contributes to the build-up of plaque in the arteries, a leading cause of heart disease. The chemicals in cigarette smoke also irritate the throat, interfere with the lung's ability to clear debris and bacteria, and promote nausea and other digestive disturbances.

Most scientists agree that nicotine is the most addictive substance used by humankind—worse than cocaine, although it works in a similar way on the brain's reward centers. (An entry for

acetylcholine: pronounced uh-settle-KOH-leen; a neurotransmitter that forms from a substance called choline, which is released by the liver

neurotransmitters: a substance that helps spread nerve impulses from one nerve cell to another

dopamine: pronounced DOPE-uh-meen; a combination of carbon, hydrogen, nitrogen, and oxygen that acts as a neurotransmitter in the brain

norepinephrine: pronounced nor-epp-ih-NEFF-run; a natural stimulant produced by the human body

epinephrine: pronounced epp-ih-NEFF-run; a hormone that increases heart rate and breathing; also called adrenaline

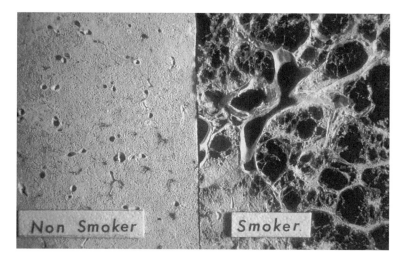

Smoking can lead to severe lung damage. On the left are the lungs of a nonsmoker; on the right, the lungs of a smoker. © *O. Auerbach/Visuals Unlimited.*

cocaine is available in this encyclopedia.) Because nicotine works so quickly and exits the brain just as quickly, it begins to induce cravings in most users within days or weeks of first use. Its effects are particularly strong on those with attention-deficit/hyperactivity disorder (ADHD), for whom it may be calming, and those with depression or a tendency to become depressed. People with those problems have a harder time freeing themselves from a nicotine addiction, so they are advised not to use tobacco at all.

Getting Hooked

Regular tobacco use causes TOLERANCE, a condition that can lead to heavy smoking or chewing, and to lifestyle changes based on that heavy use. People find themselves spending a great deal of money on tobacco products, using them recklessly (smoking in bed, smoking while driving), and endangering the health of others with secondhand smoke.

At overdose levels, nicotine causes dizziness, vomiting, muscle tremors, convulsions, and paralysis of the lungs leading to an inability to breathe. All of these symptoms can develop within minutes. Tobacco products should be kept out of reach of children and pets. Those using nicotine replacement products should never smoke or chew tobacco at the same time. In addition, great care should be taken with any insecticide or other product containing pure nicotine.

tolerance: a condition in which higher and higher doses of a drug are needed to produce the original effect or high experienced

The immediate effects of nicotine are generally mild and pleasurable; the long-term effects of tobacco use are not. Smokers accumulate a huge buildup of tar in the lungs, promoting cancer and clogging the air sacs that transfer oxygen into the bloodstream. The cancer-causing chemicals in tobacco promote growth of tumors in the mouth, on the lips, in the throat, in the lungs, in the esophagus, and elsewhere in the body. Nearly one in five deaths due to heart disease can be blamed on tobacco, and the overall death rate from cancer is twice as high among smokers as among nonsmokers.

More Dangers

People who smoke damage tiny, hair-like structures called cilia that lead to the lungs. Cilia help to remove germs and dirt from the lungs. This leads to an accumulation of mucus in the lungs and bronchial tubes—the famous "smoker's cough." Smokers also suffer more frequent and more serious cases of flu and pneumonia. Heavy tobacco use can cause men to become impotent and their sperm counts to decrease. Tobacco use has also been linked to cancers in the female reproductive organs.

Perhaps the most dangerous aspect of nicotine is the time it takes for the deadly side effects to develop. Most people begin using tobacco as teenagers, a time when they are most vulnerable to peer pressure and subtle advertising techniques. The vast majority of teenagers are enjoying the best health they will ever have in their lives. They cannot imagine growing old, developing health problems, or being at risk for fatal diseases. By the time they begin to understand how fragile the body is, they can already be deeply dependent on nicotine.

Becoming free of nicotine addiction causes immediate and long-term health benefits, including improved breathing, better sensation of taste, healthier teeth and skin, and improved strength. Quitting smoking also lessens the risks of cancer—but not entirely. Sometimes people who have not smoked in years discover that they have lung cancer. The disease is difficult to diagnose in its early stages. The very best way to avoid nicotine-related illnesses is to avoid any use of nicotine at any stage of life. If nicotine use has begun, the sooner it ends, the better the chances of living a long and healthy life.

Reactions with Other Drugs or Substances

Tobacco use causes the liver to produce more enzymes that can lower the blood levels of other medicines. Doctors should alter the doses of prescription drugs and monitor patients more carefully if those patients are using tobacco or nicotine replacement products. Nicotine should not be combined with certain asthma drugs, blood thinners, antipsychotic drugs, drugs for migraine headaches, and some antidepressants. Nicotine also interferes with some blood pressure medications such as Procardia and Tenormin. Women who are using birth control pills are urged not to smoke, because the combination of the pills and the tobacco can increase the likelihood of blood clots.

Any combination of nicotine and cocaine, opiates, hallucinogens, or marijuana can heighten the effects of the illegal drugs and possibly lead to irregular heartbeat or breathing problems. Heavy use of tobacco and alcohol further increases cancer risks. (Entries on alcohol and marijuana are available in this encyclopedia.)

Treatment for Habitual Users

Giving up the nicotine habit can be very difficult. Within hours of the last cigarette or chew, the body begins to respond to the lack of the drug. People become irritable and anxious, they overeat, they cannot sleep, and they can experience muscle tremors and a craving for tobacco. Many times, it is just easier to get another cigarette rather than to face the withdrawal symptoms.

Many self-help groups, including Nicotine Anonymous, the American Lung Association, the American Cancer Society, and the National Cancer Institute, have smoking cessation, or stopping, programs. Local- and state-funded programs also provide counselors and various treatment methods to the motivated addict who wants to quit using tobacco. These treatment programs may use hypnosis, group therapy, or behavior modification to encourage alternate behavior and help individuals combat the many facets of nicotine addiction. In many cases, health insurance companies will help pay for nicotine treatment programs.

Probably the most successful treatment methods involve nicotine replacement products such as gum (Nicorette) and skin patches (NicoDerm CQ, Nicotrol, Habitrol, and ProStep). These products recommend that the user work closely with a doctor or therapist to taper the doses of nicotine slowly. People using nicotine replacement

> ## Nicotine Withdrawal Symptoms
>
> Nicotine withdrawal causes a variety of symptoms, including:
> - restlessness
> - anxiety
> - impatience
> - anger
> - difficulty concentrating
> - increased appetite and weight gain
> - depression
> - loss of energy and interest in life
> - dizziness
> - headache
> - sweating
> - insomnia, the inability to sleep
> - tremors, shaking of limbs
> - tightening of muscles
> - cravings for tobacco.

Kreteks and Bidis

Kreteks are clove-spiced cigarettes from Indonesia. Bidis are small, flavored cigarettes from India. Both are available on the American market, and both contain high concentrations of nicotine—higher, even, than American cigarettes. These items are tobacco products, and they are habit-forming.

therapies must take care not to use tobacco products at the same time, since this may lead to nicotine overdose. They must also be aware that these therapies can be habit-forming themselves, so they must be motivated not to exceed the recommended dose on the label of the package.

Other prescription drugs used to curb nicotine abuse include buproprion (Zyban), an antidepressant, and Clonidine (Catapres), a medicine to reduce high blood pressure. Both of these products block nicotine's pleasurable effects and help a recovering user avoid tobacco products.

For most, the best way to treat a tobacco habit is to combine a nicotine replacement therapy with counseling, education, group support, and the encouragement of family and friends. A heavy tobacco user must expect that the process will not always go smoothly and must have strategies in place for times of stress. Recovering nicotine addicts usually need to alter their lifestyles in order to avoid the people and places associated with smoking. If other family members smoke in the home, this can be very challenging.

The least effective way to attempt to quit nicotine is to depend on will power or to attempt to cut back on smoking by using low-tar cigarettes or by smoking less. People who try to quit in this way usually compensate by drawing more deeply on the cigarettes they do smoke. The relapse rate for this type of cessation is very high.

Consequences

Nicotine erodes health slowly at first. Most people begin smoking early in life, when they are enjoying the best health they will ever have. Gradually, however, the consequences of long-term tobacco use become evident. People suffer from bad breath, discolored teeth, cravings, and dryness and thinning of the skin. They may develop a "smoker's cough" or a gravelly voice from damage to the larynx, the organ that produces sound in the throat. They may develop lesions—sores that do not heal or that heal very slowly—on their lips or inside the mouth. All of these are early warning signs of trouble to come.

Increased Risk of Cancer and Other Illnesses

It is estimated that one-third of all cancers and 87 percent of lung cancer in the United States can be traced directly to tobacco use. Cancer

An anti-smoking billboard shows a sickly character named "Joe Chemo" in his hospital bed suffering from cancer due to years of smoking. The character is a takeoff of the famous "Joe Camel," who was once featured on packs of Camel cigarettes. *AP/Wide World Photos.*

is an illness in which cells grow and reproduce too quickly, causing tumors inside the body. The tumors can be small at first and then grow rapidly. If the cancer reaches the lymph glands that send hormones throughout the body, the cancer can spread through the body as well. Cancer treatment generally involves surgery to remove tumors. Surgery is often followed by chemotherapy, a process that shrinks tumors but also causes nausea, weakness, hair loss, and malfunction of the immune system. Some tumors are treated with radiation to stem their growth. Radiation can cause pain and burning of the skin.

Cancer is treatable, but smokers are twice as likely to die of it as nonsmokers diagnosed with the same illness. Heavy smokers are four times more likely to die of their cancers as nonsmokers diagnosed with similar cancers.

Test your knowledge: How much do you know about Nicotine?

The National Institute on Drug Abuse of the National Institutes of Health has created this quiz for teens about nicotine and its effects. The answers follow the quiz, but don't peek. See how much you know!

1. Tobacco use can be contributed to about _____ deaths in the United States each year.

   a) 50,000
   b) 100,000
   c) 500,000

2. Smokers crave cigarettes because they _____.

   a) like the smell of cigarette smoke
   b) are addicted to nicotine
   c) like the way cigarettes make them look

3. Smoking cigarettes changes _____.

   a) the amount of a brain chemical that allows us to experience pleasure
   b) the amount of blood that flows to the brain
   c) the number of things we worry about

4. After smoking cigarettes for a while, the smoker _____.

   a) needs less nicotine to get the same feeling from smoking
   b) needs more nicotine to get the same feeling from smoking
   c) doesn't notice any change in how much nicotine they need.

5. Cigarette smoke contains _____ chemicals.

   a) 4,000
   b) 1,000
   c) 400

6. Cigarette smokers are addicted to _____.

   a) tar
   b) carbon monoxide
   c) nicotine

7. After a puff on a cigarette, nicotine is in the brain in _____ seconds.

   a) 8
   b) 18
   c) 80

8. In the brain, nicotine locks into receptors on neurons making the smoker feel _____.

   a) irritable
   b) sleepy
   c) alert and satisfied

9. After a while, the brain shuts down some receptors so a smoker needs a cigarette _____.

   a) to stop cravings
   b) just to feel normal
   c) both a and b

Answers

1. **C:** Tobacco use causes more illnesses and death than all other addicting drugs combined. Nicotine is the drug in tobacco that is responsible for addiction and keeps people smoking despite harmful effects.

2. **B:** The correct answer is b. Nicotine, the drug in tobacco cigarettes, is highly addictive. It causes changes in the brain that give smokers a strong appetite for cigarettes.

3. **A:** Nicotine boosts the amount of a brain chemical called dopamine. At first, this produces feelings of pleasure. But soon, the smoker needs nicotine just to feel normal.

4. **B:** After nicotine causes floods of brain chemicals, the brain starts to make less of the chemicals. So a smoker soon needs to smoke more to get the effects that one cigarette used to provide.

5. **A:** The addictive drug nicotine is only one of 4,000 chemicals in cigarette smoke. Many of them, such as tar and carbon monoxide, are toxic and cause diseases such as cancer.

6. **C:** Smokers are addicted to the nicotine in tobacco. However, both tar and carbon monoxide are also toxic chemicals causing many health problems.

7. **A:** After a smoker inhales cigarette smoke, nicotine enters the blood in the lungs, goes through the heart and is pumped to the brain—a journey that takes only eight seconds.

8. **C:** Nicotine is similar in size and shape as brain chemicals that regulate feelings of alertness and pleasure or satisfaction.

9. **C:** Smokers have changed the way their brains work, so that they crave cigarettes as a way to make them feel normal. Without nicotine, smokers feel irritable and depressed.

SOURCE: Adapted from "Quiz: Nicotine," in *The Science Behind Drug Abuse: NIDA for Teens,* National Institute on Drug Abuse, National Institutes of Health, U.S. Department of Health and Human Services, Bethesda, MA [Online] http://teens .drugabuse.gov/parents/documents/nicotine_quiz.doc [accessed May 24, 2005]

Long-term tobacco use is directly linked to heart attack, various lung illnesses, high blood pressure, and stomach ulcers. It also reduces the body's ability to heal broken bones, promotes arthritis, and causes bad breath and yellowing of the teeth. All of these effects stem from a product that is legal for use in the American adult population. However, the U.S. Surgeon General's warning about the various health consequences of smoking appears on all packs of cigarettes sold in the United States.

The Law

In most states, people must be eighteen years old to purchase tobacco products legally. In Alabama, Alaska, and Utah, the minimum age for purchase of tobacco is nineteen. As of the early 2000s, four other states—California, New Jersey, Illinois, and Massachusetts—were considering laws to raise the age as well. The burden of keeping underage persons from buying cigarettes or smokeless tobacco falls on the stores that sell it.

Shopkeepers risk prosecution if they are caught selling tobacco to minors. Most stores require that younger buyers produce valid identification showing date of birth. Occasionally, young undercover police officers will attempt to buy tobacco without proper identification to see if the shopkeepers are abiding by the law. A store owner who sells tobacco to a minor risks losing his or her license to sell the product, as well as fines or closure of the business.

People under the age of eighteen who get caught with tobacco products do not face criminal prosecution. However, they can be suspended from school if caught with tobacco on school grounds. Most authorities contact parents or legal guardians to report the situation. For teens who smoke, secrecy rarely lasts very long. The telltale smell of tobacco clinging to clothing and hair is hard to disguise.

Discrimination Against Smokers

In some states, private companies have introduced policies that deny jobs to smokers. The companies cite the extra burden of health care costs for their smoking employees, as well as loss of work time due to smoking breaks. Many smokers claim that this is discrimination and should not be a factor deciding employment, especially since smoking is legal. As of early 2005 no lawsuits had yet developed from the introduction of these measures, but analysts expected that legal action would soon occur.

Various states have laws that prohibit employers from discriminating against their staff for engaging in certain legal activities, like smoking, while they are not at work. According to Marshall H. Tanick in the Minneapolis *Star Tribune* "about two dozen states ... have so-called 'lifestyle rights' laws," including Minnesota, Texas, California, and Florida. Such laws prohibit employers from discriminating against "employees because of lawful off-duty conduct." Tanick noted that the 1992 Minnesota law specifically "extends to consumption of 'food, alcohol, or non-alcoholic beverages and tobacco.'" Employers can restrict the use of certain products, consumed by the employee off-duty, if use of those products interferes with the person's ability to do his or her job.

For More Information

Books

Balkin, Karen F. *Tobacco and Smoking.* San Diego, CA: Greenhaven Press, 2005.

Brigham, Janet. *Dying to Quit: Why We Smoke and How We Stop.* Washington, DC: Joseph Henry Press, 1998.

Gahlinger, Paul M. *Illegal Drugs: A Complete Guide to Their History, Chemistry, Use and Abuse.* Las Vegas, NV: Sagebrush Press, 2001.

Haugen, Hayley Mitchell. *Teen Smoking.* San Diego, CA: Greenhaven Press, 2004.

Kuhn, Cynthia, Scott Swartzwelder, and Wilkie Wilson. *Buzzed: The Straight Facts about the Most Used and Abused Drugs from Alcohol to Ecstasy,* 2nd ed. New York: W.W. Norton, 2003.

McCay, William. *The Truth about Smoking.* New York: Facts on File, 2005.

Wagner, Heather Lehr. *Nicotine.* Philadelphia: Chelsea House, 2003.

Whelan, Elizabeth M. *Cigarettes: What the Warning Label Doesn't Tell You: The First Comprehensive Guide to the Health Consequences of Smoking.* Amherst, NY: Prometheus Books, 1997.

Periodicals

"AMA Wants 'R' Rating for Movies with Smoking." *Tobacco Retailer* (August, 2004): p. 13.

Ellickson, Phyllis L., Joan S. Tucker, and David J. Klein. "High-Risk Behaviors Associated with Early Smoking: Results from a Five-Year Follow-Up." *Journal of Adolescent Health* (June, 2001).

"Fired for Smoking?: Michigan Health Care Company Has Strict Anti-Tobacco Policy." *Associated Press* (January 26, 2005).

Grunbaum, Jo Anne, and others. "Youth Risk Behavior Surveillance: United States, 2001." *Journal of School Health* (October, 2002): p. 313.

Holcomb, Betty. "The Winner." *Good Housekeeping* (July, 1999): p. 27.

Kowalski, Kathiann M. "How Tobacco Ads Target Teens." *Current Health 2* (April-May, 2002): p. 6.

"Silver Screen Smoking Is on the Rise." *USA Today Magazine* (November, 2003): p. 9.

Springer, Karen. "Smoking: Light Up and You May Be Let Go." *Newsweek* (February 7, 2005): p. 10.

Susman, Ed. "Doctors Seek 'R' for Smoking in Movies." *UPI Perspectives* (June 14, 2004).

Worth, Robert. "Making It Uncool." *Washington Monthly* (March, 1999): p. 8.

Web Sites

"2003 National Survey on Drug Use and Health (NSDUH)." *U.S. Department of Health and Human Services, Substance Abuse and Mental Health Services Administration.* http://www.oas.samhsa.gov/nhsda.htm (accessed July 30, 2005).

Billingsley, Janice. "Anti-Tobacco Programs Cut Teen Smoking Rates." *Forbes.com,* January 28, 2005. http://www.forbes.com/lifestyle/health/feeds/hscout/2005/01/28/hscout523634.html (accessed July 30, 2005).

"Campaign for Tobacco-Free Kids." *Tobacco-Free Kids.* http://www.tobaccofreekids.org (accessed July 30, 2005).

"Chimps Hooked on Smoking." *First Coast News,* April 22, 2005. http://www.firstcoastnews.com/news/strange/news-article.aspx?storyid=35962 (accessed July 31, 2005).

"Cigarette Smoking among American Teens Continues to Decline, but More Slowly than in the Past." *National Institute of Drug Abuse.* http://www.nida.nih.gov/DrugPages/MTF.html (accessed July 30, 2005).

"Cigarette Smoking Statistics." *American Heart Association.* http://www.americanheart.org/presenter.jhtml?identifier=4559 (accessed July 30, 2005).

Huggins, Charnicia E. "Lung Cancer No Longer Just a Man's Disease." *Yahoo! News.* http://news.yahoo.com (accessed June 8, 2005).

"Kicking the Habit Can Add Years to Your Life." *MSNBC.com,* February 14, 2005. http://www.msnbc.msn.com/id/6969860 (accessed July 30, 2005).

"Molecule May Be Key to Nicotine Addiction." *MSNBC.com,* November 4, 2004. http://msnbc.msn.com/id/6405269 (accessed July 30, 2005).

Monitoring the Future. http://www.monitoringthefuture.org/ and http://www.nida.nih.gov/Newsroom/04/2004MTFDrug.pdf (both accessed August 31, 2005).

National Institute on Drug Abuse. http://www.nida.nih.gov and http://www.drugabuse.gov (both accessed July 30, 2005).

"One Puff of Smoke Can Damage DNA." *MSNBC.com,* October 1, 2004. http://www.msnbc.msn.com/id/6152449/ (accessed July 30, 2005).

"Smoking Killed 5 Million Worldwide in 2000." *MSNBC.com,* November 24, 2005. http://www.msnbc.msn.com/id/6574849/ (accessed July 30, 2005).

"Study: Smoking Harms Women More than Men." *Yahoo! News.* http://news.yahoo.com (accessed June 28, 2005).

Tanick, Marshall H. "Clearing the Air in the Workplace." *Star Tribune,* April 3, 2005. www.startribune.com/stories/535/5323366.html (accessed August 1, 2005).

"Tobacco Information and Prevention Source (TIPS)." *Centers for Disease Control and Prevention, National Center for Chronic Disease Prevention and Health Promotion.* http://www.cdc.gov/tobacco/issue.htm (accessed July 30, 2005).

See also: Alcohol; Cocaine; Marijuana

Nitrous Oxide

What Kind of Drug Is It?

Nitrous oxide is a type of anesthetic, a substance used to deaden pain. It can alleviate pain without causing a loss of consciousness. Best known by the nickname "laughing gas," nitrous oxide is used primarily by dentists to keep patients comfortable during painful procedures. It can also be used in combination with other drugs as a GENERAL ANESTHETIC. When administered by trained medical professionals, the gas is considered a safe and effective form of anesthesia.

As a recreational drug—a drug used solely to get high, not to treat a medical condition—nitrous oxide is classified as an inhalant. (An entry on inhalants is available in this encyclopedia.) Inhalants contain dangerous vapors, which are gases or fumes that can be irritating or physically harmful when breathed in. Vapors from inhalants produce psychoactive, or mind-altering, effects when breathed in through the mouth or nose.

More than 1,000 different household and industrial products— all readily accessible to consumers of any age—are sniffed or HUFFED for their intoxicating effects. Glues, paints, markers, nail polish, correction fluid, and shoe polish are among the most commonly abused inhalants.

Among young teens, nitrous oxide is typically obtained from canned whipped cream available at grocery stores. Nitrous oxide gas is used to propel, or to drive out, the whipped cream from the can. Sales of nitrous oxide to older teens and adults usually occur at dance clubs and all-night dance parties called RAVES or through Internet transactions.

Overview

In the 1700s and the 1800s, chemists, doctors, and dentists in Europe and the United States experimented with three different anesthetic gases: nitrous oxide, ether (EETH-uhr), and chloroform (KLOR-uh-form). These compounds revolutionized surgical and dental procedures. While under the influence of an anesthetic gas, a patient's perception of pain is altered. Nitrous oxide, ether, and chloroform all dull or block painful sensations. They also produce a rather intense high.

Official Drug Name: Nitrous oxide, dinitrogen oxide, nitrogen oxide
Also Known As: Balloons, buzz bombs, cartridges, hippie crack, laughing gas, nitrous, whip-its, whippets, whippits
Drug Classifications: Not scheduled

general anesthetic: an anesthetic that causes a loss of sensation in the entire body, rather than just a specific body part, and brings on a loss of consciousness

huffed: inhaled through the mouth, often from an inhalant-soaked cloth

raves: wild overnight dance parties that typically involve huge crowds of people, loud techno music, and illegal drug use

Various devices used for inhaling nitrous oxide are displayed. *Photo by Erowid, © 2001 Erowid.org.*

The intoxicating side effects of the gases, however, led to their use and abuse as recreational drugs. A research report titled "Inhalant Abuse," prepared by the National Institute on Drug Abuse (NIDA) and updated in 2005, noted that "nitrous oxide is the most abused of these [three] gases."

Nitrous oxide is a gas with both anesthetic and analgesic (pain relieving) properties. It was first discovered in 1772 by British scientist, theologian, and philosopher Joseph Priestley (1733–1804). Earlier, Priestley had identified oxygen, which he termed "phlogisticated (floh-JISS-tih-kay-ted) air." The term "phlo-gis-tic" comes from a Greek word meaning "flammable."

Nitrous Demonstrations: An Unusual Form of Entertainment

Although Priestley is credited with discovering nitrous oxide, another scientist recognized the potential value of its numbing and intoxicating effects. This man was Sir Humphry Davy (1778–1829), a British chemist who experimented with the gas on himself and his friends. In a book Davy wrote on the subject in 1800, he suggested that nitrous oxide's ability to dull pain might make it a useful anesthetic in surgeries. But, as Julie M. Fenster noted in *Ether Day: The Strange Tale of America's Greatest Medical Discovery and the Haunted Men Who Made It,* "no one took his suggestion."

And so, despite Davy's writings on the subject, nitrous oxide was not put to use in the medical field for another four decades. Apparently, according to historical sources, pain was such an accepted part of medical intervention during the early nineteenth century that neither scientists nor doctors seriously considered trying to ease it. Instead, nitrous oxide, which had earned the nickname "laughing gas," enjoyed popularity as a way for the British upper classes to entertain themselves at social gatherings.

Nitrous oxide was first discovered in 1772 by British scientist, theologian, and philosopher Joseph Priestley. (Some sources cite his name as Priestly.) © *Bettmann/Corbis.*

"The gas was soon offered at dinner parties instead of wine," wrote Fenster. It was even demonstrated in theaters and at festivals. In 1824, crowds in London were amazed by a show called "M. Henry's Mechanical and Chemical Demonstrations." The highly successful performances showed the uninhibiting effects of nitrous oxide on audience volunteers eager to try the gas.

"A New Era in Tooth-Pulling!"

Meanwhile in the United States, laughing gas was featured in traveling medicine shows and carnivals. Gardner Q. Colton (1814–1898), a former medical student, made a good living by giving public demonstrations of nitrous oxide. In New York City in 1844, he organized the "Grand Exhibition of Nitrous Oxide" on Broadway, charging the then-outrageous price of twenty-five cents per ticket. Colton moved his act to Hartford, Connecticut, later that year. Dr. Horace Wells (1815–1848), a dentist in Hartford, attended the nitrous exhibition with his wife. The evening's entertainment changed Wells' life forever.

Both Wells and his wife were among the volunteers from the audience who tried the laughing gas. The couple apparently engaged in some silly antics after sampling the nitrous oxide, but Wells was actually more interested in the effects of the gas on another member of the audience. A local man named Sam Cooley had seriously gashed his legs on a piece of furniture while stumbling around the stage on his nitrous high. His knees were bleeding badly, but he felt no pain. In fact, he didn't even realize he had been hurt. Wells was stunned by the effect of the gas and concluded that nitrous oxide might be useful as a medical anesthetic. In Wells' own often-quoted words, it was the beginning of "a new era in tooth-pulling!"

In keeping with the tradition of scientific experimentation in the nineteenth century, Wells used himself as a test subject. He devised a test case involving his dental colleague and friend Dr. John Riggs, who agreed to extract a tooth from Wells' mouth. The experiment took place on December 11, 1844. Wells asked Colton to set up his nitrous oxide equipment at the office Wells shared with Riggs. Wells administered the gas himself and soon nodded off from its effects. Riggs immediately pulled a sore wisdom tooth from Wells' mouth. The nitrous oxide had worked. Wells woke up shortly after the procedure and reported feeling no pain.

Considering his test a success, Wells began using nitrous oxide—quite successfully—as an anesthetic in his dental practice. When people heard about the new dental procedure, Wells' business increased. He was confident that painful dentistry would soon become a thing of the past.

A Demonstration Gone Bad

In January of 1845, before an audience of experts from the Harvard Medical School and Massachusetts General Hospital, Wells attempted to demonstrate the anesthetizing effects of nitrous oxide. He used a bag of the gas to sedate a patient before removing a tooth. However, the bag was withdrawn too soon, and the patient awoke before the procedure was complete. The experiment was considered a failure, and Wells was devastated. He never fully recovered from the disastrous demonstration and committed suicide in 1848. More than a decade later, in the early 1860s, the medical community came to understand and accept nitrous oxide as a valuable tool. It was finally being used not as a prop in a traveling sideshow, but as the anesthetic that Wells had suggested.

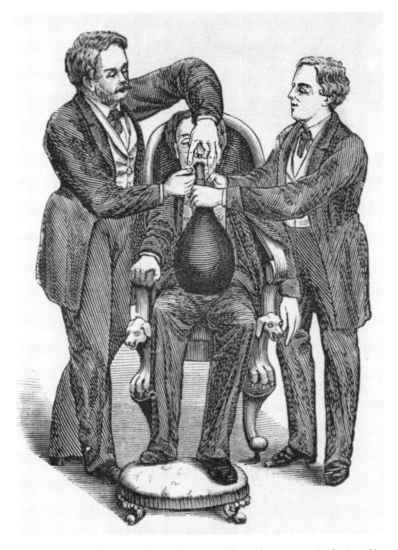

Over the years, nitrous oxide has been used in various ways. As depicted in this illustration from 1863, the gas was used as an anesthetic when preparing witnesses for trial in Great Britain. Here, one man administers the mixture from a bag while another pinches the witness' nostrils shut.
© *Bettmann/Corbis.*

Modern Uses

By 1871, companies in both the United States and Great Britain were producing compressed nitrous oxide in cylinders. As of 2003, according to the Compressed Gas Association (CGA), nearly 90 percent of the nitrous oxide manufactured

About Those Other Gases . . .

Ether is a flammable liquid with the chemical formula $C_4H_{10}O$. (Flammable means that the substance is capable of catching fire and burning quickly.) The intoxicating effects of ether have been known since the thirteenth century. It was first used as an anesthetic beginning in the mid-1800s, but its high flammability made it dangerous for medical use. The word *ether* comes from the Greek term meaning "to ignite" or "blaze."

Because ether is a liquid at room temperature, it can be swallowed, or the fumes from the liquid can be inhaled. In the 1760s, it was often dispensed by doctors by the drop onto a lump of sugar or mixed with water and used as a tonic. The use of ether as a recreational drug increased when users realized that it produced intoxication without a hangover. For a time, ether was actually consumed in place of alcohol, but many accidental fires occurred when drinkers sipped on their ether cocktails with a cigarette in hand.

It was not until the nineteenth century that ether caught on as an inhalant. So-called "ether frolics," or parties, became quite popular in the 1820s. The ether high was often compared to a spiritual experience. In fact, the term *ethereal* refers to the heavens or regions beyond the bounds of Earth.

Dr. William T. G. Morton first administered ether as a general anesthetic on October 16, 1846, at Massachusetts General Hospital. That day has since become known as "Ether Day."

Chloroform is a toxic (poisonous) liquid with a chemical formula of $CHCl_3$. This colorless anesthetic, discovered in 1833, is volatile, meaning it easily converts to a vapor. It is no longer used as a general anesthetic because of its dangerous side effects, which include serious damage to the liver.

Chloroform is an age-old tool of the trade among villains in films and television shows. In typical "bad-guy" style, a villain douses a cloth with chloroform and then approaches an unsuspecting victim from behind, placing the chloroform-soaked cloth over the person's nose and mouth. When inhaled, the fumes from the cloth quickly knock out the victim, leaving him or her defenseless.

in the United States is intended for medical and dental applications. Another 5 to 8 percent is used in the food industry. Other legitimate uses for nitrous oxide include the manufacture of airbags, semiconductors, and fuels that boost horsepower in race car engines.

However, the laughing gas parties and public demonstrations of the early 1800s evolved into a serious problem of abuse that has persisted into the twenty-first century. The gas is often sold at dance clubs and raves in balloons. Whipped cream cartridges, nicknamed "whippets," also contain nitrous oxide. These cartridges are sold through restaurant supply companies but are frequently purchased for illegal use.

What Is It Made Of?

Nitrous oxide is a compound made from nitrogen and oxygen. Its chemical formula is N_2O. The gas itself is clear and colorless, with a slightly sweet odor and taste. Nitrous oxide should not be confused with the potentially toxic gas known as nitric oxide (NO). Nitric oxide is found in the atmosphere as an air pollutant. It is also found in very small amounts in the human body, where it helps to move oxygen to the tissues and transmit nerve impulses.

Nitrous oxide is best described as a liquefied gas. It is SYNTHESIZED from a compound found in fertilizers and explosives. This compound, ammonium nitrate (NH_4NO_3), forms steam and nitrous oxide when heated. The nitrous oxide is then processed and turned into a liquid form for storage in tanks, cylinders, or cartridges.

Pure nitrous oxide is deadly. The gas must be mixed with oxygen to be used safely as an anesthetic.

How Is It Taken?

N_2O is used as an AEROSOL propellant in cans of whipped cream and some other food and beverage products. These products are a primary source of nitrous oxide for some abusers.

Depending on its intended use, nitrous oxide can be purchased in varying "grades," or degrees of purity. A food-grade version of the gas is sold to restaurants and caterers in small, bullet-shaped, metal cartridges. These cartridges are perfectly legal for use in the food preparation industry. Nitrous abusers refer to them as "whippets." One whippet delivers enough nitrous oxide to produce a three- to five-minute high. To release the nitrous oxide from a whippet, the high-pressure seal on the canister is pierced with a device called a "cracker." The resulting hole then emits a stream of nitrous oxide gas, which users inhale directly or use to inflate a balloon. Mishandling the cracker or piercing the wrong part of the canister can result in explosions and serious injuries.

Dealers often sell nitrous oxide to users at concerts, clubs, and raves. Instead of using small food-grade canisters, however, they use huge medical-grade nitrous tanks to dispense the gas into balloons. (Medical grade nitrous oxide is considered a prescription drug. These tanks can only be purchased legally by qualified medical personnel.) Nitrous-filled balloons sell for $3 to $5 apiece. One large cylinder of nitrous oxide can fill enough balloons to generate $20,000 to $30,000 in sales.

Sometimes, users fill plastic bags with nitrous oxide gas and then place the bags over their mouths or heads. This method of use carries

synthesized: made in a laboratory

aerosol: a gas used to propel, or shoot out, liquid substances from a pressurized can

Scooby and Shaggy Rile Viewers

Nitrous oxide abuse became a hot topic in 2004, when recreational use of the gas showed up in a kids' film. In a one-minute-long scene from the PG-rated Warner Bros. movie *Scooby-Doo 2: Monsters Unleashed,* one of the main characters, Shaggy, sniffs nitrous oxide from a whipped cream can and jokes about it. Seeing Shaggy do whippets is "supposed to make kids laugh," wrote Sue Marquette Poremba on the *Preteenagers Today* Web site. "It's supposed to be harmless fun. . . . That's the problem."

The scene in question begins with Shaggy and Scooby going to the kitchen. Shaggy opens the refrigerator and takes out a can of whipped cream. He shakes it up, sprays some cream into Scooby's mouth, and smiles broadly while Scooby's mouth fills up with the cream. Shaggy then takes a "hit" off the whipped cream canister. He breathes in the nitrous oxide without dispensing any cream, then hiccups. Shaggy then acts drunk and silly, saying that he needs to go outside to get some fresh air.

Concerned parents contacted the National Inhalation Prevention Coalition (NIPC) about the Scooby-Doo whippet spoof. Many were upset and believed that the film company was being insensitive to people who had lost loved ones due to inhalant abuse. One parent was especially concerned that the joke might go right over some adults' heads, yet lead children to copy the behavior. Harvey Weiss, the NIPC's executive director, brought attention to the issue in an "NIPC Inhalant Update Alert." Weiss urged Americans to view the scene from the film as a wakeup call, stating: "Our efforts should be to advance people's understanding about the dangers of inhalant use so they are recognized as a broad public health issue."

a particularly high risk for serious injury and possible death. The user can easily lose consciousness and SUFFOCATE on the bag. Suffocation can also occur when nitrous oxide is consumed in large quantities in poorly ventilated spaces, such as closed-up cars or closets.

Are There Any Medical Reasons for Taking This Substance?

As an anesthetic, nitrous oxide has many legitimate uses. Its ability to reduce anxiety, restlessness, and fear makes it especially useful in the field of dentistry. Adults and children over the age of six have been shown to experience less discomfort and mental distress when given nitrous oxide during short but painful medical or dental procedures.

American obstetricians—physicians specializing in the birthing process—used nitrous oxide as a common pain management tool for women in labor until the early 1970s. By the early twenty-first century, however, the anesthetic had been replaced by newer drugs in the

suffocate: unable to breathe; death caused by a blockage of air to the lungs

United States. However, a half-and-half mixture of nitrous oxide and oxygen was still being used in the United Kingdom to ease the pain of childbirth.

In a 2005 article for *The Age,* Julie Robotham reported on a group of Australian doctors who believed that nitrous oxide should no longer be used as a base for general anesthetics. According to an international study involving more than 2,000 patients, the use of nitrous oxide "doubles the rate of serious vomiting and PNEUMONIA after surgery," explained Robotham. Both of these side effects can result in a patient's death.

Usage Trends

Nitrous oxide is among the substances of abuse categorized as inhalants. It gained popularity on the dance club circuit because of its supposed APHRODISIAC effects. It is also preferred over other inhalants such as spray paints, shoe polish, markers, and glue because it does not leave stains on skin and clothes.

Food-grade nitrous oxide chargers, better known as "whippets," are available by the box or the case and are sold on the Internet. David Holthouse commented in a *Phoenix New Times* article, "The cardboard boxes [of whipped cream chargers] are decorated with images of fancy desserts and fresh berries, next to warnings not to ... directly inhale the contents." Whippets were blamed for the death of a twenty-year-old Virginia Polytechnic Institute student in 1999. The student suffocated after inhaling nitrous oxide from whipped cream cartridges he had purchased through an online merchant.

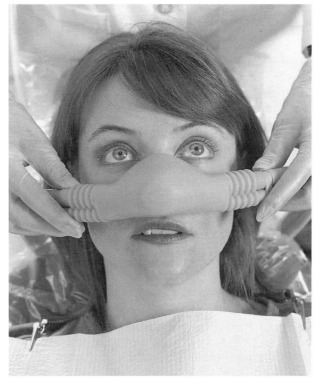

As an anesthetic, nitrous oxide has many legitimate uses. In dentistry, it is used to calm patients and lower their anxiety. © *Royalty-Free/Corbis.*

Patterns of Inhalant Abuse

The *Office of National Drug Control Policy (ONDCP)* Web site notes in its "Inhalants: Drug Facts" publication that "typically, first use of inhalants occurs between late childhood and early adolescence." According to the "2003 National Survey on Drug Use and Health (NSDUH)"—the latest survey data available in 2005—more youths age twelve and thirteen used inhalants than marijuana between 2002 and 2003. (An entry on marijuana is available in this encyclopedia.)

pneumonia: a disease of the lung, usually brought on by infection, that causes inflammation of the lung tissue, fluid buildup inside the lungs, lowered oxygen levels in the blood, and difficulty breathing

aphrodisiac: pronounced aff-roh-DEE-zee-ack; a drug or other substance that excites or increases sexual desire

Dental Highs

In an article posted on the *American Dental Associa-tion (ADA)* Web site titled "Escaping Addiction: The Door to Freedom," Dr. Thomas L. Haynes discusses the topic of addiction among dentists. "The access to large amounts of nitrous oxide," noted Haynes, along with the stress and isolation of the profession, increases the risk of abuse. "Many a dentist has been found lifeless in the office," he continued, "the N_2O mask still strapped to the face."

But general statistics on the broad category of inhalant abuse do not necessarily reflect the rate of nitrous oxide abuse. The 2003 NSDUH reports that less than one third of 1 percent of U.S. twelve and thirteen year olds reported using nitrous oxide as a recreational drug in their lifetimes. However, the rate of glue and/or shoe polish inhalation among youths in the same age group was nearly fifteen times higher than that, at about 4.3 percent.

Heavy nitrous abusers tend to be eighteen years of age or older. This may be due to N_2O's growing status as a club drug. According to NIDA, nitrous oxide use occurs frequently at raves, where it is often mixed with other club drugs such as ketamine, ecstasy (MDMA), GHB, and LSD (lysergic acid diethylamide). (Separate entries on each of these drugs are available in this encyclopedia.) By the early 2000s, nitrous oxide had gained popularity as a drug that enhanced sexual pleasure. It was even featured in a 2004 episode of the television series *CSI: Miami* as the cause of death in an otherwise healthy young woman.

Abuse in the Medical and Dental Fields

There have also been cases of nitrous oxide abuse among health-care professionals. Dentists and ANESTHESIOLOGISTS with easy access to the drug seem to be at a higher risk than the general public of developing nitrous-related dependence problems. Dependence is the belief that a person needs to take a certain substance in order to function.

Substance abuse is also especially high among healthcare professionals who administer anesthesia in a hospital setting. According to the American Association of Nurse Anesthetists (AANA), about 15 percent of anesthesia providers are substance abusers. "Nurse anesthetists are dying . . . from accidental overdose or from suicide," reported Carlos "Rusty" Ratliff in "Anesthetists in Recovery: Chemical Dependency in the Profession." Like dentists, certified registered nurse anesthetists have large supplies of nitrous oxide readily available to them. Consequently, nitrous oxide is one of the drugs these professionals may end up abusing.

"Chemical Dependence in Anesthesiologists," a document developed by the ASA TaskForce on Chemical Dependence, addresses the problem of drug abuse among anesthesiologists. Although addicted medical doctors typically become hooked on

anesthesiologists: medical doctors trained to use medications to sedate a surgery patient

OPIOIDS such as fentanyl, nitrous oxide was mentioned by the ASA as another potential drug of abuse. (An entry on fentanyl is available in this encyclopedia.)

Calling Attention to a Serious Problem

NIDA began an intensive campaign against inhalant abuse in 2005. This action was prompted by the results of the 2004 Monitoring the Future (MTF) study, an annual survey of drug use among young people in the United States. The MTF survey is conducted by the University of Michigan with funding from NIDA. Findings for 2002 through 2004 indicate that inhalant abuse among eighth-grade students was on the rise during that period. As of 2004, approximately 17.3 percent of eighth graders in the United States had abused an inhalant at some time in their lives. That represents an increase over the 2003 figure of 15.8 percent. This "upward trend in use," according to the MTF report, was accompanied by a "decline among eighth graders in the perceived risk of using inhalants."

Effects on the Body

Nitrous oxide acts as a DEPRESSANT on the human body. Once inhaled, the gas enters the bloodstream through the lungs. The blood then carries it throughout the rest of the body. It reaches the brain quickly, affecting vital functions such as breathing and heart rate. It also alters other mechanisms of the nervous system, such as the activity of NEUROTRANSMITTERS that regulate thought processes, behavior, and emotions.

A single balloon filled with nitrous oxide can bring on a short-lived but intense high. The overall effects of the gas depend largely on the user's frame of mind. It can further stimulate an already excited user, or it can sedate a more relaxed user. Symptoms of a nitrous oxide high include giddiness, a loss of balance, slurred speech, twitching, mental confusion, and an inability to feel pain. After the effects of the gas wear off, users may experience side effects such as nausea (upset stomach), restlessness, tiredness, difficulty concentrating, and the appearance of spots before their eyes.

How Nitrous Oxide Works

Nitrous oxide alters the user's perception of time. Because the effects of a single "hit" last only three minutes or so, some abusers inhale the gas many times over the course of a few hours. Such attempts to maintain a nitrous high can be fatal, since continued

opioids: substances created in a laboratory to mimic the effects of naturally occurring opiates such as heroin and morphine

depressant: a substance that slows down the activity of an organism or one of its parts

neurotransmitters: substances that help spread nerve impulses from one nerve cell to another

Dealers often sell nitrous oxide to users at concerts, clubs, and raves. Instead of using small food-grade canisters, however, they use huge medical-grade nitrous tanks to dispense the gas into balloons. Users then inhale the gas from the balloons. *Photo by Tim Sloan/AFP/Getty Images.*

breathing of the gas causes RESPIRATORY DEPRESSION. In addition, the possibility of brain damage increases when the brain does not receive sufficient amounts of oxygen.

Abusers also run the risk of vomiting and losing consciousness while intoxicated by nitrous oxide. Unconscious individuals are not able to clear their own airways of vomit. This increases the possibility of death by choking. Even if vomiting does not occur, an individual who loses consciousness from an overdose of nitrous oxide is likely to stop breathing. In addition, pure nitrous oxide takes the place of oxygen in the lungs. This process could result in asphyxiation—death or unconsciousness caused by the inability to breathe—unless the unconscious person is quickly moved to an area with fresh air. According to the CGA, death frequently occurs when abusers of the gas "attempt to achieve a higher state of euphoria [happiness and well-being]" by breathing "pure N$_2$O in a confined space—in a small room, inside an automobile or other vehicle cab, or by placing their head inside a plastic bag."

Death by overdose of nitrous oxide is very difficult to recognize. It leaves no telltale signs for a coroner or medical examiner to

respiratory depression: a slowed breathing rate; severe cases can cause a person to slip into a coma or even stop breathing entirely

identify. Under normal circumstances, blood carries oxygen to the tissues and organs of the body. But nitrous oxide pushes oxygen out of the blood. Without a sufficient supply of oxygen in the bloodstream, the tissues and organs of the body cannot function properly. Damage to the brain and other organs may result. Long-term abuse of nitrous oxide can also interfere with the production of blood cells in the BONE MARROW.

Additional Dangers

As nitrous oxide takes the place of oxygen in the lungs, a deficiency in vitamin B_{12} may result. This sparks a series of negative effects within the body. The user's red blood cell count decreases, leading to anemia (uh-NEE-mee-uh), a condition in which the blood is lacking in oxygen-carrying red blood cells. Nerve damage may also occur, leading to difficulty walking as well as tingling, numbness, or pain in the arms and legs. These side effects are usually reversible if nitrous use is stopped.

People who have a genetic disorder called phenylketonuria (fenn-uhl-kee-tuh-NORR-ee-yuh) should be particularly careful about nitrous oxide use. Phenylketonuria (PKU) is an inherited disorder that interferes with the breakdown of a certain protein called phenylalanine (fenn-uhl-AL-uh-neen). The protein is found in milk, eggs, and other foods. Individuals with PKU require a special diet that can cause a vitamin B_{12} deficiency. Because nitrous oxide can remove even more B_{12} from the bloodstream, the possibility of nerve and brain damage is especially high under these circumstances.

Nitrous users who inhale the gas while standing risk falling down and possibly breaking a limb or suffering a head injury. In addition, injury to the face, mouth, throat, and hands may occur because of the extremely low temperature of nitrous oxide. In an article for the *Phoenix New Times*, David Holthouse warned, "When N_20 is released from a whippit, it's cold enough to flash-freeze spittle." Sometimes, users who get hurt while high on nitrous oxide are completely unaware of their injuries because of the numbing effect of the gas.

Improper handling of any compressed gas tank or cylinder can also cause injuries. Attempting to inhale a gas like nitrous oxide directly from a large gas cylinder can damage the lungs beyond repair. The force of the gas entering the lungs is so powerful that the air sacs in the lungs actually burst. Victims die in a matter of seconds due to internal bleeding. Inhaling any compressed gas is especially risky for people with ear problems, as the pressure of the gas may damage the inner ear.

bone marrow: soft tissue in the center of bones where blood cell formation occurs

N₂O Plus Pre-Existing Conditions Can Equal Death

Individuals with certain medical conditions may also suffer severe and potentially fatal side effects from the use of nitrous oxide. For example, anyone with a history of PULMONARY HYPERTENSION, asthma, airway obstruction, head injury, or chest infection should not take nitrous oxide under any circumstances.

Nitrous oxide should not be given to pregnant women in the early or middle stages of pregnancy. The gas can interfere with the baby's development and may cause the mother to lose the baby before it is born. Heavy, ongoing nitrous oxide exposure during pregnancy has been shown to cause birth defects in animals.

Reactions with Other Drugs or Substances

Nitrous oxide produces effects on the body similar to those of alcohol, which is a depressant. When used along with other depressants, nitrous oxide can slow the user's breathing rate to a dangerously low—and sometimes even deadly—level.

The increasing use of nitrous oxide in combination with other club drugs poses serious risks to users. In the event of a multiple-drug overdose, emergency medical personnel may not be able to identify the mix of drugs the patient has consumed. This further complicates emergency treatment and could delay lifesaving measures.

Treatment for Habitual Users

Abuse of nitrous oxide alone has not been shown to cause withdrawal symptoms—the physiological effects of terminating use of an addicting drug. Because of this, it is not considered an addictive or habit-forming substance. At the very least, however, the gas does appear to cause PSYCHOLOGICAL DEPENDENCY. "Supposedly, nitrous is nonaddictive," wrote Holthouse, but "habitual users have a [tendency] to sit around doing whippit after whippit until all the whippits are gone, then go buy more whippits."

Nitrous oxide is eliminated from the body rapidly. However, if the patient has been abusing other drugs as well, the detoxification period, in which one rids the body of the drugs' toxins, could take up to forty days, depending on the chemicals involved. After detox, the primary goal of treatment is avoiding future drug use.

Substance abusers need to identify the underlying causes of their drug use. To curb drug abuse, they may need to alter their lifestyles substantially. This may include not going to the same clubs or hanging out with the same circle of friends if they are continuing

pulmonary hypertension: a life-threatening condition of continuous high blood pressure in the blood vessels that supply the lungs

psychological dependency: the belief that a person needs to take a certain substance in order to function

to use drugs illegally. It may mean finding a new supportive, drug-free network of friends. Nitrous oxide abusers, like other substance abusers, typically benefit from individual therapy that focuses on changing unhealthy patterns of behavior and developing better coping skills. Group therapy and self-help organizations can also assist in the recovery process. Discussing addiction in a group setting can help drug abusers gain insight into their own thoughts and behaviors through the eyes and experiences of others.

Consequences

There are few studies that focus specifically on the illicit use of nitrous oxide. Rather, the abuse of this gas is usually lumped into the general category of inhalant use. According to the 2003 NSDUH report, young adolescents who use inhalants tend to have more academic, social, and behavioral problems than those who do not. High school dropout rates and involvement in serious fights, thefts, and illicit drug use were especially high among inhalant abusers. These statistics reflect patterns seen among users of all inhalants, not just nitrous oxide.

Specifically, nitrous oxide abuse may cause mood swings and personality changes in heavy users. Users report that the gas decreases their INHIBITIONS. People with lowered inhibitions tend to take more chances and engage in riskier behavior than they would if they were not high. Nitrous oxide is also viewed as an aphrodisiac (sex enhancer) in some social circles. Some users might engage in unsafe sex, thereby increasing their risk for contracting sexually transmitted diseases, including HIV (the human immunodeficiency virus), which can lead to AIDS (acquired immunodeficiency syndrome).

The Law

Nitrous oxide is regulated by the U.S. Food and Drug Administration (FDA) as a food-grade propellant, medical-grade gas, and prescription drug. In 1971, the state of Maryland began controlling its sale and distribution. In the 1990s, in an attempt to curb the growing abuse of the gas, a number of other states followed suit. Connecticut, Arizona, Texas, Michigan, and Wisconsin were among the states that passed laws placing strong safeguards and stricter penalties on the illicit use of nitrous oxide.

Selling nitrous oxide for use as a drug carries stiff penalties. Distributors face up to 15 years in prison and fines of up to $1.5 million. In 2001, an Arizona man was sentenced to a 15-month jail

inhibitions: inner thoughts that keep people from engaging in certain activities

term and fined $40,000 for a nitrous oxide sale that resulted in the death of a Virginia college student.

Until federal legislation is passed to prohibit the possession, inhalation, and distribution of nitrous oxide for purposes of intoxication, the CGA has proposed a list of recommendations regarding its use. The main goal of these recommendations is to keep the gas from falling into the wrong hands. Among the guidelines proposed by the CGA are:

- restricting the sale of nitrous oxide to those who can prove they have a "legitimate use" for it
- encouraging legitimate users to store containers of the gas and other equipment in a secured area
- requiring medical and restaurant personnel to keep a careful count of used and unused cylinders
- reporting any thefts to the police immediately.

For More Information

Books

Brecher, Edward M., and others. *The Consumers Union Report on Licit and Illicit Drugs.* Boston: Little Brown & Co., 1972.

Fenster, Julie M. *Ether Day: The Strange Tale of America's Greatest Medical Discovery and the Haunted Men Who Made It.* New York: HarperCollins, 2001.

Lobo, Ingrid A. *Inhalants.* Philadelphia: Chelsea House Publishers, 2004.

Menhard, Francha Roffe. *The Facts about Inhalants.* Tarrytown, NY: Benchmark Books, 2005.

Periodicals

Holthouse, David. "Softly into That Good Nitrous." *Phoenix New Times* (September 29, 1999).

Robotham, Julie. "Laughing Gas Unsafe, Say Doctors." *The Age* (May 5, 2005).

White, Josh. "Virginia Student's Death Leads to Drug Conviction." *Washington Post* (October 21, 2000).

Web Sites

"2003 National Survey on Drug Use and Health (NSDUH)." *U.S. Department of Health and Human Services, Substance Abuse and Mental Health Services Administration.* http://www.oas.samhsa.gov/nhsda.htm (accessed July 31, 2005).

"About Inhalants." *National Inhalant Prevention Coalition.* http://www. inhalants.com/about.htm (accessed July 31, 2005).

ASA Taskforce on Chemical Dependence. "Chemical Dependence in Anesthesiologists." *American Society of Anesthesiologists.* 1999. http://www.asahq.org/publicationsAndServices/chemical.html (accessed July 31, 2005).

"CGA/NWSA Nitrous Oxide Fact Sheet" (November 3, 2003). *Compressed Gas Association.* http://www.cganet.com/N2O/factsht.asp (accessed July 31, 2005).

"Drugs of Abuse: 2005 Edition." *U.S. Department of Justice, Drug Enforcement Administration.* http://www.usdoj.gov/dea/pubs/abuse/index.htm (accessed July 31, 2005).

"Drugs of Abuse: Uses and Effects Chart" (June, 2004). *U.S. Department of Justice, Drug Enforcement Administration.* http://www.usdoj.gov/dea/pubs/abuse/chart.htm (accessed July 31, 2005).

Haynes, Thomas L. "Escaping Addiction: The Door to Freedom" (November, 2004). *American Dental Association.* http://www.ada.org/prof/resources/topics/topics_wellbeing_drcares_addiction02.pdf (accessed July 31, 2005).

"Inhalant Abuse: NIDA Research Report Series" (2005). *National Institutes of Health, National Institute on Drug Abuse.* http://www.nida.nih.gov/researchreports/inhalants (accessed July 31, 2005).

"Inhalant Use Is Associated with Other Substance Use and Delinquency" (March 17, 2005). *U.S. Department of Health and Human Services, Substance Abuse and Mental Health Services Administration.* http://www.samhsa.gov/news/newsreleases/050317nr_inhalants.htm (accessed July 31, 2005).

"Inhalants: Drug Facts" (February, 2003). *Office of National Drug Control Policy.* http://www.whitehousedrugpolicy.gov/publications/factsht/inhalants/index.htm (accessed July 31, 2005).

"INHALANTS.DRUGABUSE.GOV." *National Institutes of Health, National Institute on Drug Abuse.* http://www.inhalants.drugabuse.gov/ (accessed July 31, 2005).

Johnston, Lloyd, et. al. "Overall Teen Drug Use Continues Gradual Decline, but Use of Inhalants Rises" (December 21, 2004). *Monitoring the Future.* http://www.monitoringthefuture.org/ and http://www.nida.nih.gov/Newsroom/04/2004MTFDrug.pdf (both accessed July 31, 2005).

"NIPC Inhalant Update Alert." *National Inhalant Prevention Coalition.* http://www.inhalants.com/alert_update.pdf (accessed July 31, 2005).

"Nitrous Oxide Issues and Incidence of Abuse" (November 3, 2003). *Compressed Gas Association.* http://www.cganet.com/N2O/issues.asp (accessed July 31, 2005).

"Nitrous Oxide (Laughing Gas)." *MedicineNet.com,* December 13, 1998. http://www.medterms.com/script/main/art.asp?articlekey=7793 (accessed July 31, 2005).

"The NSDUH Report: Inhalant Use and Delinquent Behaviors among Young Adolescents" (March 17, 2005). *Office of Applied Studies, Substance Abuse and Mental Health Services Administration.* http://www.oas.samhsa.gov/2k5/inhale/inhale.htm (accessed July 31, 2005).

Poremba, Sue Marquette. "Sucking the Life from Your Child: The Danger of Inhalants." *Preteenagers Today.* http://preteenagerstoday.com/resources/articles/inhalents.htm (accessed July 31, 2005).

Ratliff, Carlos "Rusty." "Anesthetists in Recovery: Chemical Dependency in the Profession" (January, 1996). *American Association of Nurse Anesthetists.* http://www.aana.com/peer/recovery.asp (accessed July 31, 2005).

"Spring 2005 NIPC Inhalant Prevention Update." *National Inhalant Prevention Coalition.* http://www.inhalants.com/SPRING_UPDATE-MAY_2005.pdf (accessed July 31, 2005).

Other

"After the Fall." *CSI: Miami* (television series), CBS, November 29, 2004.

See also: Amyl Nitrite; Inhalants

Where to Learn More

Books

Balkin, Karen F. *Tobacco and Smoking.* San Diego, CA: Greenhaven Press, 2005.

Beers, Mark H., and others. *The Merck Manual of Medical Information,* 2nd ed. New York: Pocket Books, 2003.

Brecher, Edward M., and others. *The Consumers Union Report on Licit and Illicit Drugs.* Boston: Little Brown & Co., 1972. http://www.druglibrary.org/schaffer/library/studies/cu/cumenu.htm (accessed September 12, 2005).

Connelly, Elizabeth Russell. *Psychological Disorders Related to Designer Drugs.* Philadelphia, PA: Chelsea House, 2000.

Drug Enforcement Administration, U.S. Department of Justice. *Drugs of Abuse: 2005 Edition.* Washington, DC: Government Printing Office, 2005. http://www.usdoj.gov/dea/pubs/abuse/index.htm (accessed September 12, 2005).

Drummond, Edward H. *The Complete Guide to Psychiatric Drugs: Straight Talk for Best Results.* New York: Wiley, 2000.

Fenster, Julie M. *Ether Day: The Strange Tale of America's Greatest Medical Discovery and the Haunted Men Who Made It.* New York: HarperCollins, 2001.

Gahlinger, Paul M. *Illegal Drugs: A Complete Guide to Their History, Chemistry, Use and Abuse.* Las Vegas, NV: Sagebrush Press, 2001.

Gorman, Jack M. *The Essential Guide to Psychiatric Drugs,* 3rd ed. New York: St. Martin's Griffin, 1997.

Hyde, Margaret O., and John F. Setaro. *Drugs 101: An Overview for Teens.* Brookfield, CT: Twenty-first Century Books, 2003.

Keltner, Norman L., and David G. Folks. *Psychotropic Drugs.* Philadelphia: Mosby, 2001.

Kuhn, Cynthia, Scott Swartzwelder, and Wilkie Wilson. *Buzzed: The Straight Facts about the Most Used and Abused Drugs from Alcohol to Ecstasy,* 2nd ed. New York: W.W. Norton, 2003.

McCay, William. *The Truth about Smoking.* New York: Facts on File, 2005.

Olive, M. Foster. *Designer Drugs.* Philadelphia: Chelsea House, 2004.

Physicians' Desk Reference, 59th ed. Montvale, NJ: Thomson PDR, 2004.

Physicians' Desk Reference for Nonprescription Drugs and Dietary Supplements, 25th ed. Montvale, NJ: Thomson Healthcare, 2004.

Preston, John D., John H. O'Neal, and Mary C. Talaga. *Consumer's Guide to Psychiatric Drugs.* Oakland, CA: New Harbinger Publications, 1998.

Silverman, Harold M. *The Pill Book,* 11th ed. New York: Bantam Books, 2004.

Sonder, Ben. *All about Heroin.* New York: Franklin Watts, 2002.

Wagner, Heather Lehr. *Cocaine.* Philadelphia: Chelsea House, 2003.

Weatherly, Myra. *Ecstasy and Other Designer Drug Dangers.* Berkeley Heights, NJ: Enslow Publishers, 2000.

Weil, Andrew, and Winifred Rosen. *From Chocolate to Morphine.* Boston: Houghton Mifflin, 1993, rev. 2004.

Wolfe, Sidney M. *Worst Pills, Best Pills: A Consumer's Guide to Avoiding Drug-Induced Death or Illness.* New York: Pocket Books, 2005.

Periodicals

Hargreaves, Guy. "Clandestine Drug Labs: Chemical Time Bombs." *FBI Law Enforcement Bulletin* (April, 2000): pp. 1-9. http://www.fbi.gov/publications/leb/2000/apr00leb.pdf (accessed September 13, 2005).

Jefferson, David J. "America's Most Dangerous Drug." *Newsweek* (August 8, 2005).

Reid, T.R. "Caffeine." *National Geographic* (January, 2005): pp. 3-33.

Web Sites

"2003 National Survey on Drug Use and Health (NSDUH)." *Substance Abuse and Mental Health Services Administration (SAMHSA).* http://www.drugabusestatistics.samhsa.gov (accessed September 13, 2005).

"A to Z of Drugs." *British Broadcasting Corporation (BBC).* http://www.bbc.co.uk/crime/drugs (accessed September 13, 2005).

"Cigarette Smoking among American Teens Continues to Decline, but More Slowly than in the Past." *National Institute of Drug Abuse.* http://www.nida.nih.gov/Newsroom/04/2004MTFTobacco.pdf (accessed September 13, 2005).

"Club Drugs—An Update: Drug Intelligence Brief" (September 2001). *U.S. Department of Justice, Drug Enforcement Administration, Intelligence Division.* http://www.usdoj.gov/dea/pubs/intel/01026 (accessed September 13, 2005).

"Consumer Education: Over-the-Counter Medicine." *Center for Drug Evaluation and Research, U.S. Food and Drug Administration.* http://www.fda.gov/cder/consumerinfo/otc_text.htm (accessed September 13, 2005).

"DEA Briefs & Background: Drug Descriptions." *U.S. Drug Enforcement Administration.* http://www.dea.gov/concern/concern.htm (accessed September 13, 2005).

"Drug Abuse Warning Network, 2003: Interim National Estimates of Drug-Related Emergency Department Visits." *U.S. Department of Health and Human Services, Substance Abuse and Mental Health Services Administration.* http://dawninfo.samhsa.gov/files/DAWN_ED_Interim2003.pdf (accessed September 13, 2005).

"Drug Facts." *Office of National Drug Control Policy.* http://www.whitehousedrugpolicy.gov/drugfact/ (accessed September 13, 2005).

Drug Free AZ. http://www.drugfreeaz.com/ (accessed September 13, 2005).

"Drug Guide by Name." *Partnership for a Drug-Free America.* http://www.drugfree.org/Portal/Drug_Guide (accessed September 13, 2005).

"Drug Information." *CESAR: Center for Substance Abuse Research at the University of Maryland.* http://www.cesar.umd.edu/cesar/drug_info.asp (accessed September 13, 2005).

"Drug Information." *MedlinePlus.* http://www.nlm.nih.gov/medlineplus/druginformation.html (accessed September 13, 2005).

"Drugs and Chemicals of Concern." *U.S. Department of Justice, Drug Enforcement Administration, Office of Diversion Control.* http://www.deadiversion.usdoj.gov/drugs_concern (accessed September 13, 2005).

"Drugs and Human Performance Fact Sheets." *National Highway Traffic Safety Administration.* http://www.nhtsa.dot.gov/people/injury/research/job185drugs/technical-page.htm (accessed September 13, 2005).

"Drugs of Abuse: Uses and Effects Chart." *U.S. Department of Justice, Drug Enforcement Administration.* http://www.usdoj.gov/dea/pubs/abuse/chart.htm (accessed September 13, 2005).

"Eating Disorders Information Index." *National Eating Disorders Association.* http://www.nationaleatingdisorders.org/p.asp?WebPage_ID=294. (accessed September 13, 2005).

"Educating Students about Drug Use and Mental Health." *Centre for Addiction and Mental Health.* http://www.camh.net/education/curriculum_gr1to8intro.html (accessed September 13, 2005).

"The Faces of Meth." *Multnomah County Sheriff's Office.* http://www.facesofmeth.us/main.htm (accessed September 13, 2005).

"Generation Rx: National Study Reveals New Category of Substance Abuse Emerging: Teens Abusing Rx and OTC Medications Intentionally to Get High" (April 21, 2005). *Partnership for a Drug-Free America.* http://www.drugfree.org/Portal/About/NewsReleases/Generation_Rx_Teens_Abusing_Rx_and_OTC_Medications (accessed September 13, 2005).

"Health Channel—Drugs." *How Stuff Works.* http://health.howstuffworks.com/drugs-channel.htm (accessed September 13, 2005).

"Health Information from the Office of Dietary Supplements." *National Institutes of Health, Office of Dietary Supplements.* http://ods.od.nih.gov/Health_Information/Health_Information.aspx (accessed September 13, 2005).

"Herbal Supplements: Consider Safety, Too." *National Institutes of Health, National Center for Complementary and Alternative Medicine.* http://nccam.nih.gov/health/supplement-safety/ (accessed September 13, 2005).

"In the Spotlight: Club Drugs" (updated September 1, 2005). *National Criminal Justice Reference Service.* http://www.ncjrs.gov/spotlight/club_drugs/summary.html (accessed September 13, 2005).

"Index to Drug-Specific Information." *Center for Drug Evaluation and Research, U.S. Food and Drug Administration.* http://www.fda.gov/cder/drug/DrugSafety/DrugIndex.htm (accessed September 13, 2005).

Kyle, Angelo D., and Bill Hansell. "The Meth Epidemic in America—Two Surveys of U.S. Counties: The Criminal Effect of Meth on Communities and The Impact of Meth on Children" (July 5, 2005). *National Association of Counties (NACo).* http://www.naco.org/Content/ContentGroups/Publications1/Press_Releases/Documents/NACoMethSurvey.pdf (accessed September 13, 2005).

Monitoring the Future. http://www.monitoringthefuture.org/ and http://www.nida.nih.gov/Newsroom/04/2004MTFDrug.pdf (both accessed September 13, 2005).

"National Drug Intelligence Center (NDIC) Fast Facts Page." *National Drug Intelligence Center.* http://www.usdoj.gov/ndic/topics/ffacts.htm (accessed September 13, 2005).

"National Drug Threat Assessment: 2005" (February 2005). *U.S. Department of Justice, National Drug Intelligence Center.* http://www.usdoj.gov/ndic/pubs11/12620/index.htm (accessed September 13, 2005).

National Institute on Drug Abuse. http://www.nida.nih.gov/ and http://www.drugabuse.gov/ (both accessed September 13, 2005).

Neuroscience for Kids. http://faculty.washington.edu/chudler/neurok.html (accessed September 13, 2005).

"NIDA for Teens: The Science behind Drug Abuse: Mind over Matter." *National Institute on Drug Abuse.* http://teens.drugabuse.gov/mom/ (accessed September 13, 2005).

"NIDA InfoFacts: Science-Based Facts on Drug Abuse and Addiction." *National Institutes of Health, National Institute on Drug Abuse.* http://www.nida.nih.gov/infofacts/ (accessed September 13, 2005).

"NIDA Research Reports Index." *National Institutes of Health, National Institute on Drug Abuse.* http://www.nida.nih.gov/ResearchReports (accessed September 13, 2005).

"Partnership Attitude Tracking Study (PATS): Teens, 2004." *Partnership for a Drug-Free America.* http://www.drugfree.org/Files/Full_Report_

PATS_TEENS_7th-12th_grades_2004 (accessed September 13, 2005).

"Pulse Check: Drug Markets and Chronic Users in 25 of America's Largest Cities." *Executive Office of the President, Office of National Drug Control Policy.* http://www.whitehousedrugpolicy.gov/publications/ drugfact/pulsechk/january04/january2004.pdf (accessed on September 13, 2005).

"Tobacco Information and Prevention Source (TIPS)." *Centers for Disease Control, National Center for Chronic Disease Prevention and Health Promotion.* http://www.cdc.gov/tobacco/issue.htm (accessed September 13, 2005).

"Under the Counter: The Diversion and Abuse of Controlled Prescription Drugs in the U.S." (July 2005). *National Center on Addiction and Substance Abuse at Columbia University.* http://www.casacolumbia. org/Absolutenm/articlefiles/380-final_report.pdf (accessed September 13, 2005).

Organizations

Al-Anon/Alateen (Canada)
Capital Corporate Centre, 9 Antares Dr., Suite 245
Ottawa, ON K2E 7V5
Canada
(613) 723-8484
(613) 723-0151 (fax)
wso@al-anon.org
http://www.al-anon.alateen.org/

Al-Anon/Alateen (United States)
1600 Corporate Landing Pkwy.
Virginia Beach, VA 23454-5617
USA
(757) 563-1600
(757) 563-1655 (fax)
wso@al-anon.org
http://www.al-anon.alateen.org/

Alcoholics Anonymous (AA)
475 Riverside Dr., 11th Floor
New York, NY 10115
USA
In the U.S./Canada: Look for "Alcoholics Anonymous" in any telephone directory.
http://www.aa.org/

American Botanical Council
6200 Manor Rd.
Austin, TX 78723
USA

(512) 926-4900
(800) 373-7105
(512) 926-2345 (fax)
abc@herbalgram.org
http://www.herbalgram.org

American Council for Drug Education (ACDE; a Phoenix House agency)
164 West 74th St.
New York, NY 10023
USA
(800) 488-DRUG
acde@phoenixhouse.org
http://www.acde.org

American Society of Addiction Medicine (ASAM)
4601 N. Park Ave., Upper Arcade #101
Chevy Chase, MD 20815
USA
(301) 656-3920
(301) 656-3815 (fax)
email@asam.org
http://www.asam.org/

Attention Deficit Disorder Association (ADDA)
P.O. Box 543
Pottstown, PA 19464
USA
(484) 945-2101
(610) 970-7520 (fax)
http://www.add.org/

Canadian Centre on Substance Abuse (CCSA)
75 Albert St., Suite 300
Ottawa, ON K1P 5E7
Canada
(613) 235-4048
(613) 235-8101 (fax)
info@ccsa.ca
www.ccsa.ca

Center for Substance Abuse Research (CESAR)
4321 Hartwick Rd., Suite 501
College Park, MD 20740
USA
(301) 405-9770
(301) 403-8342 (fax)
CESAR@cesar.umd.edu
www.cesar.umd.edu

Center for Substance Abuse Treatment (CSAT; a division of the Substance Abuse and Mental Health Services Administration)
1 Choke Cherry Rd., Room 8-1036
Rockville, MD 20857
USA
(800) 662-HELP(4357) or (877) 767-8432 (Spanish)
http://csat.samhsa.gov or http://findtreatment.samhsa.gov

Centers for Disease Control and Prevention (CDC; a division of the U.S. Department of Health and Human Services)
1600 Clifton Rd.
Atlanta, GA 30333
USA
(404) 639-3311
(800) 311-3435
http://www.cdc.gov/

Cocaine Anonymous World Services (CAWS)
3740 Overland Ave., Suite C
Los Angeles, CA 90034
USA
(310) 559-5833
(310) 559-2554 (fax)
cawso@ca.org
http://www.ca.org/

DARE America
P.O. Box 512090
Los Angeles, CA 90051-0090
USA
(800) 223-DARE
webmaster@dare.com
http://www.dare.com

Do It Now Foundation
Box 27568
Tempe, AZ 85285-7568
USA
(480) 736-0599
(480) 736-0771 (fax)
e-mail@doitnow
http://www.doitnow.org

Europe Against Drugs (EURAD)
8 Waltersland Rd.
Stillorgan, Dublin
Ireland
01-2756766/7
01-2756768 (fax)

eurad@iol.ie
www.eurad.net

Institute for Traditional Medicine (ITM)
2017 SE Hawthorne Blvd.
Portland, OR 97214
USA
(503) 233-4907
(503) 233-1017 (fax)
itm@itmonline.org
http://www.itmonline.org

Join Together (a project of the Boston University School of Public Health)
One Appleton St., 4th Floor
Boston, MA 02116-5223
USA
(617) 437-1500
(617) 437-9394 (fax)
info@jointogether.org
http://www.jointogether.org

Marijuana Anonymous World Services
P.O. Box 2912
Van Nuys, CA 91404
USA
(800) 766-6779
office@marijuana-anonymous.org
http://www.marijuana-anonymous.org

Methamphetamine Treatment Project, University of California at
Los Angeles, Integrated Substance Abuse Programs (ISAP)
11050 Santa Monica Blvd., Suite 100
Los Angeles, CA 90025
USA
(310) 312-0500
(310) 312-0538 (fax)
http://www.methamphetamine.org/mtcc.htm or www.uclaisap.org

Narconon International
7060 Hollywood Blvd., Suite 220
Hollywood, CA 90028
USA
(323) 962-2404
(323) 962-6872 (fax)
info@narconon.org or rehab@narconon.org
http://www.narconon.org

Narcotics Anonymous (NA)
P.O. Box 9999
Van Nuys, CA 91409

USA
(818) 773-9999
(818) 700-0700 (fax)
www.na.org

Narcotics Anonymous World Services Office (WSO)—Europe
48 Rue de l'Été/Zomerstraat
B-1050 Brussels
Belgium
32-2-646-6012
32-2-649-9239 (fax)
http://www.na.org

National Association for Children of Alcoholics (NACoA)
11426 Rockville Pike, Suite 100
Rockville, MD 20852
USA
(301) 468-0985
(888) 55-4COAS
(301) 468-0987 (fax)
nacoa@nacoa.org
http://www.nacoa.org/

National Cancer Institute, Tobacco Control Research Branch (TCRB)
Executive Plaza North, Room 4039B
6130 Executive Blvd. MSC 7337
Rockville, MD 20852
USA
(301) 594-6776
(301) 594-6787 (fax)
blakek@mail.nih.gov
www.tobaccocontrol.cancer.gov or http://dccps.nci.nih.gov/tcrb

National Capital Poison Center—Poison Help
3201 New Mexico Ave., NW Suite 310
Washington, DC 20016
USA
(202) 362-3867
(800) 222-1222
(202) 362-8377 (fax)
pc@poison.org
www.poison.org or www.1-800-222-1222.info

National Center for Complementary and Alternative Medicine Clearing-house (NCCAM; a division of the National Institutes of Health)
P.O. Box 7923
Gaithersburg, MD 20898
USA
(888) 644-6226

info@nccam.nih.gov
http://nccam.nih.gov/

National Center for Drug Free Sport, Inc.
810 Baltimore
Kansas City, MO 64105
USA
(816) 474-8655
(816) 474-7329 (fax)
info@drugfreesport.com
http://www.drugfreesport.com

National Center on Addiction and Substance Abuse at Columbia University (CASA)
633 Third Ave., 19th Floor
New York, NY 10017-6706
USA
(212) 841-5200
(212) 956-8020 (fax)
www.casacolumbia.org

National Council on Alcohol and Drug Dependence, Inc. (NCADD)
22 Cortlandt St., Suite 801
New York, NY 10007-3128
USA
(212) 269-7797
(800) 622-2255
(212) 269-7510 (fax)
national@ncadd.org
http://www.ncadd.org

National Eating Disorders Association
603 Stewart St., Suite 803
Seattle, WA 98101
USA
(206) 382-3587
(800) 931-2237
info@NationalEatingDisorders.org
http://www.nationaleatingdisorders.org

National Families in Action
2957 Clairmont Road NE, Suite 150
Atlanta, GA 30329
USA
(404) 248-9676
(404) 248-1312 (fax)
nfia@nationalfamilies.org
http://www.nationalfamilies.org/

National Inhalant Prevention Coalition (NIPC)
332 - A Thompson St.
Chattanooga, TN 37405
USA
(423) 265-4662
(800) 269-4237
nipc@io.com
http://www.inhalants.org

National Institute of Mental Health (NIMH; a division of the National Institutes of Health)
6001 Executive Boulevard, Room 8184, MSC 9663
Bethesda, MD 20892-9663
USA
(301) 443-4513
(866) 615-6464
(301) 443-4279 (fax)
nimhinfo@nih.gov
http://www.nimh.nih.gov/

National Institute on Drug Abuse (NIDA; a division of the National Institutes of Health)
6001 Executive Blvd., Room 5213
Bethesda, MD 20892-9561
USA
(301) 443-1124
(888) 644-6432
information@nida.nih.gov
http://www.drugabuse.gov or http://www.nida.nih.gov

National Institutes of Health (NIH)
9000 Rockville Pike
Bethesda, MD 20892
USA
(301) 496-4000
NIHinfo@od.nih.gov
http://www.nih.gov/

Nicotine Anonymous
419 Main St., PMB #370
Huntington Beach, CA 92648
USA
(415) 750-0328
info@nicotine-anonymous.org
http://www.nicotine-anonymous.org

Office of Dietary Supplements (ODS; a division of the National Institutes of Health)
6100 Executive Blvd., Room 3B01, MSC 7517
Bethesda, MD 20892-7517

USA
(301) 435-2920
(301) 480-1845 (fax)
ods@nih.gov
http://ods.od.nih.gov/

Office of National Drug Control Policy (ONDCP; a division of the Executive Office of the President of the United States)
c/o Drug Policy Information Clearinghouse
P.O. Box 6000
Rockville, MD 20849-6000
USA
(800) 666-3332
(301) 519-5212 (fax)
ondcp@ncjrs.gov
http://www.whitehousedrugpolicy.gov/

Oregon Health & Science University, Department of Medicine, Division of Health Promotion and Sports Medicine
3181 S.W. Sam Jackson Park Rd., CR110
Portland, OR 97239-3098
USA
(503) 494-8051
(503) 494-1310 (fax)
hpsm@ohsu.edu
http://www.ohsu.edu/hpsm

SAMHSA's National Clearinghouse for Alcohol and Drug Information (NCADI)
P.O. Box 2345
Rockville, MD 20847-2345
USA
(301) 468-2600
(800) 729-6686
http://www.health.org

Students Against Destructive Decisions (SADD) National
Box 800
Marlborough, MA 01752
USA
(877) SADD-INC
(508) 481-5759 (fax)
info@sadd.org
http://www.sadd.org/

Substance Abuse and Mental Health Services Administration (SAMHSA; a division of the U.S. Department of Health and Human Services)
1 Choke Cherry Rd., Room 8-1036
Rockville, MD 20857

USA
(301) 443-8956
info@samsha.hhs.gov
http://www.samhsa.gov

U.S. Anti-Doping Agency
1330 Quail Lake Loop., Suite 260
Colorado Springs, CO 80906-4651
USA
(719) 785-2000
(866) 601-2632; (800) 233-0393 (drug reference line);
or (877) PLAY-CLEAN (877-752-9253)
(719) 785-2001 (fax)
drugreference@usantidoping.org
http://www.usantidoping.org/

U.S. Drug Enforcement Administration (DEA)
Mailstop: AXS, 2401 Jefferson Davis Hwy.
Alexandria, VA 22301
USA
(202) 307-1000
http://www.dea.gov

U.S. Food and Drug Administration (FDA)
5600 Fishers Ln.
Rockville, MD 20857
USA
(888) INFO-FDA (888-463-6332)
http://www.fda.gov

World Anti-Doping Agency (WADA)
Stock Exchange Tower, 800 Place Victoria, Suite 1700
P.O. Box 120
Montreal, PQ H4Z 1B7
Canada
(514) 904-9232
(514) 904-8650 (fax)
info@wada-ama.org
www.wada-ama.org/

Index

Volume numbers are in *italic*.

Boldface indicates main entries and their page numbers.

Illustrations are marked by (ill.).

needle exchange programs, *3*:408 (ill.)

PMA abuse, *5*:775, 780

Cancer

ecstasy for anxiety about, *3*:307, 311

fentanyl for, *3*:337, 340–341, 340 (ill.)

herbal medicine and, *3*:395

medical marijuana, *4*:501–502

melatonin and, *4*:523–524

morphine for pain, *4*:632–633, 636, 638

nicotine and, *4*:658–659, 659 (ill.)

"Candy flipping," *2*:224; *3*:305

Cannabinoids, *4*:499, 504

Cannabis sativa. See Marijuana

Canseco, Jose, *5*:870, 870 (ill.), 872

Car crashes, alcohol-related, *1*:39, 40 (ill.), 41; *4*:619

Carbonated alcoholic beverages, *1*:30

Cardiovascular disorders

alcohol and, *1*:31

diuretics for, *2*:284, 285, 286, 289

garlic and, *3*:389

ginkgo and, *3*:389

ibuprofen and, *5*:719

methylphenidate and, *5*:814

PCP for, *2*:216; *5*:761

"Carries" (Methadone doses), *4*:570

CASA. *See* National Center on Addiction and Substance Abuse (CASA)

Casanova, Giovanni Giacomo, *5*:701

Casinos, secondhand smoke in, *4*:644 (ill.)

Cassada, Joseph, *5*:743

Castenada, Carlos, *4*:558

Castro, Jessi, *1*:15

Cataplexy, *3*:366

***Catha edulis*, *2*:150–162,** 152 (ill.), 154 (ill.), 160 (ill.)

effects, *2*:157–159

history, *2*:150–153, 161

legal issues, *2*:159–162

use, *2*:151 (ill.), 154–157, 155 (ill.)

Cathine, *2*:154, 160

Cathinone, *2*:153–154, 158, 160

CBT. *See* Cognitive-behavioral therapy (CBT)

Celebrity drug-related deaths, *1*:97; *4*:620

Celexa (Citalopram), *1*:81

Central America. *See* Mexico

Central Intelligence Agency (CIA), *3*:475

See also Office of Strategic Services (OSS)

Central Narcotics Bureau (Singapore), *3*:469

Ceremonial drug use

DMT-based drugs, *2*:271–272, 272 (ill.), 273 (ill.), 274, 278, 280

ephedra, *3*:319 (ill.)

nicotine, *4*:645

peyote, *4*:548–550, 552, 555, 556 (ill.), 563, 564–565

psilocybin, *5*:792–793, 795, 798, 799

Salvia divinorum, *5*:847–848, 851–853, 858

Chamomile, *3*:384, 387

Chanu, Sanamachu, *2*:295, 296 (ill.)

Charley (Chimpanzee), *4*:653

Chat. *See Catha edulis*

Chechen rebels (Moscow theater hostage situation of 2002), *3*:336 (ill.), 337, 342

Chem-packs, *1*:66

Chemical Diversion and Trafficking Act of 1988, *2*:214

Chemical weapons

cyanide, *1*:65–66; *5*:731

ecstasy research, *3*:301

Chemicals, industrial. *See* Industrial chemicals

Chemotherapy, *4*:636, 638

Chen, K.K., *3*:317

Chest pain. *See* Angina

Chevreul, Michel-Eugène, *2*:201 (ill.), 207

Chewing of drugs

Catha edulis, *2*:152 (ill.), 153, 154, 155 (ill.), 158

vs. Palladone, *3:*426
treatment, *5:*749–750
use, *4:*536, 537; *5:*739–741,
742–745
See also OxyContin
OxyContin, *5:*738 (ill.), 747 (ill.)
buprenorphine treatment,
*4:*541–542
defined, *5:*737
history, *5:*738–739
vs. methadone, *4:*572, 573,
575, 576
Operation Dr. Feelgood,
*5:*751 (ill.)
use, *4:*530–531, 536–537;
*5:*739–741, 742, 743–745
See also Oxycodone

P

Pacifiers
with ecstasy, *3:*300 (ill.)
at raves, *5:*783, 785 (ill.)
Pain relievers. *See* Analgesics
Pakistan
heroin use, *3:*411
opium production, *5:*698
Palladone, *3:*422, 424–425, 426
See also Hydromorphone
Palmeiro, Rafael, *5:*870–871
Pamabrom (Pamprin), *2:*285
Pandemic, influenza (1918), *5:*714
Papaver somniferum. See Poppies
(Plants)
Paracelsus, laudanum invention,
*2:*188; *3:*401, 404; *4:*639; *5:*685,
698, 737
Paramethoxyamphetamine.
See PMA
Paramethoxymethamphetamine.
See PMMA
Paregoric, *5:*686, 693–694
Parker, Quanah, *4:*549, 550 (ill.),
552
Paroxetine (Paxil), *1:*81, 88
Partnership for a Drug-Free
America (PDFA)
ecstasy campaign, *3:*310 (ill.)
on inhalants, *3:*441, 450

over-the-counter drug abuse,
*5:*708
prescription drug abuse, *2:*232;
*4:*536; *5:*745, 808, 820
"Party and play" trend, *4:*595
Party drugs. *See* Club drugs
"Party packs," *1:*4
Passive smoking, *4:*643,
644 (ill.), 647
Paste form of cocaine, *2:*169
Patches, transdermal. *See* Skin
patches
Patent medicines, *5:*702–703
Patient controlled anesthesia
(PCA), *4:*533, 631, 637 (ill.)
PATS (Partnership Attitude
Tracking Study). *See* Partner-
ship for a Drug-Free America
(PDFA)
Paul, Ramón, *2:*271, 278
Paxil (Paroxetine), *1:*81, 88
PCA (Patient-controlled anesthe-
sia), *4:*533, 631, 637 (ill.)
PCP (Phencyclidine), *2:*213, 215;
*5:***756–771,** 759 (ill.), 765 (ill.)
vs. dextromethorphan, *2:*243
effects, *2:*222–223; *5:*765–770
history, *5:*756–758
legal issues, *5:*771
production, *5:*758–759
treatment, *5:*770–771
use, *2:*216; *5:*759–764
PDFA. *See* Partnership for a Drug-
Free America (PDFA)
Peer counseling, *2:*182
Peets, Joey, *3:*413
Pemberton, John, *2:*167
Pennyroyal, *3:*392–393
PEPAP (Meperidine analog),
*4:*535
Perc-o-pops, *3:*337, 338, 339,
340–341, 340 (ill.)
Percocet, *5:*737, 738, 742
See also Oxycodone
Percodan, *5:*737, 738, 742
See also Oxycodone
Performance enhancers
Adderall, *1:*15, 16 (ill.), 17–19,
19 (ill.), 21
amphetamines, *1:*56

U

V

W